Globalisation, Policy and Shipping

TRANSPORT ECONOMICS, MANAGEMENT AND POLICY

Series Editor: Kenneth Button, *Professor of Public Policy, School of Public Policy, George Mason University, USA*

Transport is a critical input for economic development and for optimizing social and political interaction. Recent years have seen significant new developments in the way that transport is perceived by private industry and governments, and in the way academics look at it.

The aim of this series is to provide original material and up-to-date synthesis of the state of modern transport analysis. The coverage embraces all conventional modes of transport but also includes contributions from important related fields such as urban and regional planning and telecommunications where they interface with transport. The books draw from many disciplines and some cross disciplinary boundaries. They are concerned with economics, planning, sociology, geography, management science, psychology and public policy. They are intended to help improve the understanding of transport, the policy needs of the most economically advanced countries and the problems of resource-poor developing economies. The authors come from around the world and will represent some of the outstanding young scholars as well as established names.

Titles in the series include:

Reforming Transport Pricing in the European Union
A Modelling Approach
Edited by Bruno De Borger and Stef Proost

Travel Behaviour
Spatial Patterns, Congestion and Modelling
Edited by Eliahu Stern, Ilan Salomon and Piet H.L. Bovy

Financing Transportation Networks
David Levinson

Transportation Networks and the Optimal Location of Human Activities
A Numerical Geography Approach
Isabelle Thomas

European Union Port Policy
The Movement Towards a Long-Term Strategy
Constantinos I. Chlomoudis and Athanasios A. Pallis

Structural Change in Transportation and Communications in the Knowledge Society
Edited by Kiyoshi Kobayashi, T.R. Lakshmanan and William P. Anderson

Globalisation, Policy and Shipping
Fordism, Post-Fordism and the European Union Maritime Sector
Evangelia Selkou and Michael Roe

Globalisation, Policy and Shipping

Fordism, Post-Fordism and the European Union Maritime Sector

Evangelia Selkou
Logistics Department, Athens 2004 Olympic Committee, Athens, Greece

Michael Roe
Professor of Maritime Policy and Logistics,
Centre for International Shipping and Logistics, University of Plymouth, UK

TRANSPORT ECONOMICS, MANAGEMENT AND POLICY

Edward Elgar
Cheltenham, UK • Northampton, MA, USA

Published by
Edward Elgar Publishing Limited
Glensanda House
Montpellier Parade
Cheltenham
Glos GL50 1UA
UK

Edward Elgar Publishing, Inc.
136 West Street
Suite 202
Northampton
Massachusetts 01060
USA

A catalogue record for this book
is available from the British Library

ISBN 1 84376 934 4

Printed and bound in Great Britain by MPG Books Ltd, Bodmin, Cornwall

Contents

Figures and Tables

FIGURES

TABLES

Acknowledgements

Rotterdam, winter 2002. Cold, windy, always damp, fog swirling in off the Maas. Ideal territory for original ideas and few diversions from concentrated research. Fortunately it was Lina and not I, marooned 10 floors up with only the maritime and logistics economies to think about. However, it was also fortunate that it was from such circumstances, the initial idea for this book developed. The central concept was entirely Lina's, although I did play a part in helping her decide which way to progress and to develop her reading of Sletmo's work on national, supra-national and international policy-making in shipping. From there the project has grown like Topsy and the result is what you, the reader, hold today.

We would both like to acknowledge the help from Edward Elgar, and Matthew Pitman, Kate Emmins and Dymphna Evans in particular. We would also like to recognise each other's substantial contribution to this book, but that is not the generally done thing at this stage. Instead we must thank the many other individuals and institutions who, commonly quite unknowingly, make us what we are, and thus are reflected in this work.

From Lina – I would personally like to thank all those who have collaborated with me over the last six years and gratefully acknowledge my debt to them. I am also grateful to Helen, Christos, Maria and Thrasivoulos who always supported me in doing what I really wished for and keep doing so. And I feel deeply indebted to all maritime researchers for their work and devoted selves in providing the infrastructure for more investigation and research in the field. I hope that this study will provide a useful basis for consideration of some of the key issues facing today's shipping industry as well as, perhaps, stimulus for further research on the topics involved.

And Mike – from my perspective the friendship, and intellectual and technical help provided by many at the University of Plymouth, has been instrumental in making this project happen – Marie Sleeman as secretarial support in the early and very latest stages and a number of undergraduate students – including in particular Dina Kottoros and Robyn Pyne who simply made me think more. And of course those whom I must thank for simply being there – the Selkos family in Maroussi and the remarkable atmosphere of Athens in general; Liz, Joe and Siân at home; and the entire squad of Charlton Athletic, without which the Premiership would be a sorry and predictable bore.

Abbreviations

AMRIE	Alliance of Maritime Regional Interests in Europe
BIMCO	Baltic and International Maritime Council
BPA	British Ports Association
CMA	Council for Mutual Economic Assistance
CTP	Common Transport Policy
CV	Commanditaire Vennootschappen
DETR	Department of the Environment, Transport and the Regions
DIS	Danish International Ship Register
DSA	Danish Shipowners' Association
DWT	Deadweight tons
EC	European Community
ECSA	European Community Shipowners' Association
EEA	European Economic Area
EEC	European Economic Community
EMSA	European Agency of Maritime Safety
EP	European Parliament
ERDF	European Regional Development Fund
ERNP	European Radio-Navigation Plan
ESC	European Shippers Council
EU	European Union
EUROS	European Register of Shipping
FDI	Foreign Direct Investment
FMC	US Federal Maritime Commission
FOC	Flag of Convenience
FSA	Finnish Shipowners' Association
FSI	Flag State Implementation
GIS	German International Ship Register
GRT	Gross Registered Tons
GWT	Gross Weight Tons
ICS	International Chamber of Shipping
ILO	International Labour Organisation
IMCO	Intergovernmental Maritime Consultative Organisation
IMDO	Irish Maritime Development Office
IMO	International Maritime Organisation

INTERTANKO	International Association of Independent Tanker Owners
ISL	Institute of Shipping and Logistics
ISM Code	International Ship Management Code
ISF	International Shipping Federation
ITF	International Transport Workers' Federation
KVNR	Koninklijke Vereniging van Nederlandse (The Netherlands Shipowners' Association)
LSM	Lloyd's Ship Manager
MAIB	Maritime Accident Investigation Branch
MARPOL	IMO Convention for the prevention of Maritime Pollution from ships
MCA	Maritime and Coastguard Agency
MOU	Paris Memorandum of Understandings on Port State Control
MS	Member States
NAFTA	North America Free Trade Association
NIS	Norwegian International Ship Register
NSA	Norwegian Shipowners' Association
NUMAST	National Union of Marine, Aviation and Shipping Transport Officers
OECD	Organisation for Economic Cooperation and Development
OETV	Offentlicher Dienste Transport und Verkehr
PSC	Port State Control
PSO	Public Service Obligations
SEA	Single European Act
SEM	Single European Market
SOLAS	IMO Convention on Safety of Life at Sea
SSA	Swedish Shipowners' Association
STCW	Standards on Training, Certification and Watchkeeping
TAA	Trans-Atlantic Agreement
TACA	Trans-Atlantic Conference Agreement
TMNS	Traditional Maritime Nations
TEN-T	Trans-European Transport Networks
UGS	Union of Greek Shipowners
UIRR	International Union of Combined Road–Rail Transport
UK	United Kingdom
UN	United Nations
UNCLOS	United Nations Convention on the Law of the Sea
UNCTAD	United Nations Conference on Trade and Development
UNCTAD Code	UNCTAD Code of Conduct for Liner Conferences
VTMIS	Vessel Traffic Management and Information Services
WTO	World Trade Organisation

1. Introduction

This book provides a contemporary and detailed analysis of a number of significant and inter-related themes. Central to the discussion is the impact of globalisation on the international shipping industry – in itself the largest logistics providers in the world and responsible for carrying at some stage, somewhere in the region of 95% of all freight products including the large majority of politically sensitive cargoes of crude oil and containers. Interwoven with this discussion is the issue of shipping policy and the relationships between policy-makers and enforcers at different spatial levels – international, supra-national and national. In such a globalised sector as shipping – where ship-owner, cargo-owner, ship registration, ship or cargo insurer, crew, officers, forwarders, legal advisers, financiers and brokers might all be based in different countries and these entirely different from the location of the ship – what is the role of national shipping policy and what relevance does it have to the growing significance of supra-national bodies such as the European Union? What role is there for international bodies such as the United Nation's International Maritime Organisation (IMO) in the policy-making process?

This book looks at how these issues relate to each other and the complex world of policy-making, governmental power and the shipping sector in an increasingly global environment in the most international of all industries – shipping. The approach is firstly to outline and discuss the progress of policy in a maritime setting and to set out its historical development. It then goes on to analyse the issues raised in the opening chapters in the context of major maritime policy developments, in particular the European Union (EU) and the complex relationships between policy jurisdictions that can emerge. New fiscal approaches to shipping – and in particular the role of tonnage tax – are used as an approach to understand these issues. This policy framework as it is constituted in 2003, just before the proposed major expansion of the organisation to incorporate ten new members from Eastern Europe, Cyprus and Malta, has emerged over very many years, from the periods of exploration and colonisation in the fourteenth to nineteenth centuries until the contemporary era, when EU integration has led to the formulation of a series of common views on the future of the shipping sector and its many related industries. However, the objective does not stop there as a substantial aim of the book is to focus upon the development of these policy issues within the continuing process of globalisation and to establish the relationship between policies for the shipping sector and the world-wide phenomenon of increasing globalisation. Shipping in many ways is *the* global industry and as such the nature of policy development is extremely complex, as all policy-making has to emerge from a spatial level of political activity – for example national or international, whilst its implementation may have to be at a different level from this. These conflicts of interest and responsibility are central to this work.

POLICY OBJECTIVES

Before we can begin to explore these issues of policy, globalisation and shipping, we need to try to answer a series of questions. Why do states have policies and more specifically why policies for the shipping sector? What is the role of the state in interfering with a commercial activity and why does the state not let those in the market organise themselves without regulation, advice and coercion?

Button (1993) provides us with a structure that helps to explain and understand the reasons for policy-making and although he specifically orientates this discussion towards the transport sector in general, much of what he says is equally applicable to the shipping sector. He identifies 13 main reasons for state policies:

1. Containment of monopoly power. The shipping sector is riddled with monopoly abuse and with tendencies that drift towards monopoly positions. These include the activities of shipping conferences in organising ship schedules, ports served, prices and quality of service, the role of cabotage protection for example in the United States where the Jones Act Provisions of 1920 continue to reserve domestic shipping trades to US flagged vessels, and to numerous cases where cargo is reserved for specific operators and owners around the world. State shipping policies commonly make these monopoly positions more extreme by protecting domestic operators (e.g. the USA) or facilitating the continuance of shipping conferences (e.g. the US Federal Maritime Commission (FMC) and the Trans-Atlantic Conference Agreement [TACA]). However, other state-like authorities like the European Union (EU) actually may attempt to control such abuses through the application of cabotage rules and competition policy in Europe.

2. Control of excessive competition. In some ways this is the reverse of the argument in (1) in that the control of excessive competition is to reduce the number of players in the market so that it becomes more stable and reliable. The result of this type of control is an inevitable tendency towards monopolisation. In shipping, trends towards deregulation in the industry, generally typified by the reduction in protected markets, may ultimately lead to cut-throat competition in, for example, the summer ferry sector in the Mediterranean. The European Union has introduced protection for such markets within cabotage rules, so that operators have a guaranteed market throughout the year and are not subject to 'creaming-off' in terms of profit.

3. Regulation of externalities. Shipping has claims to be a clean industry, especially in comparison with other transport modes, but without state intervention, the level of pollution created by the sector would be unsustainable. State interference in the form of pollution laws controlling air and water pollution, the disposal of garbage and ballast water and also controlling port activities, is widespread and enforced through Port State Control and the application of the International Ship Management (ISM) Code and IMO regulations. Market forces are unable to provide a framework to control externality production in the shipping sector and hence policies at state level and above are necessary. Safety is another issue that commonly raises its head at state level, and the maritime sector as a whole has a dubious safety record which needs constant monitoring by the state in the absence of an effective market mechanism to ensure standards. This includes the activities of ships on the high seas as well as the port industrial environment and conditions for the employment of seafarers.

4. Provision of public goods. Public goods are items where there is no practical limit to the number of consumers and identifying the amount of consumption is equally as difficult. In the maritime sector the classic example is that of the lighthouse where (almost) any number of ships can benefit from the light at any time and the 'amount' of light consumed (or the benefit from it) is almost impossible to assess. Such goods are especially difficult to place in a market framework as both conditions (restricting consumption to those who pay and charging them an appropriate amount) need to be met. Hence the state commonly takes responsibility – in shipping terms – for navigation aids of many types, for example.

5. Provision of high-cost infrastructure. Some aspects of the shipping industry are not cheap. These items include the provision of port

facilities which can be extremely expensive, along with dredging, navigation aids and other infrastructural needs. This encourages state interference as only the state may have the resources to invest at the required level.

6. Long pay-back time periods. Many of these expensive investments – especially in ports – have extended pay-back periods which may be very unattractive to private investors. This has proven to be less of a problem than expected in the privatised port market of (for example) the UK, but remains an issue where private capital is perhaps more scarce.

7. Needs. There are social objectives within shipping that commonly have to be met but which may not provide a sufficient (or any) return to the investor. Shipping services to small island communities, for example in the Mediterranean or the Scottish Islands off the UK mainland, are classic examples of where 'cherry-picking' by summer seasonal operators may occur without a public-sector obligation subsidy available. Accessibility needs of these communities can then be met but only with state involvement in the market-place. In a similar fashion, the redistribution of wealth is a common objective of governments and can be achieved at least in part, through the maritime sector. Thus, as we have seen above, general taxation based on income can be used to support those in need in island and remote communities, whilst other government support through, for example, regional initiatives, can be used to subsidise ship-building facilities and even port investments – subject of course to competition rules in areas such as the European Union.

8. National development. State involvement in shipping is commonly a result of a perceived need to support and protect an industry that both employs many people and earns considerable income for the country. This has been a well worn argument in, for example, the UK where there have been persistent calls for support to the shipping sector because of the jobs dependent upon it – particularly in the support services in the City of London – and also its contribution to the UK balance of payments – variously estimated at between £1-2 billion per annum (Gardner and Pettit, 1999a, 1999b; Gardner et al., 2001). The validity of these arguments we shall return to in a later chapter, but for the moment it is important to note that many countries around the world have adopted state involvement policies in the maritime sector for just these reasons.

9. Integration. State involvement in the maritime sector is sometimes intended as a process which can encourage and facilitate the integration of wider economic policies including attempts to

maximise regional development, to reduce levels of unemployment or to protect the environment. This commonly involves ensuring that economic investment in transport in general is co-ordinated and coupled with appropriate plans for land-use and development. Wider macro objectives, such as broad fiscal policy, can also be an objective to which the maritime sector can be seen to contribute, and the various tonnage tax proposals introduced across the European Union from around the mid-1990s can be seen as having this objective along with rather more micro aims.

10. Co-ordination. Along with the integrative policies noted in (9) above there are also more specific co-ordination issues that the state may have policies to achieve and the maritime sector is no exception to this. Thus, the Netherlands government has played an increasing role in the development of the Port of Rotterdam in ensuring that investment from both the private and public sector is co-ordinated to maximise its impact. States commonly co-ordinate rail freight investment with that taking place in state controlled ports – Poland is a good example in the 1990s – so that duplication and poor, inappropriate provision is avoided.

11. Prestige, representation and votes. There is also an argument for state involvement in the maritime sector based on the notion of its prestigious role in representing a country around the world, particularly through flying a state flag. This might require state involvement as without fiscal support, other flags (for example those of Open Registries) might be selected. Many countries now have tax regimes for shipping companies that are designed to encourage domestic registration at least in part for reasons of prestige. In a similar vein there is an argument that to retain a significant place on the international maritime stage a country needs to have a support policy for its fleet – thus sustaining it at artificial levels so that the national voice is heard at the IMO or other international bodies. Finally there is the issue of votes – and in some countries the maritime sector is important politically so that vote chasing becomes an issue which can be met by active state policies towards the sector.

12. Social conditions and training qualifications for workers at sea. Some of the earliest maritime policies in the European Union were aimed at raising the standard of working conditions and qualifications of those that work at sea, something that the market may not achieve as the linkage between commercial success and standards of training and work conditions is not always direct or clear. Other bodies such as the IMO and International Labour Organisation (ILO) also play a large role here.

13. Defence. A rather specific but common issue in the maritime sector is the strategic nature of the industry and the need therefore for the state to be involved in the policy-making process. Ports are commonly seen as strategic infrastructure which needs the state's hand behind its investment and plans and as such in most countries, even where there has been extensive privatisation undertaken, the port authorities and port land remains within the state's ownership. Good examples of this come from across Eastern Europe, where landlord ports are common; the private sector remains the main infrastructure owner. In the shipping sector the same sort of policy approach is also common – for example in the USA, the Jones Act (1920) provides for subsidies and protection to US flagged and manned vessels so that at times of strategic need, the US Navy has a fleet of commercial vessels which can be requisitioned for support. In the UK, it is one of the few supportable reasons for fleet subsidy that successive UK governments have accepted since 1979.

There are undoubtedly other factors why states develop transport, logistics and maritime policies but those noted above provide a useful framework at this stage. Considerable overlap also exists between these categories of objective and one would expect to find a number of objectives behind the derivation of maritime policies, differing in their significance in the way they are combined depending upon the situation and authorities involved.

POLICY STRUCTURES

Policy as a concept is not an easy one to define and there have been many discussions but little agreement in the transport, shipping and logistics areas about what constitutes policy and its nature. One particularly useful analysis was provided by Gwilliam (1993), who analysed the main characteristics of transport policy which were widely applicable to government and pseudo-government institutions including those of, for example, the United Nations, the European Union and the various national ministries that exist in each country.

He suggested that policy in the transport sector – which of course includes that of the maritime sector – could be divided into five areas. These were those relating to jurisdiction, the agencies of policy, their objectives, the instruments used and finally a rather distinct section relating to packages of policies. Taking each in turn:

Jurisdiction

The jurisdiction of a policy refers to the level at which it can be applied and could be interpreted broadly as a spatial interpretation of policy authority. We return to the specific spatial contexts for policies at a later stage.

Traditionally five levels of policy jurisdiction can be identified. Beginning from the most extensive and least specific there is the *multinational* (or *international*) level. Taking the shipping sector as an example, perhaps the most significant and relevant policy-making organisations at this level include the United Nations through the work of the International Maritime Organisation based in London and through the trade and development arm of the UN (UNCTAD). The IMO has played an extensive role in establishing and encouraging standards of safety and environmental quality through continued pressure on legislative authorities for higher technical standards for such things as bulk carrier design, ferry design and other technical requirements. UNCTAD has a totally different role to play in, for example, protecting developing country shipping industries (and as a by-product these countries' economic development) through the application of a Code of Conduct for Shipping and the infamous 40/40/20 rule. This is an agreement whereby national signatories of the Code agree to provide 40% of liner shipping capacity between two countries (one developing and the other developed) to each of the country fleets and 20% to cross-traders. This ensures that the inherently weaker developing country fleet retains a proportion of market share and can provide a lower grade, cheaper (and probably in many ways more suited) service between the two countries, thus preventing abuse by a developed country fleet which has the resources to win a battle for market share.

Another important international organisation that will have an increasing role to play in the maritime sector is the World Trade Organisation (WTO) – the replacement to GATT. Although progress has been abysmally slow since the conclusion of the last (Uruguay) Round of talks of GATT in 1993 (Lloyd's List, 1993), the principle has been accepted that shipping is an issue for consideration by the new WTO in its ambitions to extend and develop free trade throughout the world. Shipping is characterised by a considerable degree of interference in its markets by governments through, for example, subsidies to shipping companies, tax concessions and cargo preference as well as cabotage agreements and simply through state ownership and control. The organisation of shipping is also a prime target for state involvement in the free trade process with the continued existence of liner shipping conferences and consortia, organising services, providing joint marketing and schedules and even arranging prices. The WTO, as an international policy-making body, will be looking closely at these issues as part of its remit to extend the free trade process through the shipping sector.

The *supra-national* level of policy jurisdiction refers to that spatial level which lies between the multinational and the national – the latter is discussed below. Supra-national organisations in the maritime sector are typified by that role played by the European Union (EU) (Paixao and Marlow, 2001) and by the North America Free Trade Association (NAFTA) (Government of Canada, 1992; Gordon, 1993). Conventionally they include a number of countries allied together in some form or another, with common ambitions and may (or may not) have legislative powers and authority over and above the nation state. The EU has a multi-facetted policy stance for the maritime sector which generally forms a framework that is aimed to guide that of the nation state and which includes policy documents and legislation for the 15 member countries (2003). They are characterised by aspects of competition policy, environmental protection and safety for both the shipping and ports sectors. There is a considerably more detailed discussion of these policies in later sections of this book, but to give some idea of the extent of the EU's influence, some more recent policy initiatives have focused upon completing the internal EU market for cabotage trades (entirely within one country) by sea so that any ship from the EU now has the right to compete for domestic shipping work regardless of EU registration or ownership. It was not uncommon before the 1990s for countries such as Italy, Greece and Spain to reserve all their cabotage trades to domestic operators. The EU has also focused recently upon raising standards for bulk carriers and ferries in the light of a number of serious disasters and new legislation exists, derived from that at the multinational level of the IMO, to improve quality. Further regulations relate to environmental standards for the disposal of garbage in port, to increase competition in ports and to encourage the development of the short-sea shipping sector in competition with other, less environmentally friendly, modes.

The role of the EU in the maritime sector will if anything increase over the coming years, particularly as a series of new entrants from East Europe and the Mediterranean become members. Many of these new entrants are countries with major maritime sectors – Poland with a strong maritime tradition, a series of major Baltic ports and the largest shipbuilding industry in Europe; Latvia and Lithuania with disproportionately large shipping fleets compared with country size; Cyprus with a large Open Registry and a strong reputation in ship management; Malta with its own major Open Registry and high dependence on the sea; and a number of other countries likely to accede at a much later date but also with strong maritime interests – Bulgaria, Romania and Turkey included.

NAFTA is an association of the USA, Canada and Mexico, which together form a largely free-trade area with obvious impacts on the maritime sector. A number of discussions have centred upon the maritime implications of this agreement (Brooks, 1994; Kornegay, 1993). NAFTA, unlike the EU, has no legislative authority but does have sizeable economic impacts upon the distribution of income, consumption and economic activity. Its policy impacts in the maritime sector are thus indirect but still significant.

The *national* level of policy jurisdiction is perhaps more obvious than that at the multinational or supra-national level and traditionally has been the level which has been most significant. It is this level that is central to this book and it is the continuing discussion about its role and significance which is the central issue of maritime policy debate at this time. Sletmo (2001), Roe (2002) and Selkou and Roe (2002) have all contributed to the debate about the value and role of national maritime policies in the light of the growth of multi and supra-national bodies, and it is this theme to which we return in later chapters.

It is commonly suggested that the national level of policy-making traditionally has been the most significant of all levels as it is here that all policies have to be approved. Even the multinational and supra-national bodies such as the IMO and EU are composed of individual nation representatives, and it is the nations that decide to become and remain members of these organisations. Thus it is essentially at national level that policies are determined and put forward. Hence, for example in the UK, the representatives at the IMO and in the EU Council of Ministers are also appointed by the UK government and it is through the UK Parliament that the rules and regulations of the IMO and the EU are finally imposed.

In addition to this, the national policy-making bodies – commonly in practice, the ministries of shipping/maritime affairs, etc. – are central to decisions upon national subsidies to the sector, ownership strategies including privatisation and nationalisation and very significantly, changes in policy in terms of tax regimes and more general fiscal policy. In each country there is an identifiable, national policy-making institution at government level which plays this domestic role and that of representing the nation concerned in bodies at a multi and supra-national level.

The final two levels of jurisdiction are those at the *regional* and *local* level. These levels of policy jurisdiction are important in the maritime sector as it is here that the implications of decisions at a higher level are often imposed. Examples include the subsidies available at a regional level in ports in the remoter areas of the EU – for example in south-west UK, southern Italy and the accession countries from Eastern Europe – along with attempts to attract investment in ports by local administrations and port authorities around the world. However, despite the significance of these policy initiatives they are not the driving force behind maritime policy-making, which generally remains at the national, supra-national and multinational level. Hence we shall focus only on the latter here.

Objectives

The objectives of policy-making in the maritime sector are extremely varied and have been outlined in the earlier section of this chapter and as a result will be covered here again only superficially. This should not be taken as an indication of their unimportance, as in fact the objectives of policies should drive their character and ultimately their success or otherwise. They include such things as containment of monopoly power, regulation of externalities, welfare distribution, provision of public goods, national development and needs. One way of viewing these objectives is to divide them into two distinct categories – those directed towards the working of the maritime sector in general (for example those related to sector efficiency, environmental protection and safety) and those directed towards a policy goal in itself (for example national development, regional support and the redistribution of welfare).

Instruments

Gwilliam views the next facet of the policy process as centring upon the instruments that can be used to put policies into place. These are as varied as the objectives towards which they are directed. A classic example includes direct government intervention. In the maritime sector, states are commonly ship-owners (for example the Polish state remains the owner in 2003 of the largest bulk shipping company in Europe – 'Polska Zegluga Morska' [PZM]), port authorities (there are many examples including ports in the Netherlands, Korea, Russia), infrastructure providers – rail, road, inland waterways in most countries, and even a number of ancillary activities in some countries such as brokers, freight forwarders, haulage operators, banking and insurance providers. Undoubtedly the level of state ownership within the maritime sector has declined in the past 20 years, but state execution of maritime services remains a defining feature.

Truly private, commercial organisations are also commonly regulated by the state even where the ownership is no longer, or has never been, in state hands. The maritime sector has many examples of such regulation which is normally carried out at a national level of jurisdiction but also commonly with the authority and backing of a multi or supra-national authority. Thus Port State Control – the means by which ships are periodically checked in port that they meet a long list of internationally agreed standards and which if they fail to meet these requirements can be detained until the problems are made good – is enforced by state governments throughout the EU, under nationally agreed legislation. Banks, insurance and legal firms are normally regulated by laws passed by national governments, whilst environmental legislation in ports is similarly imposed on private (and public) sector operators (for example in terms of garbage disposal).

Fiscal measures may also be used to enforce state policies as physical or legal measures are often less effective. Here, the roles of fines or tax incentives are two opposing, fiscal measures that are commonly used by governments to achieve policies. Fines in the maritime sector can be for breaking many of the safety, environmental or regulatory laws that exist for shipping and ports. These include the notable example of the US$251 million of fines imposed in the late 1990s by the EU upon 15 liner shipping operators in the North Atlantic trade who, as members of the Trans-Atlantic Conference Agreement (TACA) and its predecessor the Trans-Atlantic Agreement (TAA), adopted a policy for uniform pricing across member operators, which was unacceptable within the terms of EU competition policy (Brooks, 2000). Tax incentives include the now widely adopted tonnage tax regimes that have proliferated around the world and particularly in the European Union during the 1990s and since then. We shall return to tonnage tax at a later stage in some detail but for now, these tax measures are an indirect subsidy to ship-owners to encourage vessels to return to or remain with a state flag through the application of corporate taxation to vessels rather than company profits (Brownrigg et al., 2001; Selkou and Roe, 2002). Ship-owners are commonly more sensitive to changes in the fiscal rather than the legal environment and as such, these types of measures have become increasingly popular with governments and pseudo-government authorities in attempting to implement maritime policy initiatives.

Industrial self-regulation is another mechanism that has a role to play in policy implementation but naturally, for a method that relies upon the industry itself to police its effectiveness, it can be less effective than state implementation. In most countries there is an organisation that represents national ship-owners – commonly 'The Shipowners' Association' – which also often sets industrial standards and attempts to impose them through coercion, persuasion and ultimately by threats of expulsion. These bodies may also be represented at supra-national level – coming together for example in the EU in the form of the European Community Shipowners' Associations (ECSA) to lobby the European Commission, Council and Parliament to achieve their preferred ends and to develop policy in a way that benefits their members. This blurring of jurisdiction level is increasingly common.

These industrial representative bodies also often play a major role in influencing the design and detail of maritime policy – with good examples coming from the UK where the Chamber of Shipping was central to government plans for the introduction of the tonnage tax regime from 2000.

Other maritime related bodies apart from the Chambers of Shipping include professional regulators such as the Institute of Chartered Shipbrokers and the Institute of Transport and Logistics. However, clearly, this process of industrial self-regulation has its limitations, biases and the bodies involved, their own agendas.

Agencies

Agencies resemble the institutions of the state policy process but are different in that they are the actual organisations that implement policies in the maritime sector. Gwilliam identifies four main groups that are applicable in the transport sector and these can be adapted to be a useful classification for the maritime industries as well.

Government departments are clearly important bodies in the state policy process and are commonly the organisations that represent nations on supra-national and multinational bodies such as NAFTA and the OECD. Clearly politicians – outside of the departmental organisation – also represent national priorities on these bodies but at different times and with different responsibilities. In many cases the politicians are the elected or appointed representatives but actually do little more than this in terms of policy development. At the European Council of Transport Ministers for example (where maritime issues are discussed and legislation approved), it is the European Commission and the domestic state departments that prepare documentation, draft legislation and advise the politicians as to what is feasible and what is the recommended action to take. A similar process occurs in most national governments where the politicians act on advice of independent, civil servants.

Quasi-independent agencies have been increasingly set up in western governments to take on the functions previously carried out directly by the state. Here the UK is a particularly good example in the maritime sector where the Maritime and Coastguard Agency is a cost centred, independent government agency directed to carry out functions related to maritime safety, protecting the maritime environment and promoting the UK register of ships. Whilst closely related to the UK government it is in theory at least, separate from it and its political influence. Government guidance is of course of importance but financial and policy independence is paramount.

Government-owned companies may also exist as well which have to operate entirely within the free market but whose main stakeholders are the state. Examples of these are becoming increasingly difficult to find but include sizeable state-owned shipping companies in Russia ('Sovcomflot') and China (COSCO). Both act with some independence from the state but at the same time have clear responsibilities in that direction – both legally to their owners, and politically. Port authorities are also commonly state-owned – with the notable exception of the UK where the large majority have been privatised – and may act as companies with state masters. Examples of state-owned ancillary companies – freight forwarders, brokers, agents, etc. – whereas once common in East Europe – are now rare.

Finally there are *trade associations*, organisations of private companies, gathered together to lobby government and other groups and to provide mutual support. These bodies – such as the International Union of Combined Road-Rail Transport Companies (UIRR), the British Ports Association (BPA) and even the European Community Shipowners' Associations (ECSA), are particularly pro-active in lobbying governments for specific policy initiatives and also play a role in the industrial self-regulation process noted above.

Packages

Gwilliam identifies a final policy category relating to the largely outdated concept of packages in policy-making which once was significant to the maritime sector but now has become blurred and rather difficult to identify. Packages refer to the contrasting approach to macro-economic strategies and politics of planned and free-market economies but with the dissolution of the Soviet empire and the regimes in Eastern Europe from 1989-1991, the role of the free market has become much more dominant. Of course there is residual evidence of planned economies – the notable example of China needs to be pointed out – but even there the role of the free market continues to grow even within a planned environment. Thus there are now many independent and privately owned freight forwarders, agents and brokers – something unheard of in the Former Soviet Union.

The remaining bastions of planned economies are few and far between and are relatively unimportant in the maritime sector – North Korea, Belarus and Cuba for example – although the role of some of the highly centralised countries of the Middle East and their not insignificant shipping interests and indirect effects upon the maritime markets through their oil reserves, should not be ignored.

One issue that always existed even when the two contrasting approaches to economic planning existed, was the clear overlap in some countries. The USA, for example, continues to preach free market policies in shipping whilst heavily protecting and subsidising its domestic shipping fleet operating on cabotage trades. The EU advocates the promotion of open competition in all markets whilst regulating for the continued existence of liner conferences and consortia, and subsidies for port infrastructure, shipbuilding and ship operating tax regimes. Such hypocrisy is not uncommon and it is here that we touch upon issues which later in this book will be discussed in some detail, relating to conflicts in policies in the maritime sector not just within jurisdictions such as the EU but also between spatial levels such as between free market initiatives at EU level and fleet protectionism at national level as is the case widely across member states.

THE STRUCTURE OF THE BOOK

As outlined earlier in this chapter, the main objective of this book is to analyse the structure of policy-making in the maritime sector taking into account the various characteristics and motivations of policy-makers and the complex relationships that exist between them. There will be a deliberate focus upon the importance of globalisation for the maritime industry and its role in the development of global markets and the future for shipping policies and perspectives thereafter. Attention will also be directed towards an examination of the relationships between policy jurisdiction levels in the light of the growth of globalisation. To illustrate the conflicts that exist in maritime policy-making and to show how these conflicts may (or may not) be resolved, there is also a close examination of one major policy thrust in the new millennium – that of the widespread adoption of fiscal initiatives – and tonnage tax as the prime example – to sustain and support shipping's role in traditional maritime countries.

Following this opening introduction to the book, Chapter 2 aims to clarify some of the most important areas for discussion and provide a more detailed insight into the issues which will be analysed in the following chapters.

This scene-setting is followed by Chapter 3, which goes on to provide a broad analysis of policy trends in shipping from the fifteenth and sixteenth centuries when the first signs of industry dependency started to appear, up until the post-war period, from 1945, when initial attempts towards achieving cost efficiency led to the mass-internationalisation of the shipping industry and many of the issues still apparent today began to emerge.

Chapter 4 provides a detailed analysis of the relationships that exist between the levels of policy implementation – and particularly the conflicts that exist between national, supra-national and international levels of policy development. The output from this discussion is the basis for the rest of the book, which then moves on in Chapter 5 to examine attempts to emphasise efforts towards a European Union shipping policy, and the main objectives and results that have occurred. This includes the tension that clearly exists between national and supra-national levels of policy-makers exemplified by the fiscal regimes now commonly applied to shipping.

Chapter 6 continues the analysis by describing the impact of globalisation on EU shipping and policies and the change in strategies and perspectives thereafter. The shipping industry is characterised by both physical capital mobility and a consequential tendency towards foreign direct investment (FDI) and it will appear that this, combined with efforts for regional integration in Europe, may sometimes contradict the industry's very nature.

Meanwhile, it appears that competition in the maritime sector continues to experience a transformation in its form and dimensions. Globalisation and capital mobility in shipping have proved to be the main forces behind the expansion of Open Registry flags and the consequent decline of traditional (typified by EU) registered shipping. However, recent trends in the European industry point towards the beginning of a new era, one that targets the elimination of substandard shipping while at the same time recognises and promotes the importance of shipping activities within the region. Thus there is beginning to form the basis for the EU to draw up new measures for the shipping sector and provide its members with the required flexibility of competing in a global environment while at the same time reducing their operating costs. One major approach to this is hoped to be the widespread application of tonnage tax across the EU. These issues will be discussed in some depth in Chapters 6 and 7.

One of the outcomes of the current study is the common observation that the industry is presently undergoing significant changes. The way or ways by which the maritime industry in general is transforming, can be seen to follow a series of structures, also recognised in other industry sectors and an analysis of these structures is undertaken in Chapter 8. Within this chapter, two partly contradictory tendencies of today's shipping industry are identified, namely, the neo-Fordist and post-Fordist dimensions with their close relationships to globalisation in shipping.

2. Setting the Scene

INTRODUCTION

There is no question that the characteristics of both national and international maritime policy have been subject to major adjustment in recent years, and perhaps in particular since the late 1970s and early 1980s, as a result of the radical economic and political changes that have been taking place throughout the world. There has been a notable reduction in the advocacy of extended nationalism and state control in the shipping sector, and this in turn is being progressively replaced by calls for further privatisation to that introduced increasingly since 1979 and further deregulatory, market economy approaches and reforms in international trade and shipping (Frankel, 1992).

These trends, which can be summarised in the term 'liberalisation', have been given perhaps greater significance because maritime transport is the largest service provider in international trade. As such it is inherently global, has widespread impact and represents a specific and extreme example of the extended process of globalisation. As of December 2001, the world merchant fleet comprised of 87,939 ships of not less than 100 gross tons, equivalent to 574.6 million gross tonnage (Lloyd's Register, 2002). It is thus not a small industry and to emphasise its role further, it is one that has shown progressive growth as the world's markets grow and as globalisation of these markets extends horizons further.

The European Union represents one of the leading players in the global market in general, demonstrated by the fact that about 90% of the trade to and from the Euro area, and about 40% of the intra-European trade is carried out at some stage of the product's journey by ship (Knoop, 2002). It is thus wholly logical to suggest that the challenges of a continuously developing global economic system will strengthen and extend the significance of maritime transport within this process of globalising trade. At the same time – and in a way that all trading markets now do – the EU depends upon increasing reliability, safety standards, environmental friendliness as well as quality and competence in shipping services in order both to preserve and to promote an industry which undoubtedly has a valuable role to play. As long as the interdependence of economies continues to grow, the globalisation of markets will also continue to intensify. If the EU is to gain the full benefits from these profound changes, substantial adaptations to its internal and external policies are necessary including those of shipping policy (UNICE, 2002). Many changes have already taken place which at least accommodate the globalising processes that are occurring, but many more will be needed particularly where conflicts between policy-makers emerge – for example at the different levels of national and international policy-making noted earlier.

Meanwhile, perhaps the supreme principle characterising today's economic and political world (and one that is a major stimulus to globalisation) remains to 'free market forces', in other words, to liberalise and to eliminate arrangements which preserve some resources or markets for the benefit of particular industries or people. For the European maritime industries, globalisation of trade represents a substantial opportunity in terms of new and larger markets in which to become involved. This suggests in turn that a main aim of the EU should be to ensure that the European maritime base is safeguarded on a long-term basis. This presents problems however in the light of increasing competition from outside the EU in the maritime sector, which has been made easier by these very same globalisation forces that have been released in recent years (Grimaldi, 2001). This book attempts to recognise these competitive trends, the problems consequently faced by EU shipping, the need to recognise increasing trends towards liberalisation in all markets and the attempts to develop maritime policies that accommodate competition, the need to protect the weakening EU maritime sector and the conflicts between policy initiators and enforcers that remain.

Governments once regularly worked against freeing up the maritime sector (and a substantial number continue with these policies despite the pressures to conform to the more fashionable liberalising trends noted above). This was commonly achieved by various combinations of regulating, protecting, subsidising and restricting the operations of foreign investors and operators. In the maritime industry a good example were the cargo reservation schemes which were advocated by some as the 'panacea of all ills' (as characterised by Frankel, 1992) in international shipping in the 1970s and 1980s. These have been progressively replaced by free market incentives and exhortations and the call for liberalisation of the shipping sector including large-scale reductions in national shipping regulations and a variety of other types of government control. Now the dominant ideology within the sector tends to emphasise that all should be free to compete on 'a level playing field' for the available markets and resources, meaning that governments are not supposed to further assist maritime firms, regions or industries.

It is a widely discussed issue that shipping is an extremely mobile, capital intensive, highly risky business and the history of shipping is full of examples which support this statement. Several factors contribute to this situation: ship-owners can be found all over the world; ships are expensive, mobile assets by definition; shipping services such as insurance, broking, legal advice, finance and freight forwarding can be provided from almost any location to any client; shipping companies vary considerably both in size and in type of operation and there is no centralised control as far as demand and supply are concerned. As such, shipping is an international industry where various players belonging to different and multiple countries commonly (in fact almost always) take part (Paixao and Marlow, 2001). The physical and capital mobility that this situation suggests and the global shipping regime which has resulted, are aspects of the external world which play a significant role in shaping or changing attitudes towards shipping policy (Aspinwall, 1995). This is true in all parts of the world and all countries, not least the region which is central to this text – that of the European Union.

DEFINING THE ISSUES

Before going on to assess the importance and impact of globalisation processes for the shipping industry in general and then the European Union industry in more detail, it is important to define and make specific the term 'globalisation'. In political, social and economic science it is extremely difficult to find an all-encompassing and widely agreed definition of the term. On the one hand, this is because the phenomenon of globalisation is a relatively new one and is still being determined by social, political, economic and technological developments that have taken place in recent years and continue today. Meanwhile, on the other hand, globalisation is subject to numerous and diverse implications in so many aspects of life, that indeed, most of the outcomes are yet to be realised making definition in terms of its outcomes a major problem (Dirks, 2001).

Despite these problems some sort of attempt has to be made. One example comes from a UK government report (UK Government Department for International Development, 2000), where the term globalisation was defined as:

'the growing interdependence and interconnectedness of the modern world through increased flows of goods, services, capital, people and information'.

Meanwhile, closer to the maritime and logistics home, Sletmo (2001) defines globalisation as the:

'triumph of markets over governments. It is the end of economic regulation by bureaucrats and the erasure of borders'.

It is commonly understood that the many narrow, nationalist views which used to exist at government policy-making level have been replaced by a general admission that the world economy is something which all nations are part of and as such each state is a part of the globalisation process. As a result, there is a collective and equal gain – a synergy in fact – which can (and normally does) result from the application of the principles of free trade. These principles manifest themselves within (for example) the European Union, in legislation that demands the free movements of capital, goods, services, labour and knowledge. These principles in turn, then will form the basis for what Sletmo defines as a 'new global prosperity' (Sletmo, 2001).

Under this perspective, industrial policies – and shipping is no exception – will have to be responsive to global needs, perhaps more accurately defined as global market calls, and be one of the major driving forces in the process of true and strong, economic collaboration across borders rather than serving the interests of nationalistic ambition and even bureaucratic elites.

Despite these clear, economic advantages and wide acceptance of the value that shipping can contribute within a free trade environment to globalisation and associated social benefits, the concept of opening up national restrictions and dismantling domestic protectionism is still not widely accepted by national governments. This is despite the fact that it is almost universally agreed that the effects of these restrictive, nationalistic practices diminish many domestic industry performances, through, for example, reductions in employment, artificial maintenance of lower safety and environmental levels and the ultimate lowering of quality standards to name but a few of the adverse impacts.

CLARIFYING THE ISSUES

Before we begin to attempt to illustrate the ways in which shipping has been influenced by globalisation trends (or indeed the way that shipping itself has influenced the moves towards globalisation), it would be pertinent to address a number of reasonable questions. For example, is not shipping already a global industry? Indeed, it is unquestionable that the shipping industry has a long and well documented history of campaigning for greater freedom for investment and the need to remove the barriers which have existed restricting access to potential, profitable fields.[1] The industry's role in the growing trends towards the process of foreign direct investment (FDI) is a long one.

---

[1] According to the Marxist theory of globalisation, this is 'the situation to which capitalism inevitably moves because the ceaseless drive to accumulate more and more capital leads to pressure to remove the barriers blocking access to more fields for investment'. Quoted in Trainer, (1999).

For many decades, ship-owners have had the opportunity to re-flag their fleets to almost any register of choice in order to take advantage of the lower labour and taxation costs which are available. The capital mobility that characterises the industry has been an inevitably crucial factor in the establishment and continuity of a global shipping regime and thus a major factor in the whole process of globalisation in more general terms (Aspinwall, 1995). Although this argument is apparently clear and difficult to deny, its development remains significant in the progress within the industry that has occurred in the later decades of the twentieth century.

Looking back throughout the history of shipping, in times like those of the colonial maritime powers, shipping has always been the only truly physically global business. However, now that undoubtedly the remainder of much of the business world is heading rapidly towards globalisation, shipping is required to play in addition, another role. It is not that shipping is now only just becoming global – we have seen that this has long been the case. It is that it is now attempting to meet the increasing needs of the markets (and perhaps more importantly the clients within this market) as they are becoming global (Parker, 1999). Moreover, the industry has a number of distinctive features, none of which is especially unique to shipping, but which in combination create a unique set of characteristics compared with other industries both within and outside the international logistics sector. These features include the fact that shipping capital investments largely consist of a number of discrete and very expensive items which in turn, have no fixed land location – in other words ships themselves. The latter constitute a very specific and unusual form of asset which by their very nature encourages an extended degree of globalisation. This feature manifests itself perhaps more than any other way in the exploitation of its unique freedom for labour employment (UK Department of the Environment, Transport and the Regions, 1999). Thus shipping not only operates in a global, business environment, but also utilises that environment in its employment of global labour markets through the flexibility offered by the international market of ship registries.

THE EUROPEAN UNION CONTEXT

The European Union context for shipping is perhaps the best example of where these globalisation trends can be seen operating in the late twentieth century, and this book makes no apologies for using this context for many of its examples. This is not to say that the process of globalisation and shipping is not happening everywhere – by definition it must be or not at all as globalisation must be worldwide, however the EU market-place is undoubtedly at the forefront of the processes of globalised shipping and the inter-relationships between the global business environment and the shipping sector, and hence can be taken as both typical of today's trends and the likely developments elsewhere in the decades to come.

The EU Common Transport Policy (CTP) has made significant progress since the mid-1980s in parallel with further development of the EU in more general terms (Commission of the European Communities, 1995b). The key objective of the CTP is to ensure that the EU, currently as the world's largest trading bloc (and with the expansion due to take place in the early twenty-first century, for the foreseeable future), can continue to rely on efficient and safe transport services. This objective has led to the development of a series of specific policies to cover each sector of the transport industry where action at the European level is most appropriate. These EU policies have inevitably had to incorporate both the impact of globalisation on the shipping industry and the effects of the shipping industry on globalisation itself.

In the maritime sector, the CTP aims to ensure that EU ship-owners operate on a world market without significant barriers and disadvantages – it is consequently global in nature, character, form and content. It also aims to 'promote the competitive position of Community ship-owners, the employment and skills of Community seafarers, safety at sea, and to safeguard the marine environment' (Coleman, 2000).

For many years at the end of the twentieth century, shipping and the international business environment in which it has to work, is presently characterised by excess capacity. This is particularly the case in the liner sector but evidence of this global over-capacity is also apparent in the bulk and ferry sectors. This implies that there is commonly intense competition on the supply-side, and also a tendency towards strong bargaining power on the demand side. Eventually, the inevitable consequence is a downward pressure on the price level for services with a series of knock-on effects, not least of which is the need to constrain costs by adopting certain global policies towards labour, bunkering, construction and other globally available services. The cost structure of shipping companies is thus crucial in remaining competitive. However, in the EU, this cost structure is strongly influenced by factors that are beyond the control of the shipping companies themselves and commonly are only affected to a substantial extent by the policies of states to which the shipping companies may be associated. Thus shipping policy within the EU is a major factor in the inter-relationship between the shipping industry and the global markets for their services and the services they use. These complex inter-relationships are also affected considerably by government attitudes to the industry and its markets and the institutional framework that exists. European Union countries are characterised by a high standard of living compared with the world average, even with the entry of East European states in the coming years and extensive (and expensive) social security systems. As a result, both the high net wages and social security payments that contribute to a strong disadvantage in labour and social costs for European based ship-owners, compare unfavourably with those costs which derive from non-European (usually Third World) countries or from disinvestment from the EU area to lower cost locations – much of which is more possible in the shipping industry than any other.

The trend to flag out (in other words to register ships owned in the EU to flags outside of the EU with lower labour and social costs) and in addition, the threat of the loss of maritime activities through management relocation, have stimulated European governments to reconsider their shipping policies (Van der Linden, 2001). The Netherlands and UK initiatives, for example, have proven to be partly successful in halting the trend towards higher costs, particularly after the introduction of a series of tonnage tax regimes in the EU which in effect provide an indirect subsidy to EU based ship-owners whilst allowing these same companies to benefit from global rates of labour and social costs (rather than those currently operating in the EU). These trends will be discussed in more detail within the European shipping policy context in later chapters, but for now need to be noted as a major trend within the industry. The main characteristic of the maritime industry is that it operates in a global environment and is consequently put under permanent competitive pressure from low-cost Open Registers – that is those located outside the traditional register regime. This has created an extremely mobile industry (perhaps the most mobile of all industries) able to avoid many of the requirements and controls (and consequently high costs) by registering vessels in other countries (Coleman, 2000).

NEO-FORDISM AND POST-FORDISM IN SHIPPING

Linked to the discussion above, this book will go on to examine models of shipping development and activity which provide a convenient and useful basis for examining and understanding shipping at the turn of the millennium. In particular, aspects of neo-Fordism and post-Fordism as applied to international shipping will also be examined as these models provide an analysis of the structure which underlies the trends towards the globalised economy. As such, they can help us to understand the tensions that have begun to arise between national policy-making and that of supra-national and international policy-making, typified by that between EU member states and the EU itself. This is particularly evident within the shipping industry where the nature of the business, as we have seen above, is inherently mobile and global, therefore making policy application more difficult in an effective way.

National shipping policies, as a result, may conflict with those at other levels in an environment where application and enforcement is near impossible and certainly very difficult. In later chapters, it will be clear that the globalising world economy is characterised by two partly contradictory tendencies. On the one hand we can identify neo-Fordist development, characterised by the principle of *comparative advantage* of lowest possible input costs – in shipping, typified by the advent of flags of convenience – which emerged intensively during the 1970s. This process of neo-Fordism was largely made possible by developments in transportation and communication technologies and was eventually promoted even further by liberalisation and deregulation of international trade and financial markets (Asheim, 2001).

On the other hand, the post-Fordist tendency is largely observed as currently a growing force within the world economy, inevitably affecting the shipping industry. post-Fordism development is also characterised by increasing global competition but is derived from the far more dynamic principle of *competitive advantage*, focusing on:

'making more productive use of inputs, which requires continual innovation' (Porter, 1998).

It is both obvious and accepted widely that all maritime regulations must be considered in an international context, because of the very international nature of shipping itself. However, in terms of the establishment of the Single European Market (SEM) for example, the EU had initially addressed shipping issues from a very narrow regional point of view and continued to do so for a number of years as the end of the millennium approached. However, the EU maritime strategy that emerged in the mid-1990s began to recognise the international character of shipping and many pending regulatory proposals from the European Commission were consequently withdrawn in the light of this recognition of a flawed strategy for the industry which was likely to lead to its demise within the EU (Danish Shipowners' Association, 2001). Despite this, there have been recent attempts to revert to traditional (pre-1995) thinking in Brussels, which are causing concern in the shipping industry, and it has often been the case that EU proposals have resulted in increasing and considerable worries among both senior business figures and civil servants who attempted to criticise:

'the increasing centralisation of power in Europe' (Lloyd's List, 2001dddd).

The shipping industry more generally is central to world trade, carrying as it does approximately 90% of international trade. It also has a long history and experience of both national and international regulation and as such it is paramount that policy-makers recognise and understand the complexities that exist within this area (Alderton and Winchester, 2002b). The neo and post-Fordist models can help to understand these processes and clarify the issues.

The following chapters signify an attempt to present and examine some of the core aspects of the globalised shipping arena, the extent to which global tendencies percolate down to the level of the national governments and affect the formation of shipping policies, both at national and supra/international level, using developments within the EU as a prime example. The following chapter goes on firstly to look at the development of shipping policy in general, as a background to the more detailed and up-to-date study that follows.

3. An Overview of National Shipping Policies – History and Development

INTRODUCTION

We shall begin with a West African proverb:

'Rain does not fall on one roof alone.'

Indeed, global economic changes are heavily inter-related and shipping is one of the main driving forces which lie behind this complex arrangement and interaction that inevitably occurs.

Shipping is an industry which of necessity, operates on an international basis, selling its services worldwide, as well as 'buying' factors of production, such as insurance, fuel and the ships themselves, on a world market (Goss, 1987). In practice, shipping is extremely sensitive to the widely recognised cyclical fluctuations of world trade, the effects of which are transmitted to shipping and shipbuilding, often with highly beneficial or disastrous consequences (Cafruny, 1987).

Shipping, of all industries, can be viewed as indeed perhaps the most international of all. Several factors contribute to this situation which have been identified by many authors: ship-owners are spread all over the world and although there are well known concentrations in London, Piraeus, Oslo and. elsewhere, they can in fact be found almost everywhere; shipping companies vary considerably both in size and in type of operation and their international activities drive this variation; and there is no clear and well defined controlling mechanism as far as demand and supply are concerned (Paixao and Marlow, 2001). In addition, as we have seen already, the great array of ancillary (but vitally necessary) activities typified by shipbroking, freight forwarding, bunkering, agents, financing and legal support, are also international businesses commonly far removed from the ships or their owners. Thus a Greek owned vessel may well be financed in New York, insured in London, flagged in Cyprus, bunkered in the Baltic, with agents in each port it visits and a multinational crew from the Philippines and Korea.

No other industry approaches the international characteristics and problems that this implies.

For most traditional maritime nations such as Greece, the UK, Norway and the USA, shipping was characterised (and still commonly is) by government attempts to provide the necessary legislation and resources to safeguard the stability and progress of their nationally flagged and owned fleets. Such attempts have in general focused on the expansion of the domestic registered fleet and its capability in fulfilling the nation's commercial, economic, strategic, political and international obligations (McConville, 1999). Furthermore, most traditional flags, such as those of the UK and other EU countries, and the respective trades unions and governments, have generally attempted to ensure that most of the crew working on domestically flagged vessels usually have much the same nationality as the ship (Goss, 1987). This may not be for economic or even safety/environmental reasons, but often for political or commonly traditional objectives. As the historical development of these flagging policies of governments is closely related to the present domestic policy outcomes, the following sections will attempt to trace these policy developments from the earliest days. From there it will be possible to understand better the position that shipping policy finds itself in today.

THE KEY ASPECTS OF SHIPPING POLICY – AN HISTORICAL VIEW

The Freedom of the Seas Concept

During the period of exploration and expansion which characterised developments in the fifteenth and sixteenth centuries, emphasis was placed not only upon the development of private commercial law as applied to trade and the shipping sector but, more particularly, upon the development of the 'public law concept' which suggested that along with commerce and trade went issues relating to the ownership of the seas (Farthing, 1987).

Indeed, when at that time, the Spanish complained to Elizabeth I of England about violations of the Spanish *mare clausum* ('closed seas'), the English authorities replied that it was:

'contrary to the law of the nations'

to forbid the British from trading in these regions since:

'The use of the sea and the air is common to all: neither can any title to the ocean belong to any people or private man.'

According to Farthing (1987), the statement quoted above must be regarded as one of the first which recorded the principle of the freedom of the seas, although he continues that at that time it was no more than a unilateral declaration by a sovereign state, rather than a more broadly accepted policy as such. However, the principle was to become the foundation of many policy measures for the future in the maritime sector.

Freedom of the Seas – The Conflict Between Shipping Liberalism and Interventionism

The sixteenth and seventeenth centuries will be remembered as the post-mercantilist period in Europe and will always be associated with the Dutch commentator Grotius. During this period, a number of European traditional maritime nations developed a strong presence in shipping and trade for the first time and the prospect of not embracing free trade and freedom of the seas would have limited their further growth (Odeke, 1984).

At the end of the sixteenth century, the freedom to navigate the oceans was far from universally accepted, and in many cases not even formulated in any specific way. However, in the sixteenth and seventeenth centuries, there was the clear rise of Dutch maritime interests, and a sizeable increase in the strong presence of the Dutch as a major commercial, trading and maritime nation (Farthing, 1987). At the same time, the English (later British with the incorporation of Scotland from 1707) continued to create new regimes suiting the requirements of their own trade and shipping industries (Cafruny, 1987).

The Navigation Acts of the United Kingdom, which had been used to protect and promote British shipping for nearly three hundred years, were repealed, accompanied by the substantial development of British capitalism. As a consequence, there was no longer a need for restrictions on trading by any nation and there followed the growth of a tendency towards the free trade principle.

This movement towards the acceptance of the 'freedom of the seas' principle more widely was highlighted in a legal form by the Dutch philosopher Grotius who emphasised that:

'navigation was free to all, no country could lay claim to the seas on the basis that their navigators were the first to sail on it' (Farthing, 1987).

The Need for Maritime Power

Odeke (1984) observes that there is a distinct role of the freedom of the high seas doctrine which can be explained by the so-called 'laisser-faire' attitude of the traditional maritime nations (TMN). In particular, the principle is characterised by commercial implications and should have the result of producing more than satisfactory results for *all* parties, provided that both the buyers and sellers in the market have roughly equal bargaining power.

On the other hand, he continues that in a political sense, the doctrine of the freedom of the high seas is quite different. The real freedom of the high seas principle is emphasised as the right of all commercial vessels assuming their lawful and peaceful origins, to sail the high seas and enter territorial waters:

'without let or hindrance, and to find a safe harbour in case of trouble.'

In other words, the principle implies that perfect conditions of equality exist and includes:

'...the rights of all nations, developed or developing, to establish and/or develop, national merchant marine fleets of their own, irrespective of their means' (Odeke, 1984).

Whilst this statement is one that largely relates to economic objectives, expressly associated with the laisser-faire doctrine, the 'political' freedom of the sea is at least in theory, a real freedom. In practice, and that means effectively in commercial terms, it is nothing more than the freedom to exploit the resources that are represented by the oceans rather than being some higher ideal relating to the principles of liberty, communal ownership and generosity (Odeke, 1984).

The initial development of the freedom of the seas principle was not aimed at contributing to the creation of a liberal strategy in shipping, but rather to promote the self-interests of the traditional maritime nations of the time. However, one effect of its development was to highlight the major importance of liberal strategies in the shipping and international trade sector and to introduce a new range of ideas and perspectives for the maritime sector in the coming period.

The Wave of Shipping Liberalism

The immediate result was the wave of shipping liberalism that characterised the last two decades of the nineteenth century. However, political and economic forces which developed within the same period were to lead to the downfall of the laisser-faire regime and introduce a new phase of international political economy. This new phase was important due to two main factors related to political and economic trends of the time and the immediate years to come:

1. The intensification of international rivalry, characterised by expansionist colonial policies and efforts to end British dominance.
2. The increasing concentration of capital, both nationally and trans-nationally, combined with the greatly enlarged role of the state in economic affairs (Cafruny, 1987).

Liberalism in a Non-Liberal Framework; Modern Capitalism and State Intervention in Shipping

Between 1880 and the late twentieth century, the trend towards shipping liberalism was transformed into one that was characterised by the increasing formation of cartel arrangements and the extended role of state intervention (Odeke, 1984).

The tendency towards concentration of ownership and the intensification of international rivalry that was outlined earlier, had both significant and direct impact upon shipping and related shipping policies. Political reasons, such as the maritime rivalry that existed between the UK and Germany during the late nineteenth and early twentieth centuries, led some traditional maritime nations to attempt to develop closer relations between domestic export firms and ship-owners. An example of these attempts is the one made by the German government which, in an effort to strengthen its national shipping industry, facilitated mergers and promoted cargo-reservation schemes, including the reservation of human cargo (Cafruny, 1987). Whereas cartel arrangements and their way of functioning is, even today, a matter of debate, they were not considered to be a breach of the freedom of the seas as they could serve in achieving economies of scale. On the other hand, cargo reservation as well as flag preference schemes can commonly be seen as an erasure of laissez-faire due to their restrictive and protectionist character

Although the post-World War II period appeared to contain some degree of liberalism within the international trading community including the shipping sector, the level of truly free trade was undoubtedly rather limited. Commentators at the time put this down to the intense need for the restructuring of national fleets which led to support measures and other protectionist measures used to prevent serious damage to the fleets.

These trends led, in turn, to a tendency towards an intensification of shipping subsidies and the deliberate development of national fleets. These subsidies were not always as clear and simple as they were sometimes made to sound but from an economic perspective, a subsidy is:

'a payment to individuals or businesses by a government for which it receives no products or services in return' (Odeke, 1984).

In absolute terms, the purpose of aid of this sort would be to maintain a *specific* industry – in this case shipping – at a cost that society:

'...can readily afford but that cannot otherwise be profitably supplied at this price' (Odeke, 1984).

The important assumption is normally, however, that the industry to which the aid/subsidy is to be provided should be defined as vital to the public welfare and/or national interest. Otherwise the free market should be allowed to prevail.

Subsidies can be either provided directly or indirectly. Direct or indirect subsidies in the shipping sector have been a traditional way of government intervention, especially since World War II. In this respect, direct aid to shipping would include the subsidy of coastal or island services or ship construction subsidies given by the traditional maritime countries in order to protect their national shipbuilding industries from intense competition abroad. Indirect subsidies, which are given by a number of countries, would mainly include cheap loans and accelerated depreciated provisions although a range of other fiscal incentives and supports can be envisaged and as we shall see in later sections, have been used in increasing amounts (Sturmey, 1962).

Under the definition noted earlier, of what can be considered to be a subsidy, falls any form of financial aid or fiscal relief directed towards the shipping industry. The main reasons given for the application of such types of fiscal benefits to national shipping were the perception of national governments that there was an essential need for the maintenance, establishment and development of domestic merchant fleets in the context of intense pressure from other fleets worldwide. Financial aid was thus normally considered to be a tool to assist in sustaining the prosperity of what was viewed as a vital national, maritime industry. Its success was measured as being the relief of the industry's financial problems commonly through lowering high operating costs, such as labour costs or making more readily available, access to cheap capital. However, the full range of shipping subsidy types is both highly varied and extensive.

Although nowadays, both operational and construction subsidies would be characterised as being direct, and cargo preference as a form of flag discrimination, for many years they were all classified as just subsidies (Odeke, 1984). As Sturmey (1982) observes, subsidies were then considered as:

'...the lesser evil forms of intervention; they do not directly impose trade barriers, their effects are most easily gauged, and they discriminate equally against all foreign ship-owners. Whether direct or indirect in form, subsidy levels constitute an easily quantifiable form of government intervention in shipping.'

The Position Between the Early 1950s and the Mid-1960s

So far, the discussion has examined some of the major turning points that the shipping industry has experienced from the period when discovery and colonisation were the main drives for the establishment of merchant fleets and the industrialisation of shipping, up until the period after World War II, where the needs of the shipping industry were increasingly realised by national governments with all the interventionist measures that this realisation suggested. The post-World War II period could be said to be particularly important for the domestic shipping industries of the world, especially due to the increased nationalist tendencies that grew within the sector during that period and which, in turn, led to protectionist practices and policies, increasingly until the late 1950s and into the 1960s (Sturmey, 1975).

However, assessing whether and to what extent discriminatory practices were successful for the establishment and growth of national fleets is not the main purpose of this study. On the one hand, they might have led to the maintenance of national fleets and safeguarded national employment to a certain extent, but on the other they may have encouraged the continuation of an inappropriate system of transport provided by an expensive and inefficient domestic supplier. It is, however, the purpose of this book to examine the future of shipping policy in the light of trends towards globalisation rather than whether a system of support through national policies has been or could be effective.

Over the years, various reasons and arguments have been expressed in order to defend or encourage the development of national shipping policies and their natural tendency towards fleet support. Quite obviously, it is uncommon (if not unheard of) to find national policies that are aimed at dissolving national fleets and thus we are largely safe to equate national policies with some sort of intervention on behalf of the domestic fleet. Meanwhile international and supra-national policies may well take a much broader viewpoint in that they are attempting not to artificially support a domestic flag but to achieve the much more sizeable aims of efficiency, and a safe and clean industry.

A review of the incentives which are considered to be the main features behind the continued development of national shipping policies has been presented by Goss and Marlow (1993; quoted in Sletmo, 2001). Some of the reasons given for the maintenance of a national shipping policy in the light of global trends and developments include the protection of an infant industry (in the sense that 'young' industries require protection at an early stage if they are to survive to compete), contribution to the national balance of payments, defence reasons and the need for a maritime policy that aims to highlight the nation's presence internationally and assure its participation in international policy decisions (Sletmo, 2001). Nevertheless, it is widely agreed by those outside the national policy-making institutions that the main consideration of a national shipping policy should be that shipping is an industry with origins based on free trade and that protectionist policies will only serve in damaging its liberal and global nature.

Sturmey (1975) provides the following definition of a national shipping policy:

'A nation may be said to have a shipping policy when it encourages, permits, or formulates measures to interfere with or control the free play of market forces in regard to the employment of shipping. The interference or control may extend from *ad hoc* measures to a carefully planned and continuous policy.'

This process of domestic interference was common in the mid-1960s but was a result not so much of the threat to domestic fleets but more in terms of a blinkered view by policy-makers that fleets merited support as representatives of a nation's status. With the rise of flags of convenience which was just about to take place, the incentive moved from one of fleet promotion to fleet survival.

A NEW ERA IN THE INTERNATIONALISATION OF SHIPPING – FLAGS OF CONVENIENCE

The gradual development of a global environment for trade has been well documented and will not be repeated here. In the shipping sector, perhaps the most obvious manifestation of the globalised trends occurred with the dynamic growth of flags of convenience (or more formally termed Open Registries) from the 1960s onwards. This is not to ignore the importance of internationalisation in the shipbroking legal, financial and other aspects of the industry but it is the emergence and subsequent dynamic growth of Open Registries that typifies these trends.

There has long been a tradition that the *law* of the sea has been grounded in the notion of the freedom of the high seas (Alderton and Winchester, 2002b). This freedom has historically, three underlying principles:

- a ship of any nation can navigate the oceans freely;

- the ship's national state has exclusive rights over the ship; and
- no other nation can exercise dominion over that ship.

Freedom is thus the dominant, guiding principle of the law of the sea. However, the United Nations Convention of the Law of the Sea (UNCLOS, 2001) recognises that each state has a right to establish the conditions for the granting of its nationality to ships, including that:

'regulations covering these conditions would address administrative, technical and social policy matters, including the seaworthiness of the vessels and the manning and training of crews' (OECD, 2002).

Changing a vessel's registry from a national to an Open Registry flag has long been a worldwide phenomenon (Haralambides and Yang, 2003). The earliest examples of such a phenomenon were usually where the decision to re-flag was taken for political or military reasons, whilst the more recent examples are much more likely to be on economic grounds (reduced taxation, simplified administration and cheaper labour costs in particular) and reflect the globalised nature of an industry which can effectively choose any country in which it wishes to register its assets whilst remaining formally (and financially) located elsewhere. However, it is only between 1918-1939 (i.e. the period between the two world wars) that a number of nations specifically developed as 'Open' Registers, in other words states that would accept the registration of vessels from any other nation with almost no restrictions.

The use of Open Registries or flags of convenience actually dates back to 1922 when the USA took the initiative to allow registration of US ships in Panama (Haralambides and Yang, 2003). In this period, a treaty between the USA and Panama exempted shipping profits from taxation and this, combined with laws that had, up to that time, raised labour costs in the USA, gave further incentives to US owners of ships to flag to Panama. The first European ships were also re-flagged to Panama during the same period and by 1939, the Panamanian register was already characterised as 'convenient' in shipping circles. However, the actual term 'flags of convenience' was not used until the early 1950s, following on from the ITF (International Transport Workers' Federation) Campaign Against Flags of Convenience at its 1948 World Congress in Oslo, Norway (Alderton and Winchester, 2002b). In particular, the ITF regarded and continues to regard flags of convenience as ones:

'where the nationality of the owner is different from the country of registration'.

In this way, any vessel can be declared registered with a flag of convenience, regardless of the flag chosen or its characteristics, if the nationality of the owner is different from the flag flown by the vessel (Dickinson, 2001). Registries have been declared as flags of convenience on the basis of the Rochdale criteria from The Committee of Inquiry into British Shipping (Rochdale Committee, 1970), some of them being:

- The register is open. Anybody can own a vessel on the register.
- Entry and exit from the register is easy.
- There are low or no taxes on shipping.
- The country does not need the tonnage, that is there is no essential domestic need for that register.

Crewing by non-nationals is freely permitted and there is no infrastructure or political will to enforce the national or international standards that have been adopted or prescribed. This is a very strict interpretation of Open Registries and more commonly, they are defined in terms of safety record or their administration as well as the degree of separation between ownership and country of registration.

UNCLOS (2001) (as well as the earlier 1958 Convention on the High Seas), which was mentioned earlier, gave great weight to the idea of a 'genuine link' between the ship and the flag of the vessel. However this genuine link is not accurately defined and this has allowed, if not encouraged, various interpretations of these links to prevail. One interpretation is that:

' . . . the link can be purely economic, rather than social or national, naturally preparing the ground for the further growth of Open Registers, since these can issue flag registration on the payment of a fee. In this sense, the genuine link is reduced to one of client and service provider, leaving the associated obligations of the flag state highly questionable' (OECD, 2002).

The last 50 years or so have seen the evolution and growth of the flag of convenience system, to the extent that, by January 2001, 46.5% of the world fleet was registered under an Open Registry flag. In Figure 3.1, Panama appears to be the most popular shipping register, with all top four countries (Liberia, Bahamas, Malta and Cyprus) at the beginning of 2001 being flags of convenience. Greece, although not a flag of convenience, also appears in the top five registration flags, with a 6% registered fleet, similar to Malta.

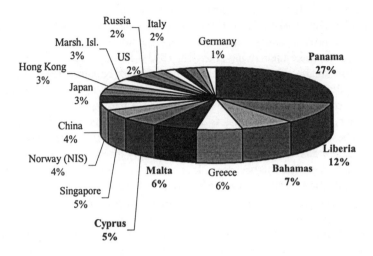

Source: Lloyd's Register of Shipping (2002) *World Fleet Statistics 2001*, Annual Report, p.10.

Figure 3.1: Merchant Fleets of the World by Registration

Flags of Convenience and Employment Implications

As we noted in an earlier section, Open Registries owe a considerable part of their increased widespread popularity in the later decades of the twentieth century to the relatively simple regulation process and the fact that they charge low or no corporate taxes. Nevertheless, an additional factor that makes these countries attractive in vessel registration is that there are also no restrictions on the hiring of crews in terms of their nationality (and therefore in terms of their cost). Thus ship-owners can easily hire crews of *any* nation they choose, opening up the market to one that is intensely global and shifting the balance of choice away from national issues associated with registries to one of international comparative cost. Thus these flags of convenience have increasingly expanded recruitment into Third World countries, particularly in their search for cheap labour. India, the Philippines, South Korea and Indonesia represent today's major suppliers of seafarers to these vessels. This has led to the creation of a large number of crewing agencies that have gone into business by supplying low-cost labour to operators of these vessels. Of these, the Philippines have become the greatest supplier of world maritime labour.

The employment implications that arise from the operation of flag of convenience vessels are related to the extent to which the crew of the ship is protected by legal jurisdiction, the recourse they have if their employment agreement is broken, as well as the on-board conditions within which these people have to make their living (Forsyth, 1993). This is partially a result of lower union membership levels than those of their counterparts from the more developed nations. However, a generalisation of Open Registry conditions should be made with care since there are many internal differences that appear within Open Registers themselves (Alderton and Winchester, 2002a). These factors have become central to the ship registration issue. The shipping sector has, as a result, become increasingly globalised in the process as national registration becomes less attractive and the market for international labour easier (and more beneficial) to enter.

It is widely recognised that since its first appearance, this process of flagging-out (i.e. the change of a ship's registry from a national flag to an Open Register) has been an important focus of debate in international shipping circles (Bergantino and Marlow, 1998). Figure 3.2 shows that by 1st January 2002, the foreign flag share for selected maritime nations had increased dramatically, especially in countries such as Japan, Greece, Germany and Norway, although the reverse effects can be observed for nations like Hong Kong and the UK. Thus shipping had become even more globalised and further detached from the shipping policies of any particular nation.

The rapid increase in this trend, especially during the 1970s, continued through the 1980s and from 1998 the fleet of the major flag of convenience countries surpassed that of the traditional maritime countries for the first time. By growing flag of convenience fleets we mainly refer to the top eight Open Registry flags, namely Liberia, Panama, Bahamas, Cyprus, Malta, Saint Vincent, Bermuda and Cayman Islands, of which the major ones included only Liberia, Panama, Bahamas and Cyprus (Institute of Shipping Economics and Logistics, 2002). The emergence of this extensive network of Open Registry fleets and their impact upon the national and traditional maritime nations and their respective shipping policies has been drawn to the attention of the industry for a variety of reasons. Firstly, Open Registry fleets have grown at a faster rate than any other fleets in the world. Secondly, there is a general belief that the expansion of these registries has limited the growth of the fleets in other traditional maritime countries, and has caused the decline of these fleets, with associated consequences for national defence, balance of payments and the growing decline of national trained crews. Finally, the occurrence of several incidents involving environmental disasters in recent years has largely increased public awareness of the flag of convenience issue (Bergantino and Marlow, 1998).

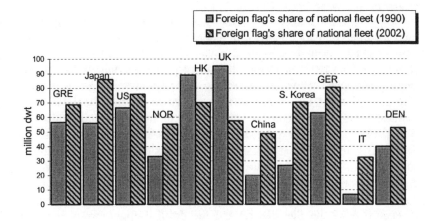

Sources: Data for 1990: Sletmo, G.K. and Holste, S. (1993) Shipping and the competitive advantage of nations, *Maritime Policy and Management*, 20, 3, 243-255 and UNCTAD (1991) *Review of Maritime Transport 1990* (New York: United Nations), Table 5, p.12.
Data for 2002: Institute of Shipping Economics and Logistics (2002) *SSMR Market Analysis 2002: Ownership and Patterns of the World Merchant Fleet*, University of Bremen: ISL.

Figure 3.2: The Role of Flagging-Out in Selected Maritime Nations. Comparative Statistics 1990-2002

CONCLUSIONS

What can be drawn from the analysis that has been undertaken so far with regards to the evolution and development of shipping policy and in particular the recent growth in Open Registers? Perhaps it is the intense need of ship-owners to work towards cost minimisation and thus exploitation of the cost benefits that these registries can offer at almost the exclusion of any other issue. Clearly ship-owners and shipping companies are intensely interested in the financial consequences of their decisions (Marlow et al., 1997). It is important to recognise that these ship-owners have the freedom to choose the flag flown by their vessels for their own commercial reasons and that this choice will bring commercial benefits to the companies concerned in most cases – or otherwise they would not do it. However, there are also negative issues here, not only in terms of the results these decisions may have for national economies (and in particular for national fleets), but also in terms of the incentives and benefits given to the shipping sector by the national governments themselves in an attempt to reverse the ship-owner decisions (Alderton and Winchester, 2002b).

Despite these commercial trends, many people believe that nationally registered fleets are an important ambition and thus require national shipping policies to ensure they are retained in the context of Open Registry pressure (Gardner et al., 2001; McConville, 1999). Up until the late 1980s, national ship-owners, with vessels registered domestically (or with these ambitions), saw little prospect for change in the political or economic climate of the traditional maritime countries with regards to the ship registration issue (Eyre, 1989). However priorities and incentives, particularly within the European Union shipping sector, were about to change. Consequently we shall turn to the policies that have emerged with regards to flagging, efficiency, state support and fiscal incentives within the EU to examine the conflicts that exist between the globalised nature of international shipping (exemplified by the flag debate) and the detailed application and role of national shipping policies. How have these tensions between spatial levels been resolved (if at all) within the EU? However, firstly we must examine in some more detail the issues of policy-making in the shipping sector at different spatial levels to provide a conceptual background to the debate that follows.

4. International, Supra-national and National Shipping Policies[*]

INTRODUCTION

The international shipping industry is characterised by a number of very particular characteristics which make it unlike almost any other industrial or commercial sector. In particular it is intensely mobile – both in the physical sense in that the main items of infrastructure – the ships – can be transferred with relative ease to a very large number of world locations constrained only by size – and in terms of the capital which these items represent, which involves no physical movement of assets necessarily but does involve usually a transfer of ownership, registration or other features to whatever location makes most financial sense. These two characteristics are intrinsically tied together in that the capital mobility of shipping is enhanced by the physical mobility of the assets, which makes any sort of 'compulsory national association very difficult' (Roe, 2002) and as a consequence, the practical application of a national shipping policy at best a problem and at worst, impossible.

These two features of mobility that apply to the shipping sector are also fundamentally important when it comes to the issue of policy, how it is applied and whether it works, and in this chapter we shall be examining from where policy derives and in particular the relationship between shipping policies at different levels of imposition and origin – those at international, supra-national, national, regional and local levels. The issues of mobility which we have outlined above are one of the major features of the sector which drives shipping policy at each of these levels, although not to the exclusion of a large range of other factors which need to be incorporated in any analysis.

This chapter will also place the assessment of shipping policy in the context of the growth of globalisation as a broader concept and its close relations, foreign direct investment and strategic alliances/joint ventures as outlined in the work of Frankel (1999), Ryoo and Thanopoulou (1999),

---

[*] This chapter is derived from Roe (2002)

Thanopoulou (1995), Peters (2001), Randay (2001), Sletmo (2001) and Slack et al. (2002). These globalisation developments are trends which the shipping industry has experienced often before any other sector and which are typical of the complexities that surround policy relationships in the industry.

This chapter is structured into a number of related themes. The first outlines the development of assessments of shipping policy and evaluates the range of different studies that have taken place across the world and the common themes that have emerged from these studies.

The second part of this chapter develops a model for the main themes that underlie the emergence of shipping policy development at this time and which are most significant in directing the detailed shipping policy initiatives that have arisen in the late twentieth and which continue to emerge in the early twenty-first centuries. It also incorporates the development of a new shipping policy model that attempts to reflect all the influences that drive and direct policy-making at each level and which provides a novel analytical framework for the discussion that follows.

Using this new model, the third part attempts to introduce the concepts of spatial policy levels – those at the international, supra-national, national, regional and local level – and incorporates examples of policy activities which take place at each. Here, the specific problems which can be associated with developing effective and spatially inter-linked policies for the shipping community begin to become apparent, particularly in the context of tensions between national and international/supra-national policy initiatives.

Policy initiatives rely in any sector upon the role of interest groups – including for example, state and local government, the shipping and other related industries, shipping and other sectoral employees, pressure groups both in favour and against the sector, etc. – and shipping is clearly no exception. As a result, the fourth section looks at the role of interest groups using a model of interest group participation in policy development outlined by Aspinwall (1995) and other work by Lu (1999), and how these affect the inter-relationships between the spatial levels that we have identified.

The following part of this chapter takes the work by Ledger and Roe (1993) and analyses the contextual factors that have had an influence upon the shipping industry in the process of policy development. During the discussion a number of examples further illustrate the problems of maintaining consistency between shipping sector policies, particularly across the spatial levels outlined in an earlier chapter.

The final part of this chapter examines the development of globalisation and begins to look at how it has impacted upon shipping industry policies and their continued development. To be more specific, it attempts to focus upon the problems of reconciling linkages between the spatial levels of policy that exist and an industry that works outside many of the constraints that these policy levels might impose upon the sector.

A SPATIAL PERSPECTIVE TO SHIPPING POLICY

Shipping policy is a focus of interest that has been widely studied over the past decades, where attention has tended to concentrate upon a very large number of issues. These include ship and port subsidies, maritime safety, the maritime environment, seafarer and officer employment, taxation and the fiscal environment, inter-modalism and its impact on shipping and a very large number more. Here, the focus will be upon an examination of the spatial implications of shipping policy, as one of the key themes of this book remains the intense difficulties inherent in co-ordinating and making effective the different levels of policy-making that have been identified

One of the difficulties of attempting to provide a comprehensive assessment of shipping policy is that a wide interpretation of the concept would result in such substantial sources of material and breadth of discussion that little would be achieved towards the process of clarifying the issues and providing an analysis of policy as a whole or its component parts. The result is that the discussion in this chapter is focused deliberately upon the main publications which relate to specific spatial regimes. The regimes chosen have stemmed from those defined earlier in the book relating to international, supra-national and national boundaries. The discussion is deliberately limited with respect to the regional and local levels of influence if only because they would tend to generate too specific a discussion of policy implications which would not be useful here. However, the importance of policies generated and imposed at these lower levels of the spectrum should not be overlooked nor understated. They will be incorporated in the discussion further at a later stage in the text.

The research publications which are discussed in this section are not claimed to be exhaustive nor comprehensive, but they are indicative of a variety of the trends in spatial shipping policy that exist. The interested reader would be wise to read further using these sources as a first step, in any attempt to grasp the full sweep of shipping policy literature.

Issues central to international shipping policy-making have been thoroughly considered through many papers and over many years. The more significant works include those by Gold (1981) who discussed the international maritime sector in general, Schrier et al. (1985) covering liberalisation in shipping, Behnam (1994) with an extended consideration of the role of UNCTAD in the shipping sector, Moyer (1977) and his detailed work analysing the impact of shipping subsidies, Frankel's (1989, 1992 and

1999) works relating the sectors of shipping, logistics and ports, Yannopoulos (1989) and generic shipping policy issues, Odeke's (1984) highly considered work on protectionism and shipping, Li and Wonham's (2001) discussion of a variety of specific policy issues relating to safety, and the earlier seminal work by Goss (1982).

Meanwhile, examples of work which focus particularly upon shipping policy at the supra-national level can be found within the extensive discussion that has occurred concerning the involvement of the European Union in shipping policy including the important works by Bredima-Savopoulou and Tzoannos (1990), Wang (1993), Hart et al. (1993), Peeters et al. (1995) and Aspinwall (1995), and a number of others which tend to be briefer but remain significant including those by Van der Linden (2001) and Paixao and Marlow (2001). In addition, the impact of supra-national issues and the conflicts they stimulate at national level are discussed in detail in Brooks (2000) with particular reference to liner shipping policies and the difficult relationships that exist between the USA, Canada and the EU in this sector. There is also an extensive number of other publications which dwell on the specific nature of shipping policy at the EU level and the complexities of imposing such policies on nation state members who are often fairly ambivalent about co-operating with their senior partner. Aspinwall's (1995) work here is particularly significant as it considers the relationships between the various policy-making actors on the EU stage in the shipping sector including national governments, pressure groups, EU politicians and officers and the industry itself.

In Eastern Europe, the works by Ledger and Roe (1993, 1995) and Roe (1998) dominate the discussion of shipping policy in a context where there is no over-riding supra-national authority (unlike for example in Western Europe in, for example, the European Union – although this situation will change in 2004 with the planned accession of a number of Eastern European countries to the EU that year), but where regional commonalties are adequate to suggest that a supra-national consideration of policies and policy operationalisation is appropriate. Once again the problems of introducing a series of common-themed policies for the widely distressed shipping industries of Poland, Romania, Bulgaria, Ukraine, Russia, Estonia, Latvia and Lithuania in the light of common approaches to EU accession, in addition to the need to meet a set of widely applied rules and requirements of the EU, is clearly apparent.

This is particularly the case where national demands (and even regional and local ones within a country) conflict with the more over-riding needs and demands of a future supra-national authority. This is commonly the situation in Eastern Europe where the poor state of the national shipping industries contrasts severely with the protected status enjoyed up to 1989/1991.

Domestic help to these industries is often a political necessity at home but one which has no place within the soon to be imposed EU, supra-national, shipping policy framework.

Other neo-supra-national, shipping policy work is characterised by that of Hawkins and Gray (1999, 2000), Sun and Zhang (2000) and Hawkins (2001) for the Asia-Pacific region, which again lacks a supra-national shipping authority to give it coherence and even less so than East Europe, lacks the over-riding driving force of potential EU membership which acts to compel national policies to work with each other and at different levels. On the one hand this reduces the conflict between policy-making levels as there is no requirement to act in collaboration, but on the other hand the implied co-ordination that exists within the region has its own pressure effect that in turn can lead to conflict.

At a national shipping policy-making level, the quantity of published research is quite extensive and only a limited number of sources are noted here for a restricted number of (significant) countries. Clearly many others exist. In the context of UK policy, much research has been completed recently following the introduction of a new tonnage tax system for ships registered with the UK – an issue itself that raises conflicting views with respect to the harmonisation requirements of the EU (although the Commission has recently issued new guidelines for state support to the maritime sector which have made it quite clear that support of this type is acceptable under the Treaty of Rome). Relations with neighbouring countries and the international (for example through the effect upon flags of convenience) and regional (for example the employment) implications are also of significance here. Particularly notable publications include those by Brownrigg et al. (2001) and broader policy discussions can also be found in Colvin and Marks (1984), Gardner and Pettitt (1999a) and Gardner et al. (2001).

The breadth of discussion of shipping policies in a wide range of other countries is sizeable. For example, Poland receives detailed attention from Walenciak et al. (2001) and Wrona and Roe (2002); Taiwan from Lu (1999); Iran from Mimiran, (1994); the USA from Whitehurst (1983) and Sletmo and Williams (1981); Nigeria from Omosun (1987) and Nasiru (1994); Japan from Goto (1984); Turkey from Yercan (1999), Yercan and Roe (1999) and Barla et al. (2001); China from Flynn (1999), Sun and Zhang (1999) and Lee et al. (2002); and Korea from Kokuryo (1985), Lee (1996, 1999) and Song et al. (2001). There are many others from many countries of the world, which emphasise the overall significance of the national level of policy-making that exists for shipping, and its importance in relationship to other spatial levels that have been identified earlier, in particular its role in formulating and driving policy at the international and supra-national level.

Significant Factors that Impact upon Shipping Policy

Hoyle and Knowles (1998) provide a substantive basis with which to analyse the generic factors that underlie the emergence of overall transport policy at the beginning of the twenty-first century. It is convenient to use these factors as a framework to help to understand the development of shipping policy as part of this process throughout the world. From there it will be possible to go on and look at the development of shipping policy at the different spatial levels that exist before attempting to analyse the problems that manifest themselves when linking these policy levels together. These linkages are essential in ensuring that the policy framework as a whole works efficiently and effectively and as noted in the introductory paragraph to this chapter, the connections between shipping policy levels are where the greatest stresses occur in applying policy within any spatial context.

The work of Hoyle and Knowles (1998) was directed in particular at understanding and illustrating transport activity from a spatial perspective and for this reason is particularly suited to the discussion here. However, it is important to make clear that they were not considering policy-making and its application, nor the shipping sector in any specific way. During the discussion, they identified five factors that we can apply to the shipping sector and the emergence of policy within it. These are discussed in some detail in the next section.

The Factors Driving Shipping Policy

The issues governing the emergence of shipping policy can be summarised as follows:

1. *An historical perspective* – the shipping sector is, in part at least, directed by its past, either the immediate past or by events and issues which occurred further back in time. Thus traditional trading routes (for example the North Atlantic liner route or the Gulf-Far East crude oil trade), the location of port facilities (for example Rotterdam, Hamburg and Genoa) and the existence of historical maritime seats of power (for example London, Piraeus and New York) are all established features of the shipping market-place. Any policy development in the sector has to take the existence of these features into account. This does not mean that new trade routes, new ports or new maritime powers do not or cannot emerge – take North Sea oil, the Port of Fos/Marseilles and the rise of China as a maritime force as examples – however the established and existing network of trade patterns, centres of port activity and centres of

power are heavily influential. Successful maritime policies have no choice but to accept that these influences exist and that policy will also tend to emerge most powerfully and frequently from the myriad of locations associated with them.

2.   *Nodes, networks and systems* – the maritime sector is essentially characterised by a combination of nodes (ports), networks (trading routes) and systems (the organisation and infrastructure that connects the other two features together – including communications, financial agreements, a legal framework, shipbrokers, freight forwarders, brokers etc.). Policy-making ultimately is about organising and directing these three items and the environment that it creates within which each has to operate. This environment might be characterised by encouragement for the activity concerned to take place in a certain location, for a particular trade or for this activity to take place at a certain time (for example favourable tax regimes in EU member states for shipping including tonnage tax systems), or to control unwanted activity (for example the control of sub-standard environmental or safety practices). Policy-makers need to understand the series of inter-linkages that commonly exist if the policies they create are to be specific, meaningful and to achieve largely what they are specifically aimed to do.

3.   *Modal choice, intermodalism and flexibility* – the shipping industry takes place within a highly competitive commercial environment, not just characterising the industry itself but also in terms of competition with other modes. Within Europe, short-sea shipping faces severe and intense competition from trucking services which operate across the whole continent and are based throughout most countries, whilst even international rail freight services are increasingly competitive as developments in East European rail infrastructure continue to be introduced and new investments such as the Channel Tunnel and the Oresund link become fully operational. Shipping policy-makers need to understand the increasing choices available to shippers which places shipping in a new commercial environment throughout Europe – and also incidentally elsewhere in the world where the protected markets that used to commonly exist for the maritime sector have now largely dissolved. In addition, within Europe, the concept of intermodalism continues to expand and develop, with the prolonged support of the EU, so that shipping is now commonly seen as one link within a complex and extensive intermodal chain – including trucks and trailers on ferries, rail ferry operations, containerised services and the multitude of specialist

facilities needed to ensure an adequate inter-linkage. Policy-making in shipping has much to do here to ensure that developments are co-ordinated and that the shipping industry plays its full role within the overall transport system.

4.   *Deregulation and privatisation* – both deregulation (the reduction or removal of state control and influence and the consequent tendency towards reduced bureaucracy and increased freedom of commercial activity) and privatisation (the partial or complete transfer of ownership from the state to the private sector) have been major trends worldwide in many economic sectors for some years now. Shipping has been no exception to this trend and there is clear evidence that the process continues unabated. The substantial developments in deregulation (especially in ports but also in the organisation of the maritime sector) and privatisation (of state-owned ship-owners, brokers, freight forwarders, port industries and the like) in East Europe have provided many examples of both trends (Ledger and Roe, 1993). Elsewhere the privatisation of ports, state shipping companies and ancillary activities coupled with the attempts by (for example) the EU to reduce state interference through relaxing cabotage rules and reducing/controlling state subsidies have been quite clearly apparent. Shipping policies have reflected these trends since the early 1980s and it appears, will continue to do so. Rather curiously, in a number of other ways, the need for tighter safety and environmental controls in the shipping sector and the desire to see reduced state interference has raised government involvement in policing the industry's activities. The state now though has the role of ensuring that within the new liberalised and deregulated market, standards of safety, the environment and commercial honesty are maintained despite the removal of authorities and owners, one of whose main functions was to sustain these standards under the old regulated regimes.

5.   *Holism* – shipping policies need to recognise that shipping is part of a much wider human activity that is very closely linked with a large multitude of other economic, social, political and technological developments that both influence the shipping sector and are heavily influenced by it. Thus shipping policy-makers have to understand that (for example) changes in financial policy in the EU or in the political context for the US Federal Maritime Commission (FMC) will have a substantial impact upon the shipping investment and operational climate and probably necessitate these factors being incorporated into the shipping policy formulation process. Shipping is an holistic activity that cannot be separated out from the

complexity of the real world – but this, in turn, makes policy-making both difficult and at times, very slow.

Shipping Policy and the Identification of Spatial Levels of Both Origin and Implementation

Policy in the shipping sector both emerges and is applied within the industry at a wide variety of spatial levels. These have been noted earlier in this chapter and are summarised in Figure 4.1, which attempts to indicate the main features of the shipping policy framework and the factors which influence those policies that emerge along with the players involved in its development. These spatial features can be divided into five levels forming a distinct hierarchy. This, in many ways, is simply a convenience as in the real commercial world there remains considerable overlap and confusion between them – but at the same time, there are undoubtedly clear distinguishing features of each which are significant for the process of policy derivation and implementation and which have their own distinctive impact. These differing spatial policy levels and the problems that emerge of co-ordinating and making consistent the policy initiatives across and between them, is the core theme of this chapter and has been identified as a highly significant issue in earlier work by Cafruny (1985, 1987, 1991) and Aspinwall (1995), amongst others. The following discussion focuses on the relationships between these levels and the difficulties that this can sometimes present to the policy-maker and to the industry itself.

At the apex of the hierarchy of spatial levels there are *international policies* which are derived by a number of international shipping-related organisations which should, at least in theory, provide an overarching structure for the policies derived at lower, spatial levels. Within the shipping sector, significant international policy-making institutions include the United Nations International Maritime Organisation (IMO), responsible amongst others for policies towards safety and the environment in shipping generally, and the Organisation for Economic Co-operation and Development (OECD), which is made up of representatives of the developed countries of the world and which is active particularly in shipbuilding policy worldwide (although it also concerns itself with liner shipping competitiveness).

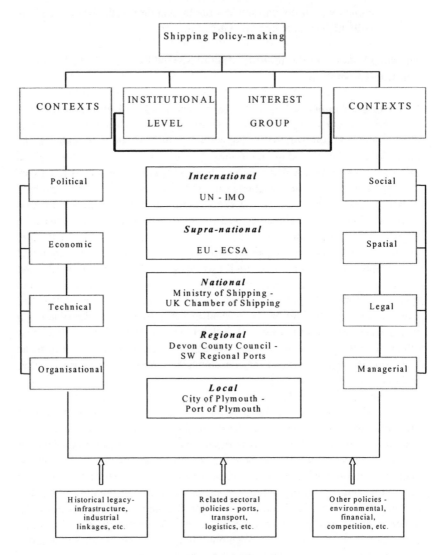

Figure 4.1: The Context for Shipping Policy-making

In each case, there is no legal requirement for countries (and therefore the industry itself) to abide by the policies which have been derived, and no powers of law-making rest with these organisations. However, at the same time, membership by individual (and powerful) nations is very extensive and its continuation (and that of sustaining an international reputation) requires that these international policies and recommendations are followed. Hence in terms of influence they are highly significant organisations.

The policy framework at the international level provides the broader agenda for what emerges at the next level – *supra-national* – typified by the activities of the EU. This organisation generates shipping policies that are applied to all member states, backed up by laws that are normally superior to national (member state) legislation where there is any conflict (Brooks and Button, 1992; Kiriazidis and Tzanidakis, 1995; Paixao and Marlow, 2001).

EU shipping policy is therefore highly significant as it supersedes any conflicting national legislation and thus is a major driver of policy within the sector. Member states have no choice, once policy and legislation is agreed, but to follow the general trend and direction of the EU as a whole. Clearly they do have a role to play in the generation of this policy and thus commonly agree its direction and trend, even where there may be disagreements over detail.

Various other supra-national regimes exist including the North America Free Trade Association (NAFTA) consisting of the USA, Canada and Mexico, with a series of maritime, logistics and transport related policies but no specific law-making powers (Brooks, 2000), and in historical terms, the Council for Mutual Economic Assistance (CMEA) which represented the countries of the Former Soviet bloc (including the USSR, Poland, Hungary, Romania, Bulgaria, DDR and Cuba amongst others), but which again had no legislative powers (although considerable persuasive ones). Useful discussion of its role as a policy-making body can be found in Chrzanowski et al. (1979) and Ledger and Roe (1996).

If we take the EU as an example, the policies which continue to emanate from the deliberations of the European Commission (and more specifically DGVII – responsible for Transport and Energy Policy), the Council of Transport Ministers and the European Parliament, are normally designed to interact with international policies of (for example) the IMO. Thus, recent EU legislation, which is aimed at enforcing the use of double-hulled tankers in EU waters, along with other environmental and safety measures, has deliberately avoided any technical conflict between the different spatial levels represented internationally and supra-nationally, although there remains some dispute over timing. Of course, this may not always necessarily be the case where the maritime interests of the EU conflict with those of the wider global framework and it is clear that sometimes, severe divergences of policy-outcomes producing inter-spatial inconsistency, can produce tensions that may be very hard to reconcile. The development of policies over implementation of the UNCTAD 40/40/20 rule for liner shipping by the EU during 1979 reflected these tensions as the EU's overarching commitment to free trade and economic liberalisation was severely tested by UNCTAD's demands for market interference on behalf of developing countries. An agreement was eventually reached within the EU and the 40/40/20 rule was accepted, but the difficulties of achieving consistency in maritime policies across international/supra-national/spatial boundaries where the agendas were fundamentally different, were clearly apparent.

This discussion of supra-national policy-making should also make reference to the problems of compatibility with the national policy level, particularly again with reference to the EU and the difficulties experienced in reconciling EU policies on (for example) state aids and cabotage, with the desires and agendas that exist in differing member states. These stresses are notably apparent in the context of the EU. Aspinwall (1995) provides detailed reference to the prolonged discussion that took place before Greece would agree to the opening up of shipping cabotage markets within the EU to all ships of EU flag. The agreement that was reached eventually contained a series of safeguards for socially vulnerable markets (e.g. the Greek Island trade where seasonality of demand could lead to some islands losing shipping services at times of low demand to shipping companies from around Europe 'creaming off' the profitable peaks). Also introduced were extended delays in implementation of the new policies to give the shipping industry time to adapt to the proposals. The concessions that were agreed had the notable effect of diluting the overall ambitions of the EU to open all shipping markets to all ships and operators that were both safe and environmentally friendly and reflected a clear divergence in policy ambitions between the supra-national and national interests that existed. The role of shipping state aids has also presented a similar set of difficulties and the EU Commission has compromised in its fundamental principles of liberalising markets so that some vestiges of state aid remain in place at a national level in most member states, albeit controlled in their amount, characteristics and methods of application.

Figure 4.1 also indicates the presence of two more levels of policy-making in the shipping sector which have yet to be discussed but which may also at times play a significant part in the conflict between spatial levels – those at *regional and local* level. These two levels, typified by regional governments (for example Noord Brabant in the Netherlands) and city governments (such as that in Le Havre or Dunkerque in France) once again should aim to derive shipping policies that are compatible with the levels that lie above them at the national, supra-national and international level.

To not do so almost inevitably will lead to problems of policy implementation. Thus, for example, a regional maritime policy-making authority within the EU might find problems in complying with EU policies restricting state aid to shipping when the local, perhaps economically dominant ship operator, needs substantial regionally derived financial support to remain in business. Similarly, city ports operating at a local level need to match their policies with their regions where they are located but at times political differences (manifesting themselves as different spatial policies) can interfere substantially with this process.

Interest Groups

The discussion so far has focused mainly upon the role of the state at each spatial level in the derivation of shipping policy and has emphasised both how important and also how difficult it is for policy-making at these different levels to work together and to ensure that policy created at one level is co-ordinated with that at each of the others to generate meaningful and consistent initiatives.

Figure 4.1 also includes examples of the more significant interest groups that have a significant role to play in the creation and application of shipping policies. These interest groups represent those parts of the broad shipping industry which are active within the sector and who are both the generators and those most affected by the policies that are created. Examples of some of them have been discussed above. Thus at the international level, the International Maritime Organisation (IMO) is a major interest group which acts as both a creator and absorber of international shipping policy measures. Meanwhile, at the supra-national level, an organisation such as the European Community Shipowners' Association (ECSA), based in Brussels, Belgium, and representing ship-owners throughout the EU, is a highly significant interest group that attempts to place pressure upon EU and national policy-makers to take greater account of their views. At a national level, the UK Chamber of Shipping plays a similar role in relation to the UK government (and in turn is a member of ECSA), but also in discussion with other interest groups (e.g. the European Shippers Council or the UK seafarers union, NUMAST). Similar relationships exist at local and regional level for all port authorities, environmental pressure groups, local truck haulier associations, etc. in every country, each of which has a voice feeding into the policy-making process to a greater or lesser degree.

These voices will act across each of the spatial levels – thus, for example, the UK Chamber of Shipping (representing UK ship-owners) will input policy initiatives directly to DGVII of the EU – and not just to their representative spatial policy-makers (in this case the UK government ministry responsible for shipping). The situation thus gets increasingly complicated as consistency and compatibility vertically up and down policy-making bodies at state level, now has also to function horizontally with interest groups and also in a sense, diagonally with groups at different spatial levels.

There is also a very substantial number of interest groups dependent upon each policy level and issue, each inter-relating with the other to a lesser or greater extent and this may be in opposition or in collaboration – this latter feature will also vary with the issue concerned.

The Contexts

The last piece of this increasingly complex puzzle which constitutes a spatial representative model of shipping policy is provided by the series of contexts within which each of these policy initiatives and relationships must operate and which in turn impact upon their development, potential and success or failure. A number of these can be identified following the earlier work of Ledger and Roe (1993), and these are incorporated within Figure 4.1. They include the following:

Economic: this context refers to the impact of economic related factors upon the derivation and characteristics of shipping policy for any particular spatial regime (international, supra-national, etc.). Thus this context would normally include (for example) the impact of the introduction of the euro in the 12 EU states, the general condition of the world economy at any particular time upon the shipping sector, the specific implications of the steel scrap market upon the shipping industry, the strength of the US$ in the world economy, various economic crises as for example in 2002/2003 in Argentina and Venezuela, and the effect of the continued efforts towards the development of free markets in Eastern Europe from 1989 onwards. It is clearly a highly significant and wide-ranging context that is difficult to incorporate in its entirety and understand its full implications but which is fundamental to decisions upon shipping policy at all levels and all circumstances.

Legal: this context refers to the legal framework within which the shipping sector is obliged to operate. This will inevitably include national laws and regulations as well as normally, those of a supra or international nature – for example, shipping operators which are based within countries within the EU or operating to and from any EU ports are obliged to comply with not only the legislation relevant in their home state but also the large multitude of EU regulations and directives that have been imposed upon this sector. These include, for example, the substantial pieces of legislation which refer to safety in the ferry and bulk carrier industries, competition rules for the liner shipping sector and rules for the operation of cabotage services. The competition rules which are applicable to liner shipping are a very good example of where differing legal regimes can apply to the same industrial sector dependent upon the spatial level that is under consideration. There are domestic laws in, for example, the United Kingdom or Germany, that control numerous aspects of shipping activity and impacts that these activities might have upon the local environment (local government pollution controls), port safety (port regulations), seafarer employment (income tax regulations and social security rules) and taxation (UK tonnage tax). Meanwhile, at the EU level there is a series of further regulations that apply to the competitive conditions between liner operators, agreements which are applicable to liner consortia and conferences and the penalties that can be applied by the European Commission (including the frequently discussed 4055-4058/86 Regulations, which are analysed in more detail in Chapter 5). At the same time, at an international level, the industry is subject to the rules and policies of the IMO in terms of ship safety, seafarer training and environmental protection amongst other things.

The legal framework is in a state of constant change at each spatial level as a response to a myriad of social, political and economic pressures and it is within this context that some of the more significant failings of co-ordination between these levels are apparent.

Managerial: this context refers to the relationship of the internal structure that exists within shipping companies to the policy framework that is imposed for the sector from the governmental level. Clearly, the size and complexity of shipping company organisations and the changing range of interests that shipping companies have incorporated into their activities have an important impact in terms of broader policy-making and its implementation. The latter issue is particularly significant as shipping companies increasingly integrate within the market-place vertically, absorbing logistical functions traditionally carried out by separate organisations but now incorporated within one company structure. Thus, for example, the Danish company Maersk's recently developed interests in the full range of logistics from shipping to trucking and agency work to air transport has implications for state and neo-state policy-makers and vice versa in that it is no longer shipping policy which is solely important but a range of policies from competition to industrial, transport to regional development and so on. This increase in the diversity of functions taken on by traditional shipping companies, makes life more complex for all those concerned with policy-making and implementation and has also increased pressure on the industry to conform to a considerably wider range of policy initiatives and priorities.

The problems faced by the TACA members in the liner shipping market on the North Atlantic is evidence of this in that they have fallen foul of competition policies of the EU in the area of inland trucking. The issue here was that members were accused of being anti-competitive for complete transport journeys, as their strategies included the inland parts of container journeys to and from ports and not just the shipping links. These shipping links are permitted under Regulation 4056/86 of the EU, to be part of a conference agreement and thus (with some restrictions) to have prices and quality of service agreed across operators as part of a shipping conference. Inland transport sectors are not covered by 4056/86 and hence there arose conflict as ship operators (such as Maersk/Sealand but also many others) ran foul of the discrepancy between the new logistical environment incorporating shipping, trucking and much more, and the legislative framework of the EU (relating only to the shipping element of a journey).

It is only whilst the economic and logistical benefits of vertical integration for shipping companies remain greater than the potential complexity that comes with it (and the risks of falling foul of legislation) that the changes in managerial context and the trend towards vertical integration in logistics policy will continue. Whilst these stresses continue to develop, shipping policy initiatives will also have to continue to incorporate the new environment that has emerged.

A further example of complexity that changes within the managerial context has brought centres upon conflict within the liner industry again in the North Atlantic market between the state-like organisations of the EU and the FMC in the USA. Each has differing views upon the acceptable nature of liner conferences (and even whether they should exist at all) and also the option of including inland transport within overall conference legislation (Brooks, 2000). These differing opinions may place liner shipping companies within difficult circumstances as they strive to remain within the law of each organisation at the same time as competitive within the market-place.

Organisational: this context refers more particularly to the structure and characteristics of the shipping industry as a whole rather than internal company activities and two important trends here stand out in relation to policy-making at all levels – those of privatisation and globalisation. Following the demise of the Soviet empire throughout Eastern Europe and with it the highly important role of state-owned shipping companies in these countries (Wrona and Roe, 2002), and combined with the trend of a general divestment of state-owned assets around the world in all sectors, the shipping sector as a whole has seen a considerable trend towards increased private ownership. The importance and impact of state policy-making for the shipping sector has undoubtedly lessened as a result, as governments become distanced from day-to-day company decisions, finance and operations.

Meanwhile, at the same time, there has been a resultant increase in the impact of supra-national and international policy-making in the shipping sector, with the aim of increasing control over the external effects of the industry. Shipping has tended to find itself increasingly released from public sector obligations and this has had some detrimental effects as well as beneficial ones. This is evidenced in the increased activity in shipping policy-making of, for example, the EU, the FMC in the USA and the United Nations IMO in the fields of safety, environment and competition. The prime objectives are to protect public interests in areas where the market has little or no interest and there are very few natural mechanisms in a privately dominated market which can ensure that high levels of safety, low levels of environmental pollution and healthy competition between players in the shipping industry are maintained.

One significant problem that emerges here between spatial policy-making levels is that commonly it may be advantageous for (say) competition policy to be neglected at a national level as this may ensure a strong international presence for a domestic fleet. Thus, for example, subsidy for domestic shipping fleets may be made available in some form by state governments whilst its application is being strictly controlled at a supra-national level – for example, the EU may have policies and guidelines to restrict subsidy to shipping companies whilst national governments may see a political and economic necessity to provide such support.

In terms of globalisation, the substantial growth of this trend has markedly changed the nature of the shipping industry worldwide and in all sectors including bulk, liner and ferry, which although each has always operated within a global market, until recently was much more nationally dominated and controlled. Thus, the UK privately owned shipping company P&O has been a major bulk, ferry and liner operator worldwide for many years but more recently has found it necessary to enter a series of global strategic alliances and to merge (for example) its liner operations with Nedlloyd of the Netherlands. Policy-making in the shipping sector is directly affected by this type of merger and trend, particularly at the domestic and state level as, in the example cited here, national shipping policies in the UK and the Netherlands may conflict (for example in terms of subsidy), causing at best confusion within the sector and possibly considerably worse. In addition the increased impact of flags of convenience and international registers for shipping can confuse the picture further. Nationally based shipping companies now have to work more and more within an internationally derived policy framework whilst, for example, international and national policies towards training, labour and employment clearly may conflict with the requirements of each other.

Political: the political context is one from which all shipping policies have to emerge. It is rarely if ever the case that a single technical, economic or legal framework exists that stimulates or controls shipping policy formulation. In practice, the political characteristics and nature of any specific policy is normally the most significant context of all. Substantial political changes (for example those that occurred in Eastern Europe between 1989-1991; the various Arab-Israeli conflicts; or the effects of the World

Trade Centre incident in September 2001) are often of somewhat less significance than the political relationships between players both within and close to the sector. A good example, described in some detail by Aspinwall (1995), refers to the political relationship between the European Commission (the executive body of the EU) and the Council of Ministers (currently still the main legislature of the EU) concerning the introduction of Regulation 4056/86. This regulation effectively permitted the existence of liner conferences for shipping operators working into and out of EU ports, something that under the extensive competition rules promoted within the Treaty of Rome should be thoroughly illegal. The European Commission's view was quite clearly that this should not be permitted, but they were over-ruled by the Council of Transport Ministers in 1986 who, under intense pressure from the commercial shipping industry and acting in a political rather than a legal or economic context, legislated for their existence. An internal political conflict resulted in a policy that conflicts with all other industrial sectors within the EU (none other has such an exemption from competition law) and which has presented a continuous series of difficulties in co-ordinating different policy level initiatives since then. Other political pressures which have been significant at EU level in overtly affecting policy-making include the concessions granted to Greece over the delay in imposing shipping cabotage laws and the continued existence of subsidies for shipping operations against all principles that the EU tries normally to uphold. Recent examples of where stresses have emerged here in recent years centre around the various forms of tonnage tax that have been introduced throughout most EU member states as a way of aiding domestic shipping fleets. Such political concessions do nothing to create a consistent and meaningful policy framework for the shipping sector as a whole, evidenced in the continuing friction between the European Shippers Council (ESC) and the European Shipowners' Association (ECSA) over the existence of liner shipping conferences and the maintenance of higher freight rates that the former believe is an inevitable consequence.

Social: this context refers to a multitude of highly complex relationships between the shipping industry and the wider society in which it has to operate.

These issues commonly include the significance of maritime employment and the policies which are aimed at its promotion or reduction. This forms a major strand within maritime policy-making at local, regional, national and supra-national levels in particular. Considerable recent debate has also focused within the EU upon the introduction of new tax regimes by member states for shipping, partly at least aimed at encouraging or sustaining employment levels, in particular the tonnage tax now found in the large majority of member states and to which considerably more reference is made later in this text. In addition, there has been a large number of policy initiatives concentrating upon seafarer training, conditions of service and the environment, all with strong social implications. Certainly at all levels, these social implications stemming from a particular policy need to be noted by politicians as they choose shipping policy initiatives, as the relationship between the two is always a close one and the political and economic impacts amongst others can be sizeable.

Spatial: this context considers the issue that all shipping policies are not only derived at a variety of spatial levels as we have been discussing in earlier sections – that is, international, supra-national, national, regional and local levels – but also are affected and influenced by a wide variety of spatial issues. These might well quite commonly include issues relating to peripherality – a major theme within the EU – whereby the disadvantage felt by peripherally located regions and states (for example many of the accession countries of Eastern Europe; or the economically disadvantaged areas of southern Italy, much of Greece, Ulster and Portugal) can be reduced through policies which promote improved transport links including those by ship and those which pass through ports. By aiming to improve these links, the friction which stems from a peripheral location can be substantially reduced. Examples come from port developments in Southern Italy, improved intermodal links through the UK and new ferry links between Scotland and the Netherlands, each receiving funds from the EU.

Meanwhile, other spatial contextual influences include the promotion of short-sea shipping across Europe by the EU with the aim of reducing dependence upon pollution-generating road transport, and a variety of regional policies to improve the lives of island based communities in the Mediterranean, around Scotland and in the Baltic. The latter is evidenced in the EU through the design of the cabotage regulations which allow countries to protect selected domestic routes, with the agreement of the European Commission, for social reasons and thus are not forced to open them up to wider European competition.

A very large number of other spatially related issues are significant to the shipping sector – including regional policies designed to develop economically backward areas and the consequent industrial and commercial impacts that result; the effects of the emergence of new countries in Europe including those of Russia, Belarus, the Ukraine and the Baltic States of Latvia, Lithuania and Estonia and their relatively important shipping fleets and transport activities; and the effects of the construction of new port facilities including, for example, those for oil export in the eastern Baltic Sea which recently has seen new developments of this sort in Russia, Latvia and Lithuania.

Technical: this context refers to the changes in technical facilities and activities which have both direct and indirect effects upon shipping and its related industry. Shipping policies need to take account of these changes and this will include a multitude of new safety and environmental regulations at international, supra-national and national level aimed to accommodate the continuing growth in ship size both in the container and bulk vessel sectors. Significant changes in ferry design and the need for and imposition of improved technical and safety rules have stimulated further regulations in particular within the EU and following the 'Estonia' and 'Herald of Free Enterprise' disasters in the Baltic Sea and at Zeebrugge respectively. The growth of new port facilities and continual changes in modal choice also have had their effect and the continued growth in road transport and the construction of new pipeline facilities have implications for policy-makers in the shipping sector. The EU's promotion of intermodalism as a concept also has impacted technically upon the shipping policy sector.

These eight, major contexts provide an external framework within which all shipping policy has to be placed at all levels – policy-making which tends to try and ignore their influence will have no chance of succeeding. The relative significance of each of these contexts will be dependent upon the spatial level concerned and the issue involved as well as a host of other inter-connected factors but undoubtedly in the very large majority of cases, each context has a significant role to play. Some are ever-present and always central – particularly political issues – but also the respective legal framework that exists and the economic relationships that are maintained between the shipping industry and its broader setting.

In addition, shipping policy cannot ignore the much wider context in which it has to be introduced and in which it is implemented. Thus shipping policy at all levels has to accept that there are other policies – including industrial, financial, environmental, competition, infrastructure, energy and so on – with which it is required to co-ordinate and of which it has to be aware. Failure to do so again will result in conflicts developing between policy-makers and other players within the shipping sector and therefore must result in ineffective policy-making. In addition, shipping policy needs to recognise the role that other transport modes play and the fact that policies for one mode may well conflict with those for another – for example, the promotion of road transport through continued road building and subsidised taxation for trucks will have an inevitable impact upon the short-sea shipping industry. Clearly and probably ideally, the separate modal policies should be integrated into one whole, but this is often made difficult as there always remains competition between the different modal interests and structurally these policies will commonly emanate from entirely different government ministries. Finally, shipping policy, if it is to be fully effective, has to be aware of its inheritance in terms of industry structure, ownership, tradition and significance. These in turn will affect its role and potential in terms of policy success.

CONCLUSIONS

This chapter has discussed shipping policy and has focused in particular upon two features which are common to virtually all regimes and locations – the extreme complexity of the variety of influences that control both its character and successful implementation, and the significance of ensuring that there is compatibility across all spatial levels if shipping policies are to have any chance of being effective. There is nothing more likely to inhibit the success of shipping policy initiatives than to have conflicting policy ambitions at each spatial level – national, supra-national and international – something for example, that has characterised the industry in conflicts between Greece and the EU over cabotage trades, and also between the USA's FMC and the EU over liner conferences and their operations on the North Atlantic.

This consistency across spatial levels needs to be maintained in the context of policies emerging in other areas as well – for example the environment and economy – or else conflicts will again emerge which will effectively inhibit the achievement of the objectives at which the policies are aimed. There are many examples of national governments promoting both short-sea shipping through tax concessions, as well as trucking through taxation subsidies, whilst both continue to operate within the same markets in competition with each other.

Such conflicts of interest that occur frequently within the shipping policy arena have been made more significant and also more difficult to resolve with the trend towards increased globalisation of markets and the impact that this has had upon the already highly internationalised shipping industry and its increasing moves towards further international joint ventures and more strategic alliances. In effect, it is now really only at an international level that shipping policy can ever be truly and comprehensively effective. Thus the EU may have ambitions to open up and liberalise markets and can insist upon high environmental and safety standards for shipping, but it is prevented from fully achieving these ideals and implementing appropriate policies because to do so would destroy EU shipping fleets within a global context. This is a consequence that would be politically and socially unacceptable throughout the EU area. Thus the EU agrees to compromise upon issues such as flags of convenience (which in many ways it should welcome as a consequence of a free market) by allowing member states to subsidise their own fleets through low taxation regimes compared with other comparative industries – thus breaking their own Treaty of Rome competition law principles. The very international and mobile nature of the shipping industry makes this conclusion almost inevitable. Similar forms of compromise can be seen in the cases of liner shipping, cabotage and manning rules. Meanwhile, Port State Control offers an interesting example of where the EU has achieved much of what it wishes within an international framework but at a supra-national level – in that by enforcing higher standards upon ships of all nationalities entering EU ports, then safety and environmental standards across the EU are maintained even where the ships concerned are operated under a legal regime outside of the EU. Of course this has little impact upon vessels that never enter EU ports, but in many ways this is of no significance to the EU member states, particularly in the political short-term.

At the international level – say at the United Nations IMO – it would in theory be possible to achieve agreement across all nations for rules that then could be universally applied at all spatial levels, right down to regional and local. Such agreements are very difficult (if not impossible) to achieve and conflicts between policies imposed at differing levels remain and will do so whilst nations, ship operators, local interests and others see benefits in imposing their own policy initiatives. The globalisation of a highly complex and mobile industry which is characterised by a very large number of international interests and heavily entwined with other industrial and commercial sectors – as shipping is – makes policy-making a frustrating and difficult business but one which perhaps more than any other, reflects the complex pattern of commercial interests that exist throughout different regions of the world.

5. The European Union and Shipping: A Case Study of Policy-making

INTRODUCTION

This chapter will present some of the major stages in the development of the maritime policies of the European Union which emerged up until the late 1990s. More recent policy developments which have occurred since then and applied in the early twenty-first century, and especially those related to state aids, will be examined in depth in Chapter 7 as they provide an extensive case study of the complex relationships that exist between the various spatial levels of policy-making in the maritime sector in this region.

The European Union was chosen as the policy-making body to help understand the process of maritime policy creation. This was because it represents an ideal forum where the complex inter-relationships between the various levels of policy initiative, which have been discussed earlier, are clearly apparent. It represents both a dynamic area for the maritime sector and a good example of where policies have to interact. Thus the relationships between the member states and the European Union itself are central to the derivation and effective implementation of policy. It is upon these inter-relationships that we will focus the discussion.

However, to do this effectively, we must first gain a clear understanding of the major maritime policies which the EU has pursued over its lifetime and in particular over the more recent years until the late 1990s. The maritime policy of the EU showed sporadic progress until the 1980s (for example see Walter, 1960, 1963; Little, 1962; Despicht, 1966a, 1966b, 1966c, 1966d; Strom, 1966; Goergen, 1972; McKenna, 1972; Beagley, 1973; Lazarus, 1978; Holst, 1982) after which it developed considerably, and it is this later period upon which we will concentrate in the coming chapters. This chapter will examine the build up of policy until the late 1990s when, at the turn of the century, a change in approach can be seen which was central to the national/supra-national conflicts which exist within the EU. The following chapters go on to look at the most recent developments which hope to resolve these conflicts and to provide an effective policy framework for the maritime sector in the coming years ahead.

The European Union's single market programme, officially launched with the publication of a comprehensive White Paper by the Commission in 1985, has proved to be of tremendous importance for Europe's economic and political development. The willingness of the member states to transfer significant legislative powers to Brussels has been vital in the overall development of a single market for the EU's economy. A milestone in this respect was the Single European Act (1986), which introduced the concept of qualified majority decision-making into the European Council of Ministers – the main legislative-making body of the EU at the time. This replaced the ubiquitous unanimity previously required for all legislative measures having as their objective the establishment and functioning of this single internal market and thus facilitated the development and implementation of EU legislation for the majority of issues including those relating to the maritime sector.

A step further towards integration was taken in 1992, when the member states approved the Maastricht Treaty which gave the European Parliament real powers to influence legislation in the same areas under the 'co-decision' procedure (Lyons, 2000). Prior to this, the Parliament was largely a discursive body with little direct influence upon the policies of the EU, but following the Maastricht Treaty, the Council and Parliament shared the process of legislative power and as a consequence increased the democratic and integrative potential of the organisation. Policy thus became the output of not only the administrative process of the Commission, nor of the private political discussions of the Council, but also the elected politicians of the Parliament.

THE EARLY EU MARITIME POLICIES

Meanwhile, in more specific terms, for many years the European Community (EC), later the European Union (EU), did not have a shipping policy of any real substance (Paixao and Marlow, 2001). Gwilliam (1979) criticises the efforts of the EC towards a common transport policy through the 1960s and 1970s as being 'cruelly disappointing'. This mainly resulted from the differences in the primary policy objectives that existed between the Community and the member state countries and epitomised in many ways the spatial conflicts in policy-making that frequently emerged (and still emerge) in the EU. Thus maritime affairs were seen to be a member state issue up to this time, with EU focus at a supra-national level targeted upon the wider concerns of land-based transport with its predominant internal implications for the economies of the member states. Maritime affairs were viewed as essentially 'overseas' and thus not central to the formation of an internal market.

Shipping had been mentioned in the 1956 Treaty of Rome but only once in Article 84, which read:

'The provisions of the Title shall apply to transport by rail, road and inland waterway.
The Council may, acting unanimously, decide whether, to what extent and by what procedure appropriate provisions may be laid down for sea and air transport.'

The inclusion of the wording in the second paragraph is widely attributed to the influence of the Netherlands who wished to sustain free trade in shipping and thus attempted to exclude shipping policy from the requirements of the Treaty. Their success was clear when no unanimous decision directly relating to shipping was passed until 1977.

In fact the first policy document (although not legislation) produced by the European Commission directly upon shipping matters had only been presented the year before, some 19 years after the EU's formation. This 1976 Communication (Commission of the European Communities, 1976) accepted that there were certain problem areas concerned with Community relations with non-member countries, mainly caused by the unfair pricing competition from Eastern Bloc countries' liner fleets and it suggested measures to try and meet these problems. At that time, all players in the shipping market were witnessing events whose impact will be examined in more detail in the following chapters. In brief for the moment, these were characterised by the volume of shipping under EC flags and the size of seafaring employment decreasing substantially and certainly more severely than in most other countries of the world. The effect of non-member competition from Eastern Bloc fleets (predominantly from the USSR, Poland, DDR, Romania and Bulgaria) was a major factor in this decline (Bergstrand and Doganis, 1987).

Changes in policy attitude towards favouring the inclusion of shipping within a legislative framework only emerged from 1973 and the joining of the EEC by the United Kingdom, Denmark and the Irish Republic – each with reasonably substantial maritime interests. The European Commission meanwhile, stimulated by the new members' support, brought a test case to the European Court of Justice concerning the freedom of movement of labour – in this case seafarers – under Article 48 of the Treaty. The Court agreed with the Commission (that seafarers were included) and by implication there was a need for an EEC maritime policy to be developed. By coincidence, within two days, the UNCTAD Code of Conduct for Liner Shipping had been agreed and this presented the EEC with its first maritime policy issue.

The UNCTAD Liner Code and the Brussels Package

One distinct feature of particular importance to EC policy at the time was the introduction of the UNCTAD Liner Code in 1974. Up to this time there was a series of well-known and documented debates over the organisation of liner trades in terms of conference agreements among contracting operators, characterised by the agreed frequency and allocation of sailings, loyalty arrangements and deferred discounts if shippers made exclusive use of conference services. The deteriorating situation in terms of relationships between shipping companies, shippers and national maritime administrations, resulted in a series of disputes concerning the role of market forces and the position of state maritime policies. These disputes led to several governmental and intergovernmental inquiries and investigations (Pallis, 2002). At that time, the European Community's view was that the regulation or liberalisation of conferences by the EC would destroy the conference's traditional ability to determine freight rates in an artificial way (i.e. to avoid the influence of the market upon pricing, quality and supply), which thus assured their market shares. This effective control of the markets by liner conferences was felt to be to the detriment of the liner (and particularly the shipper) market overall. However, regulation of such conferences and thus liberalisation of the liner shipping market by the EC would lead to increased competition in trades where European firms were dominant at the time. In the face of such a situation, the EC (but also in fact the entire group of OECD countries) preferred the certainty of the UNCTAD Code to the potential threats of a much more liberal and completely open-conference regime (Cafruny, 1987). Thus liner shipping policy was markedly affected by member state influence rather than supra-national imposition and in particular, that of a series of sizeable shipping companies whose role in national policy-making was indisputable (if subtle). This included Maersk (Denmark), P&O (UK), Hapag Lloyd (Germany), CGM (France) and Nedlloyd (Netherlands) amongst others. The rules of the Treaty of Rome would suggest that the EC should have imposed its supra-national authority over member states' (and their shipping company) preferences and outlawed liner conference practices. The UNCTAD Code controlled the conferences' market shares in developing market trades but also formalised their existence – something made even more concrete in 1986 as we shall see later.

More specifically, the most important element of the UNCTAD Code to all those involved in liner shipping, and not just the EC shipping companies, was the 40/40/20 cargo sharing agreement. This established the right of national lines of each trading country to participate equally in the transport of generated liner traffic by allowing 40% of the cargo to be carried by the flag of the exporting country, 40% by the importing country, while the remaining

20% of the traffic share would be safeguarded for third flag carriers. The Code also included criteria and procedures for freight rate determination and rules for the settlement of potential disputes between ship-owners and shippers (Aspinwall, 1995; Pallis, 2002).

The situations under which the Code was or was not supported varied for each of the different European Community countries – in fact it was agreed individually by France, West Germany and Belgium, rejected by the UK and Denmark and Italy, whilst the Netherlands and Luxembourg abstained. However, the Commission felt that common (and unanimous) action on the Code was necessary for both political and legal reasons. Eventually, the Commission recommended that member states should sign the Code, and in 1977 the proposal for a regulation embodying this and the Code's acceptance was submitted to the European Council of Ministers. The proposal would form the basis of a Community-wide conditional acceptance, which was formalised in Regulation 954/79 (Aspinwall, 1995).

What the Code actually aimed for was the maintenance of an open trading regime between the OECD countries, while allowing for the 40/40/20 agreement with the developing countries. However, these kinds of practices were in direct conflict with the already well established EEC Rules of Competition (Articles 85-94, EEC Treaty of Rome, Part 3, Chapter 1, Section 1) prohibiting cargo-sharing, flag discrimination, maritime subsidies and other related restrictive shipping practices (Odeke, 1984; Aspinwall, 1995).

Whilst at that time, Community countries continued to have a varied view on the Code's practices, there was also the need for the member states to establish a common approach on these matters and on the overall aspects of transport policy, always of course in line with the Treaty of Rome. The countries decided there should be a common accession to the Code and this immediately led to the 'Brussels Package' in 1979 (Odeke, 1984; Cafruny, 1987; Aspinwall, 1995).

The proposed common policy approach was embodied in a Council Regulation, intended to secure that there would no longer be any discrimination between shipping lines of the EEC or the OECD which put these discriminatory practices into force. While it cannot be said that all countries from either the EEC or the OECD had enthusiastically accepted the Code, it has been argued (by Odeke, 1984 in particular) that the main drive for the former was at least in part related to the organisation's determination to exclude the substantial amounts of USSR shipping tonnage which was entering EC trades. The USSR was commonly felt to be able to compete unfairly in the liner trades because its shipping industry was entirely state-owned and had no commercial basis to its operation, unlike shipping from elsewhere. Although the growth of Soviet shipping was substantially bigger than from elsewhere, these claims of unfair practices have not been entirely substantiated by the investigations of the time and may have just been a political manoeuvre by those politically opposed to the USSR regime (Bergstrand and Doganis, 1987). One of the purposes of the Brussels Package, nevertheless, was to change the conditions for European and world shipping (including that of the Eastern Bloc) and promote an increasingly liberal trade environment, largely free from cargo-sharing arrangements.

OTHER EARLY MARITIME POLICY ISSUES

A number of other policy issues also featured in these early days of maritime policy-making in the (then) EEC (Bredima-Savopoulou, 1981a, 1981b; Bredima-Savopoulou and Tzoannos, 1990; Erdmenger and Stasinopoulos, 1988). They focused upon a series of maritime social policies, the right to establishment for shipping companies, competition rules and safety and pollution issues.

The *social issues* were mainly related to the free movement of workers, the harmonisation of employment conditions across the EEC, issues relating to social security, and the relationships of conditions of employment for overseas seafarers compared with those from the EEC. They thus derived from the original European Court of Justice case noted earlier. These issues in turn had emerged from the 1980 Hollesen study for the European Commission examining the employment of seafarers and which itself had emerged as a result of the earlier court decision. It revealed considerable differences between pay and employment conditions for seafarers from different member states. A particular concern was the fact that these differences were not a consequence of the characteristics of member states' labour markets but were simply inconsistencies within the overall EEC market. These inconsistencies were compounded by a resistance to movement of labour despite the court ruling, caused by trades union resistance and the failure to recognise seafarer qualifications across member states. In general terms this suggested the need to get away from member state policies for seafarer employment and a primary role for supra-national policies to guide the industry and protect the individual.

The issues relating to *right to establishment* derived from Articles 52-58 of the Treaty of Rome which makes it illegal to discriminate in terms of nationality concerning the right to establish companies in another member state. In shipping policy this focused upon registration more than anything else at that time.

Finally, as mentioned above, the European shipping market in the late 1970s was facing major difficulties in terms of *competition and safety and pollution*, whose impact would be influential for many years to come. These mainly centred upon the decline of the Community's member states' shipping fleets accompanied by severely pessimistic signs concerning EU seafarer employment. As a response to these negative trends, the objectives of the maritime policy of the EC at the time were identified by Paixao and Marlow (2001) as being:

- The provision of shipping services independent of the place where the company was set up.
- The safeguarding of free access to a free world shipping market.
- The promotion of fair competition.
- A guarantee in the long term of entrepreneurial skills, taking into consideration the aspirations of the developing countries that wished to join this economic activity.
- The promotion of social conditions for seafarers.
- The maintenance and improvement of safety standards and protection of the environment.

Even though only limited progress was made, the policy programme continued, with more countries with maritime interests (for example Greece, Spain and Portugal) joining the Community by 1986, adding further pressure for the accomplishment of more effective solutions to the severe problems and threats to the European shipping market. This also placed more pressure on reconciling some of the differences which were clearly apparent between the ambitions and desires of the member states and the EC itself.

The Four Council Regulations of 1986: The 'First Package'

One of the immediate results of the accession of the new member states with increased maritime awareness was the adoption of four new Council Regulations on 16th December 1986. This is frequently regarded as the starting point of systematic and meaningful EU involvement in maritime affairs. Similar to previous EU actions, these four Regulations were mainly concerned with aspects related to the 'external relations' of shipping, promoting at the same time a new stage of co-ordination between the member states' policies, thus signifying the initiation of a supra-national approach to maritime policy within the EEC (Pallis, 2002).

The 1986 package of measures (Bredima-Savopoulou and Tzoannos, 1990) consisted of the following Regulations which were directed at the liner shipping market:

- Council Regulation (EEC), No. 4055/86 applying the principle of freedom to provide services to maritime transport between member states and between member states and third countries.
- Council Regulation (EEC), No. 4056/86 laying down detailed rules for the application of Articles 85 and 86 of the Treaty to maritime transport.
- Council Regulation (EEC), No. 4057/86 related to unfair pricing practices in maritime transport.
- Council Regulation (EEC), No. 4058/86 concerning coordinated action to safeguard free access to cargoes in ocean trades.

The main aims of these measures were to improve the competitive structure of the European liner shipping industry and its ability to counteract unfair competition from third countries (Brooks and Button, 1992). The adoption of the 1986 package by the Council at a Community level was based on an open-market, non-protectionist philosophy and at the time was considered to be the basis of a policy package of legislation in the context of European shipping in general and liner shipping in particular (Commission of the European Communities, 1997).

The scope of each Regulation was as follows.

4055/86 was directed towards ensuring the freedom to provide liner services. This was for intra-EEC trades and applied to nationals and shipping companies of member states established within the EEC. Its purpose was to prevent any member state from discriminating in favour of or against any shipping companies on the basis of their nationality and as such represented a direct move towards an EEC view of maritime policy as against a national perspective. A supra-national policy was thus beginning to emerge to supersede existing national policies.

Both intra-EEC trades and those between EEC members and countries beyond the EEC were included. Unilateral cargo restrictions had to be eliminated by 1st January, 1993 along with any other existing discriminatory cargo-sharing arrangements. In terms of future arrangements, both bilateral and cargo sharing agreements would only be permitted by the EEC where no other effective means of trade existed.

Interestingly, it also applied to companies established outside the EEC area where the company was controlled by EEC member state nationals and where the shipping company was operated in accordance with the legislation of that member state. In effect, the EEC was applying maritime policy to member states and their nationals even when they were located outside the EEC area, and applying these policies over and above those of the member states themselves.

4056/86 was undoubtedly the most contentious and radical of the four Regulations and to this day remains hotly disputed by shipping companies and shippers alike. The basic aim was to apply the competition rules of the Treaty of Rome (as detailed in Articles 85 and 86) to the liner shipping industry but to do so in a way that was adapted to the specific needs of the industry and accommodated the supra-national aspirations of the EEC at the time. The details of the Regulation are outlined in the next section but for the moment it is important to note that it was subject to considerable debate and unusually, was adopted by the Council (and hence became law) despite the opposition of the Commission who felt that it was in fact not in accordance with the requirements or philosophy of the Treaty of Rome. This disagreement between the Council and Commission remains to this day a serious and real one that has affected relationships between these two bodies and the nature of subsequent maritime policies in many areas.

The Regulation itself applies to all international liner services that serve EEC ports other than those of a tramp nature. Its contentious part is that which relates to the bloc exemption provided to liner conferences from the competition rules of the Treaty of Rome. The Treaty, by all accounts, makes agreements such as liner shipping conferences (whereby prices, quality of service and other operational arrangements between competing liner shipping services are fixed in advance between operators) illegal except for the existence of this Regulation. No other industrial or commercial activity within the Community has such an exemption.

Although the exemption is granted subject to certain conditions and obligations (for example that conference agreements are relatively transparent and open to new members), it remains essentially an anomaly, a supra-national maritime policy applied across all EU countries and their national maritime policies, which permits liner shipping companies to arrange prices, routes, ports of call, quality of services and marketing agreements. The justification for the Regulation from the Council was that in a unique industry it provided a balance between the needs of the ship operators and the shippers, ensuring stability whilst also providing a relatively competitive environment.

Breaches of the Regulation can be investigated by the Commission (and have been from time to time) and extensive fines on shipping companies can be imposed. The well-documented TACA case is clear evidence of this (Brooks, 2000), where disputes over the fixing of inland shipment prices by the TACA North Atlantic conference were eventually declared illegal and resulted in substantial fines for operators. Final clarification of what was permitted was not achieved until 2003.

In policy terms it represents a clear supra-national policy in that individual member states and their respective liner shipping companies are subject to policy on competition and conference agreements which over-ride any local initiatives or desires. National priorities are subject to detailed supra-national, EEC legislation that makes no provision for member state differences or for the later policy of 'subsidiarity' which followed the 1987 initiatives towards the Single European Market, aimed at increasing the amount of national input into Community policy. More on this issue will be discussed in later sections.

4057/86 was aimed at dealing with unfair pricing practices in the liner trades. It empowered the Commission to impose a compensatory duty upon non-EEC ship-owners if the following conditions were cumulatively present:

- There were unfair pricing practices present. These were defined as where there was price undercutting of EEC liner shipping services made possible by non-EEC shipping operators receiving non-commercial advantages such as subsidies, preferential legislation, guaranteed cargoes etc. Although initially aimed at Eastern Bloc, state-owned shipping fleets, due to the regime changes which occurred in this region between 1989 and 1991, it was actually countries in the Far East (and more specifically South Korea) that were the target.
- These unfair pricing practices were causing injury.
- The interests of the EEC make EEC intervention necessary.

The procedure was dependent upon complaints from the industry about supposed practices which would then be investigated by the Commission. The Commission then would impose compensatory duties if the complaint was found to be justified. The imposition of duties required a Council decision within two months of the Commission notification. Account had to be taken of the existing shipping policies and external trade considerations.

Compensatory duties would normally be imposed on each container landed in the EEC which would redress the difference in costs which the overseas ship-owner faced.

Once again we see a definite policy at supra-national level that in effect takes account only of the needs and demands of the Treaty of Rome and takes no account of national policy interpretation. There is no scope for local interpretation dependent upon local circumstances.

4058/86 was aimed at co-ordinated action using diplomatic initiatives or countermeasures in cases where third countries restrict access to ocean trades by EEC shipping fleets. This covered all shipping activities – liner, bulk and tramps – passenger and freight vessels. It was designed to work against governments that distort competition by giving preferential treatment to their own ship-owners through flag discrimination.

Co-ordinated action by the Commission can only follow a request from a member state, which in turn has to be followed by a proposal to the Council within four weeks. The Council has the duty of specifying the developments that have generated the need for countermeasures, their extent and duration. If the Council fails to act within two months then national action by the member state is allowed.

Unlike the other three Regulations, 4058/86 clearly encompasses both national and supra-national policy provisions. Member states have to generate the original complaint and may well be involved in taking action if the Council fails to move quickly enough. In some ways this Regulation provides an early example of an increased involvement of member state policy-making within the EEC framework that was to develop much more extensively in the late 1990s and is discussed in more detail in later chapters.

While this First Package achieved some of its objectives in defining the beginning of a policy package for the EEC shipping industry and liner shipping in particular, and also introduced an initial strategy for a supra-national policy structure under which national policies might develop, the measures failed to stop the decline of the Community-registered fleet. The share of the world fleet registered within the European Community dropped to 15.4% in 1988 from 32.3% in 1970. The Community fleet tonnage was practically halved between 1975 and 1988 (Table 5.1), whereas in 1990 (Figure 5.1), the foreign flag share of the national fleets for the six most important European maritime nations ranged from 6.8% (Italy) to 95.2% (UK) (Brooks and Button, 1992).

The 'Positive Measures Package'

In 1989, a second maritime package of policy proposals, the so-called 'Positive Measures Package', was brought forward by the European Commission for discussion and it was hoped would form the basis for the development of legislation. This package of proposed measures for a common shipping policy was designed to complete the Community Shipping Policy, particularly the internal dimension. The document entitled 'A Future for the Community Shipping Industry' contained an analysis of the world shipping industry and four draft positive measures (Aspinwall, 1995). By that time, the problem of addressing the decline in the competitiveness of Community shipping fleets in the world markets had become even more obvious (Brooks and Button, 1992).

The main proposition of the 1989 package of measures was the creation of a Community ship registry, also known as EUROS (European Register of Shipping). The next three proposals included recommendations to establish the effectiveness of a port state control regime among EC member states aimed at policing the quality of shipping through a process of ship inspection and detention in Community ports, and a further regulatory attempt at opening the discussion upon cabotage definition for a Community ship-owner – a necessary first step before full cabotage liberalisation could be established as envisaged by the Treaty of Rome (Aspinwall, 1995).

The EUROS register was designed as a second, parallel register for all national registers of the Community in order to offset the benefits offered to ship-owners from Open Registry countries (Paixao and Marlow, 2001). The main obligation of EUROS registration related to minimum crewing requirements, specifically that the officers and at least half of the crew members should be Community nationals. This obligation would, of course, impose increased operating costs for the Community ship-owners compared with Open Registry conditions, placing them at a competitive disadvantage. In a cost assessment study conducted by Kiriazidis and Tzanidakis (1995), the crew cost differences between an EC and a third country flag were estimated. Employment costs proved to be very sizeable. For a 1500 gt container vessel, a Third World crew would cost US$350,000 per annum, whereas for a Netherlands crew the expenses were estimated to be approximately US$1,286,000 per annum. The application of EUROS was, however, to be voluntary.

Table 5.1: Merchant Fleets as a Percentage of Total World Tonnage 1975 and 1988

Merchant Fleets	1975	1988
Flags of Convenience	25.9	35.0
Rest of the World	9.20	24.3
Other OECD	28.4	18.4
European Community	30.8	15.4
CMEA	5.50	6.90

Source: Hart et al., p85 (1993).

Some benefits were attached to registering with EUROS including sole access to EC cabotage markets and to EC aid contracts and a more favourable state subsidy scheme offered to those shipping companies with EUROS registered fleets. However, the Commission failed to explain why these benefits could not be achieved without introducing the EUROS register and ship-owners remained highly sceptical of the proposal. More specifically, cabotage liberalisation was seen as a natural consequence of the freedom to trade within the context of the European single market whilst continued conflict between those nations who were unwilling to lift their domestic cabotage restrictions implied that a further benefit of the proposed EUROS flag was lost at least for the time being (Hart et al., 1993). Meanwhile, state subsidies to shipping as well as privileged aid contracts were at that time also in conflict with the Commission's arguments about cargo reservation schemes concerning third countries (Aspinwall, 1995; Kiriazidis and Tzanidakis, 1995; Pallis, 2002).

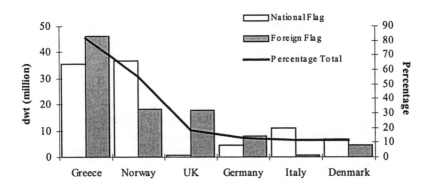

Sources: Sletmo, G.K. and Holste, S. (1993) Shipping and the competitive advantage of nations, *Maritime Policy and Management*, 20, 3, 243-255; UNCTAD (1991) *Review of Maritime Transport 1990* (New York: United Nations), Table 5, p.12.

Figure 5.1: Flagging-Out in Selected Maritime Nations, 1990

Despite the fact that this was the peak of the flagging-out crisis in the Community and ship registration decline was at its most severe, the Commission had produced an over-ambitious proposal (i.e. EUROS) for the shipping sector, unpopular with the industry and member states and thus doomed to failure. It took some time, but was eventually realised by the Commission that there was no desire from the industry or member states to proceed with the European flag idea and the proposal was withdrawn under the direction of the Commissioner for Transport (BIMCO, 2000; Pallis, 2002). This represented a victory for the industry as much as anything but also, to a limited extent, one for member states over the Commission and thus national policy over supra-national.

In addition to the EUROS proposals, a number of other policy measures were promoted at the same time as part of the 'Positive Measures' package. Although these measures included consideration of manning and research, technical harmonisation for ship transfer between EU registers, a series of social measures, enforcement of ILO and IMO standards, food aid and shipping and the definition of ship-owner status, undoubtedly the most significant of these focused upon cabotage and guidelines for state aids to the shipping sector (Commission of the European Communities, 1989). In terms of this last policy area, a series of guidelines were issued in 1989 which member states were required to follow when considering subsidies to the shipping sector. These will be of some considerable importance in the later discussion of national/supra-national policy balance in the maritime sector in recent years. Revised guidelines were issued in 1997 and 2003 which were fundamental to this balance and which made the original 1989 guidelines redundant (Lloyd's List, 2003z; Tradewinds, 2003). We will return to these new guidelines in the next two chapters.

Cabotage

The first stage of EEC shipping policy – dominated by the four liner shipping Regulations discussed earlier – had recognised the need to remove shipping cabotage restrictions within the Community so that all EC ports were open to all EC shipping in all trades, without restriction by nationality of flag, owner or crew. However, no agreement had been reached and so it was left to the 'Positive Measures' package to accommodate this issue. The initial proposal was that only EUROS flagged vessels would benefit from freedom of trading between all EC ports but, as we shall see later, with the failure to implement EUROS this proposal was dropped in favour of widespread cabotage freedom application.

The cabotage issue centred on the numerous restrictions that existed in many countries of the EC, upon which flagged ships could operate in the maritime domestic trades – between ports of the same country. These restrictions were clearly in direct contravention of the Treaty of Rome but were widely applied in Italy and also the Greek Island trades as two good examples. The resolution to the problem took some time to be reached but eventually Regulation 3577/92 was agreed in 1992. This Regulation was characterised by a considerable number of derogations reflecting the contentious nature of the cabotage issue and also an increasing recognition of the EC that national opinions and thus policies needed to be accommodated. Supra-national requirements could not just be imposed without taking into account member state priorities as well.

The Regulation stipulated the following:

- From 1st January 1993 the freedom to provide maritime transport services within a member state was to apply to all EC ship-owners who have their ships registered in and fly the flag of a member state.
- Maritime cabotage included: mainland cabotage (the carriage of passengers or goods by sea between ports situated on the main territory of a member state; off-shore supply services between the mainland and structures located on the continental shelf of that member state; island cabotage (the carriage of passengers or goods by sea between ports situated on the mainland and one or more islands of that member state or between islands of the same member state).

Community ship-owners were also specifically defined and were to include those based in member states with effective control based in the member state or those located elsewhere but where their vessels flew a member state flag and the company was controlled by member state nationals.

There was also extensive discussion of public service obligations (PSO), which were to be the main basis for derogations. A member state could impose a PSO as a condition of a cabotage service (thus reserving the service to the member state fleet) with the permission of the Commission and under strict and well-defined conditions.

Specific derogations delayed the imposition of the Regulation as follows:

- Mediterranean coast plus France, Spain and Portugal.
  Cruise services – until January 1995.
  Strategic goods (e.g. oil and drinking water) – until January 1997.
  Small vessels (<650 gt) – until January 1998.
  Passenger and ferry services – until January 1999.
- Mediterranean Sea, Canary, Azores and Madeira Islands, Ceuta and Melilla, French Atlantic islands, French overseas departments – until January 1999.
- Greece. Vessels <650 gt and all passenger and ferry services – until January 2004.

These derogations were an important indicator of the difficulties faced by the EC in reaching any agreement on cabotage and this reflected the growing power of member states in the development of maritime policy in the EU. In fact some of the member states (notably Greece) actually opened up their markets to all other member states before the deadline was reached. However, the trend towards a growth in the significance of national policies was noticeable.

MARITIME POLICY MEASURES DEVELOPED AT THE TURN OF THE MILLENNIUM

Following the two packages of the late 1980s, a veritable cascade of maritime policies emerged during the 1990s which together can be viewed as a coherent thrust in maritime policy-making and which can be drawn together for discussion in terms of the national/supra-national conflict. Only some of the more important policies will be discussed here and, as noted earlier, the discussion of state aid to the maritime sector (which should be viewed as a major policy element) and its impact upon the national/supra-national dichotomous discussion will be examined in depth in later chapters.

In 2002, the Commission stressed that the key priorities of the EU maritime policy would consist of ten major strands:

1. Enhancing the competitiveness of EU shipping.
2. Continuing to open up the markets for ports and shipping as a cost effective alternative to long-distance road haulage and to eliminate infrastructural bottlenecks.
3. Strengthen control of all vessels in EU waters to ensure strict enforcement of international laws and standards for safety and the environment.
4. Develop EU initiatives for global solutions, complemented by EU-wide measures where appropriate to improve maritime safety and the environment.
5. Improve security for passenger and goods transport on ships and in ports.
6. Develop short-sea shipping and improved connections of ports to inland transport networks as a contribution to sustainable development and the promotion of 'motorways of the sea'.
7. Strengthen the rights of passengers.
8. Enhance the status and attractiveness of maritime professions to retain know-how in Europe.
9. Increase transparency of information as an aid to safety and as a means of monitoring the implementation of EU maritime policies.
10. Develop technology to strengthen maritime safety and environmental protection (Commission of the European Communities, 2002b).

These were the main maritime drivers behind the broader EU White Paper of 2001 'European Transport Policy for 2010; Time To Decide' (Commission of the European Communities, 2001a). Thus the EU maritime policy could be summarised as addressing the economic inefficiencies associated with congestion on major transport routes and the bottlenecks caused by natural barriers, and in particular a more specific aim to shift goods and passengers from roads to other modes whilst meeting the demands of citizens for safe, reliable and environmentally friendly transport. Sea transport is seen as playing a key role in achieving these objectives.

This set of policies was drawn together into three main thrusts:

1.   Stimulation of the competitiveness of European shipping.
2.   The development of a seamless door-to-door Europe-wide freight network.
3.   European initiatives to raise the standards of maritime safety and environmental protection.

The Competitiveness of European Shipping

This forms a major strand to the European maritime policy and one that is inherently tied up with the issues of national and supra-national policy interaction and as such will be discussed in more detail later in this chapter and beyond. However, the essentials of recent legislative initiatives will be outlined here for completeness and to be noted at this stage. As we have seen already, since the beginning of the 1980s (and possibly even earlier), European shipping has been faced with increased competitiveness, particularly in international freight markets. This has been in part at least because of the opportunity for third country operators to benefit from cheaper labour, tax incentives and sometimes, lower safety standards. The result has been the rush to flag-out from Europe. A consequence has been the significant decline in the number of European Union seafarers – a feature which the EU is committed to reverse to ensure that the know-how loss that this implies will not occur.

This know-how is believed to be important because of the extensive ancillary maritime activities to be found in such locations as London and Piraeus which some commentators believe is highly dependent upon a regular supply of EU ex-seafarers (Gardner and Pettit, 1999a; Gardner et al., 2001). Leaving aside for the time being the question of whether this is in fact the case, the EU has accepted that to ensure a flow of EU ex-seafarers then the 'playing field' for EU based international operators has to be levelled artificially. The rules to direct the market intervention that this suggest can be found in the 1997 Communication of the Commission on state aids to the maritime sector. These rules have been reviewed once more in 2003 and will be examined in detail in a later section which will assess the EU versus nation state issues which they imply.

Meanwhile the number of EU seafarers employed on EU flagged ships has fallen by 50% since 1985 with obvious employment implications but also potential impacts on safe and environmentally friendly shipping which are not always associated with non-EU seafarers. The EU as a consequence has taken steps to preserve and develop home-grown resources of skill and experience. In 2001, the Commission adopted a communication on the training and recruitment of seafarers. The main points were:

- Implementation of existing legislation on living and working conditions on ships.
- Voluntary agreements to give priority to the employment of European seafarers on European ships.
- Measures to raise awareness of seafaring careers and to improve the social status of maritime professions.
- Dissemination of best practice among national maritime education systems.

The EU also believes that the economic and social development of outlying regions – and particularly island communities – relies upon good transport links to markets and thus reliable ferry services to the mainland. Regulation 3577/92 relating to cabotage in shipping, and which has been discussed above, is the main legislative approach to this issue with a number of special conditions and derogations for island services.

In more general terms the EU expressed its commitment to the World Trade Organisation GATS negotiations on maritime transport services. In connection with this and in meeting the requirements of the Treaty of Rome, the EU stressed its application of the principle of unrestricted access to its maritime markets and promoting the participation of international operators. Externally it continues to attempt to remove obstacles to the access of EU shipping operators to cargoes or other maritime services. This latter objective remains the main thrust behind Regulations 4057/86 and 4058/86 in the liner trades.

Bilateral agreements between the EU and third countries normally provide for equal treatment for EU flagged and operated ships in ports. In this sense the issue of national policies have been over-ridden by those of the supra-national power where conflicts arise.

Internationally agreed conventions on safety and the environment (in effect those of the IMO) are fully endorsed – once again placing any conflicting national policies secondary to the supra-national need. However, recent national policy-making by France following the Prestige pollution incident, in banning entry into French waters of single-hulled tankers before the introduction of IMO and EU legislation which does the same, suggests some success at national level over that of supra-national.

Finally, and rather a diversion within this section, is the increased role of maritime security for both passengers and freight following the events of September 2001. The EU is planning a number of measures to increase security levels, particularly for containers. These measures will follow those agreed by the IMO.

Short-Sea Shipping and Seaports

The EU believes that short-sea shipping is fundamentally efficient, cost-effective and environmentally friendly. It is an important component of the EU transport system accounting for 43% of the total tonne-kilometre intra-EU freight movement in 2000 and continues to grow in size. However, road transport is both larger and grows faster.

Congestion on road and rail within the EU costs about 0.5% of total economic output and short-sea shipping offers a means of overcoming some of the problems that this implies. However, it remains underused and also is not as well integrated into the transport chain as it could be. Therefore the EU has a role in promoting its use. Both technical and practical obstacles are apparent and so the Commission was attempting to identify the most significant bottlenecks which inhibit the use of short-sea shipping and also to suggest proposals to overcome them.

Examples include Directive 2002/6/EC standardising reporting formalities for ships at EU ports and the Marco Polo Programme was established with a budget of 115 million euro over 5 years with the aim of shifting 12 billion tonne-kilometres from road to rail, inland waterway and short-sea shipping. Further to this, ports need to be improved with faster turnaround times and more transparent charges. In addition a number of policy proposals exist and are summarised as follows.

Ports and the trans-European transport network

EU ports provide the vital link between inland and short-sea shipping networks and between the mainland and islands. Their ability to handle freight is consequently important for the development of short-sea (and deep-sea) shipping.

The Trans-European Transport Networks (TEN-T) were established in 1996 as a series of continent-wide corridors (crossing numerous EU borders and member states) which initially ignored the role of ports within them but following revision and extension in 2001, now include them as specific nodes to be improved alongside airports and rail and road links. They are a clear expression of supra-national transport policy with implications for national transport policies.

Motorways of the sea

Since the 2001 White Paper on Transport (Commission of the European Communities, 2001a), EU maritime policy has also extended to the need to establish what was termed 'Motorways of the Sea' as part of a way of relieving pressure on roads including the Alps, the Pyrenees and Benelux. The first stage is envisaged as improving the services provided by ports including their linkages to inland transport.

Port services

An increasingly contentious area in 2001-2003 were the proposals to streamline the services provided by ports including pilotage, cargo handling, towage and mooring. Free markets for these services in theory existed but in practice differed in their extent across the EU. As a consequence the Commission put forward a proposal for a Directive on Port Services in 2001 which was then open for discussion and comment. Its main objective was to increase market access to port services of this type to increase competition and quality and to lower price.

The proposals have met with much opposition from the port sector across Europe, partly from interested parties fearing for their long-established monopoly positions but also from some member state governments (in particular the UK) where ports were already entirely privatised but in such a way that opening them up to further competition would be to the severe disadvantage of the new owners.

This element of the 'Ports Package' has clear supra-national/national implications and resistance to its proposals for time-limited contracts and competition in all activities was received variably across the EU. In late 2003 it remained subject to severe pressure for change from member states' governments and the industry and was ultimately rejected by the European Parliament.

In addition the EU ports package has contained a review of current charging practices in ports and the role of state aid in port finances. The implications of the variable regimes in member states which emerged has clear ramifications for member state/EU policy relationships. The EU has, however, made it clear that it does not intend to regulate the ownership or management of ports but to ensure that aid and financing are both transparent and fair.

Research and development
The EU has been funding research in both shipping and ports since 1994, focusing particularly upon safety and the environment and the operational and technical systems needed to ensure that the sector meets necessary standards in the context of developing seamless door-to-door transport networks.

Maritime Safety and Pollution

Maritime safety and pollution forms the third and largest group of policies of the EU. One of the effects of the 'Erika' incident, where 20,000 tonnes of heavy fuel were washed onto the French shore from the stricken oil tanker in December 1999, was an incentive for the EU to tighten existing maritime safety and environmental legislation and subsequently to introduce considerably more. As a consequence the EU has adopted 20 pieces of maritime safety legislation covering all key areas.

This legislative programme was, of course, built upon measures that already existed. In 1993 the Commission had issued a communication entitled 'A Common Policy on Safe Seas' (Commission of the European Communities, 1993) which outlined a framework to eliminate ship operators which placed the environment and safety at risk to gain competitive advantage. This communication and subsequent legislation has been based around four main principles:

1. Convergent application of internationally agreed rules on maritime safety and environmental protection – essentially those of the IMO and ILO.
2. Uniform enforcement of these rules in EU waters.
3. Complementary EU measures where international rules are deemed insufficient.
4. A stronger role for the EU in the international scene.

Following the 'Erika' incident, the EU published a package of proposals to enforce maritime safety in EU waters – *Erika I*. This included:

*   Strengthening the existing Directive on Port State Control. Increased numbers of ships were subsequently inspected and a blacklist produced of those to be refused access.
*   Strengthening the existing Directive governing the activities of classification societies when conducting safety checks on ships for flag states. The quality requirements of classification societies was raised; continued operation within the EU of these societies is

dependent upon meeting these standards; and the societies are now monitored rigorously.

- It brought forward the timetable for the phasing out of single hulled tankers. The IMO regulation that existed was to phase these vessels out by 2026 but the EU introduced legislation to move this forward to 2015. This issue has now been partly overtaken by events surrounding a further oil tanker spill from the 'Prestige' in 2002 which has seen France ban single hulled oil vessels with almost immediate effect.

These proposals were all adopted by Council and Parliament in record time in December 2001. Member states were to introduce national legislation to enforce the rules as soon as possible. There are clear implications here for the international/supra-national/national policy debate including the role of the EU over national safety policies, the importance of IMO legislation in all this and the rejection of the EU timetable by a member state (France). Currently (November 2003) there are three dates for phasing out single hull tankers in different parts of the EU and beyond with clear (or perhaps rather confusing) implications for ship-owners, the markets and policy-makers.

Erika II was a second package of maritime safety proposals which was proposed in December 2000 and approved in June 2002. Here three more measures were put forward which were mainly practical solutions to underpin *Erika I*:

1. The creation of a European Agency of Maritime Safety (EMSA) with the aim of monitoring the effective application of EU maritime safety rules. This new agency will collect information, maintain a database, audit classification societies, facilitate the exchange of good practice, provide technical assistance for safety and marine pollution prevention and organise Port State Control inspections.

2. Monitoring traffic passing through EU waters. Member states will be given strengthened powers to intervene where there is a threat of accident or pollution. Vessels in EU waters will be required to fit automatic identification systems and voyage data recorders (black boxes). Data on dangerous cargoes will be shared and ports will be given the authority to prevent vessels leaving in times of bad weather. Member states will be required to provide places of refuge for vessels in distress.

3. Improvement in the mechanism for the payment of compensation to victims of oil spills, raising the upper limit to be paid in the event of major spills in European waters and setting appropriate penalties to be imposed on those causing pollution through negligent behaviour.

Erika II raises even further questions about the relationship between the EU as a supra-national authority, and the member states in the context of maritime policy. In particular the new powers to be afforded to the European Agency of Maritime Safety take away traditional responsibility for such affairs from member states and aim to harmonise procedures. There is no doubt that the application of Port State Control procedures has been highly variable between member states and this in particular has been the main incentive for this part of the *Erika II* package.

However, in other ways the role of member states will be strengthened especially through the new powers granted in terms of monitoring of traffic and their intervention when pollution or safety is threatened. The result is a balance between the two forces of national and supra-national with the potential of achieving the best of both policy-making strategies.

The importance of safety does not stop there in terms of EU maritime policy and some of the issues which are central to both *Erika* packages have been subject to considerably more discussion.

The EU notes that maritime transport is heavily regulated from a safety and pollution perspective at the international level – primarily through the work of the IMO. In recognition of this the EU has proposed that it should become a full member of the IMO in the near future in addition to the member states themselves, which would be an unusual combination of two policy-making levels and might present some difficulties in the years to come where conflicts occur.

The EU's major international concern is that the international regulations that do exist are not necessarily applied harmoniously or effectively. In particular, a number of Open Registries and other flag states do not implement or enforce the agreed safety standards, a situation which has led the EU to its policy on Port State Control. Directive 95/21/EC of June 1995, which established common procedures for the inspection and detention of ships calling at EU ports, was an early result (Commission of the European Communities, 1995a). Under the Directive, at least 25% of all ships calling at an EU port must be inspected although it is left to the member state to decide which these should be. However, under this Directive, many of these inspections were inadequate and consequently, under *Erika I*, the number of thorough inspections is to rise considerably. Certain ships will also be targeted such as chemical tankers, single hull oil tankers and older vessels.

Most inspections are carried out on behalf of member states by classification societies. The fundamental role that such societies play means that the EU allows only 12 out of the 50 societies that exist to conduct such inspections, based upon the new, strict quality control procedure for classification societies.

Supra-national policy here over-rides that of the member states except in allowing classification societies to choose the vessels to be inspected. This has not in itself been a contentious transfer of policy power as it is widely agreed that the harmonised outcome should be for the benefit of all concerned (except the unscrupulous ship-owner of course).

Meanwhile the EU has also taken note of the fact that 80% of all maritime accidents are caused by human error and hence the training of crews and their conditions on-board vessels are fundamental issues in relation to safety. The issue is essentially two-fold: some 10% of all maritime certificates are false or obtained fraudulently and there is a lack of uniformity in training and certification. As a consequence the 1994 Directive 94/58/EC gives the force of EU law to the IMO International Convention on Standards of Training, Certification and Watchkeeping for Seafarers (STCW). The Directive was revised both in 1998 and 2001. In addition, two Directives from 1999 regulate seafarers' working hours and provide for the monitoring of working hours by port states. The role of Port State Control helps here as well in inspecting the quality of accommodation on-board ships. Therefore, here we have international policies taken up supra-nationally and imposed upon nations within the EU but with some flexibility given to the member states as to how they interpret the rules and apply them as long as the rules are met.

In terms of the passenger ferry industry, and following a number of ferry accidents in the 1990s, the EU has acted comprehensively to harmonise and strengthen their policy for member states. The first Regulation dates from 1995 on the safety management of roll-on/roll-off passenger ferries. This made the IMO International Ship Management (ISM) Code mandatory for all ferries calling at an EU member state port.

Three further Directives from 1998 and 1999 were also adopted:

1. Harmonisation of Safety Standards for all ferry types relating to vessel construction, stability, fire protection and life-saving equipment.
2. Registration of passengers and crew requiring a full count of all those on-board passenger ferries before sailing.
3. A specific and mandatory inspection process for all passenger ships on regular services. The member state has the responsibility that the vessel complies with the safety certificates of its flag state.

Meanwhile, in March 2002, the Commission put forward a Communication containing proposals to enhance the safety of passenger ships (Commission of the European Communities, 2002a) which included:

1. A proposal for a Directive introducing specific stability requirements for all roll-on/roll-off passenger ships operating international services.
2. A proposal to strengthen and simplify the existing Directive on safety rules for passenger ships operating domestic routes.
3. Announced the Commission's views on the regulation of liability of damage caused to passengers on ships.

The EU has also been active in terms of the safety requirements for specific ship types. In terms of bulk carriers, the EU has been conscious of the increasing losses which have been partly attributable to inappropriate loading and unloading in ports. The result has been the 2001 Directive based upon the IMO Code of Practice for the Safe Loading and Unloading of Bulk Carriers which includes promotion of quality assurance in port terminals (Commission of the European Communities, 2001b). In addition there are a number of Directives specifically targeting safety of fishing vessels.

The EU's role in maritime pollution control policy has been extensive. In 1993 the Directive on Hazardous Materials was passed and introduced the first attempts to make all ships in EU waters carrying polluting or dangerous materials notify relevant authorities. A more comprehensive system of information control, traffic management and prevention pollution has now been developed. Provisions within *Erika II* for traffic monitoring will help in this process.

In terms of the deliberate discharge of polluting substances by ships at sea, a Directive on port-reception facilities for ship generated waste and cargo residues was adopted in December 2000 (Commission of the European Communities, 2000a). All ports now must provide appropriate facilities and ensure that they are used and ships are charged for this facility.

In July 2002, the Commission proposed measures to prohibit the use of environmentally harmful anti-fouling paint on ships which would lead to a ban on the use of certain compounds on EU ships with almost immediate effect and those of other ships in EU waters from 2008. In addition it was noted that ships' contribution to air emissions was rising and the EU has proposed that low sulphur fuel should be used in all regions of high sensitivity. Finally, the illegal discharging of oil and other polluting substances is covered by the Marpol Convention but the EU claims that the rules within this convention are widely ignored. The EU is to propose new measures to increase its effectiveness in EU waters and to introduce sufficiently severe penalties.

In the navigation field, the *Erika II* proposal for a European sea traffic monitoring system was underway by 2002 and in addition, two further navigation aids were being developed:

- Vessel Traffic Management and Information Services (VTMIS) supported by 10 million euro of EU funding is attempting to progressively integrate coastal and port vessel traffic services, distress and communication systems and other automatic telecommunication applications.
- The European Radio-Navigation Plan (ERNP) was launched some time ago in 1992 to develop radio services which could accommodate the needs of increasing volumes of traffic.

Finally, and on a broader safety note – but no less significant – the EU has encouraged the maritime industry since 1997 to develop quality measures and in 1999, twenty-nine international and European industry associations have signed the Maritime Industry Charter on Quality aimed at eliminating unsafe shipping. The most notable outcome of this has been the establishment of a new database – Equasis – in May 2000, which contains the details of 66,000 vessels – in effect the entire world fleet of merchant vessels over 100 grt. Information on the database includes ship characteristics, inspection reports for the previous five years, classification and other certification, insurance and P&I cover and other vessels operated by the same organisation. This information is transparent and reliable and hence can help the industry make safer shipping choices.

Many of these safety initiatives of the EU have been initiated in the context of supra-national policy-making but nonetheless, commonly are not a contentious part of the national/supra-national debate. In many cases they simply confirm existing international regulations accepted by the member states or are so clear in their creation of a safer and cleaner environment that the policy argument is largely irrelevant. Some exceptions do exist (e.g. there are contentious issues within Port State Control), but it is more often the issues relating to competition in shipping and ports that have thrown up the debate.

Perhaps the most interesting area of policy conflict (and the way attempts are being made to resolve it) stems from issues to do with state aid and it is to these issues that we return in a later chapter in more detail. For now, we will conclude this chapter by a discussion upon the growth of globalisation and its impact upon policies for the shipping industry in the EU in a climate of debate about the existing and developing relationships between the supra-national policies of the EU and the national demands of its member states.

THE EMERGENCE OF GLOBALISATION –
COMPETITION FORCES AND REACTIVE POLICIES

The situation which characterised the European Community shipping market in the late 1980s can be broadly explained through examination of the effects of three main factors:

1. The emerging importance of shipping services for the increasingly global economy along with the increasing presence of newly industrialised countries in the shipping market and the impact of these new economies on costs.
2. The fierce competition between European Community (later European Union) registered ships and vessels registered elsewhere (most notably Open Registry vessels).
3. The failure of either member states or supra-national EC policies to reverse the decline of European shipping.

Meanwhile, growth in the developing world economy since the early 1980s has been mainly due to the increased significance of the service sector, whilst growth in demand for primary commodities has generally slowed in relative terms. In addition, competition in the industrial and shipping services sector was becoming even more apparent with the emergence of a range of newly industrialised countries establishing both production and transportation services. These included in particular countries such as Korea, Malaysia, China and Thailand. As a consequence of the trend of large multinational companies towards seeking low-cost global production facilities, a gradual shift in the nature of trade between Europe and the newly industrial countries occurred, a shift involving a reduction in bulk and considerably more containerised traffic. This relocation of production also favoured the newly industrialised country shipping fleets as compared with those from the traditional countries of the EU. The former not only were based in the countries to which production had moved but also were commonly flagged with Open Registries with consequently much reduced costs compared with those fleets from the EU.

In addition, between 1980 and 1988, world seaborne trade decreased by 9%, however world fleet capacity fell by only 5% – in 1988, the estimate of excess capacity was around 20% (Brooks and Button, 1992). Much of this excess in fleet capacity was to be found in the more expensive, traditionally flagged fleets – including those of the EU.

The slight increase in the level of freight rates in the second half of the 1980s was not enough to raise profit margins and thus lead to higher investment in new vessels. The inevitable consequence was the ageing in particular of the EU flagged fleet in most vessel categories. This steady ageing of the traditional European fleet led to doubts about the fleet's safety standards as well as questions of its future potential (Kiriazidis and Tzanidakis, 1995).

Until 1988, Open Registers had grown to accommodate 35% of world shipping (Brooks and Button, 1992), further increasing to 38.2% of world tonnage since 1991 (Kiriazidis and Tzanidakis, 1995). Flagging-out implied a direct competition between EU registered ships and third country vessels not only in international trades but also in most trades within the Community. It also implied the loss of not only economic but also potentially military resources. Moreover, in many years flagging-out was followed by relocation of ancillary activities such as ship management to countries outside the EU, leading to an even greater loss of employment, both on-board and on-shore, with all the related consequences, such as the loss of maritime know-how and less incentives for Europeans to join the maritime profession.

All this was possible in part at least because of the continued effects of globalisation in trade and markets. Of course, the specific nature of the shipping industry also had its impact – in particular the mobility of infrastructure, personnel, regulation and finance that has characterised it for many years – but the trends towards global sourcing of an increasing number of industrial products and the intensification of the use of cheap, Second and Third World labour in the production of goods for First World markets had its own impacts upon the shipping sector as well, leading to increased demand for maritime transport. This in turn had its regulatory and policy impacts and it is these issues that interest us, particularly since as the shipping industry became more globalised and affected by international policies, the conflicts between the spatial levels of policy-making became more apparent.

Thus international policies to combat and regulate pollution, safety, personnel and investment (e.g. from the IMO) have become increasingly common and necessary whilst the demands for supra-national interference (e.g. from the EU) have increased at the same time that traditional national policy bodies (e.g. the EU member state) have attempted to retain their own influence. These conflicts are what we shall go on to examine using the EU's attitudes to state aids to shipping as an example.

State aids provided by individual nation states have been something that has characterised the world shipping industry since it developed and are commonly viewed within countries as necessary and acceptable (even obvious). The EU has a different view in its search for policy harmonisation to meet the demands of a free and single market outlined in the Treaty of Rome, and this has caused some intense difficulties. Failure to address these difficulties adequately has led to the decline of the EU ship and seafarer as we have seen. Meanwhile the EU has also decided to impose EU-wide policies on the member states that match those of the main international regulatory body, the IMO, with further conflicts of policy emerging from this.

The result at the end of the 1990s was recognition by the EU that some sort of new balance was necessary between these conflicting issues and this new policy initiative was characterised by the state-aids package of 1997. We shall see in later chapters how this has led to the proliferation of one measure in particular across the EU – the use of a specific shipping tonnage tax – and whether this has had the desired effect for all those concerned.

CONCLUSIONS

This chapter has attempted to consider EU maritime policy as it had developed by the turn of the century. These policy initiatives present an interesting example of the introduction of supra-national measures in the context of traditional national maritime policies of the member states and in the light of a developing international regime for the sector. The problems of these spatial inter-relationships and how they are beginning to be resolved (or otherwise) are the central theme of this analysis and of the chapters to come.

EU maritime policy up to the early 1990s had succeeded in addressing a number of major problem areas of shipping within the Union in the context of the demands of the Treaty of Rome. The most notable driver behind policy was a combination of the need for improved safety and environmental structures along with the obvious and severe decline of the EU fleet. These two themes are of course highly related and EU maritime policy has been characterised by attempts to deal with these issues on a concerted basis. However, as the year 2000 approached, the continued reduction in the number of both EU flagged ships and seafarers was proceeding unabated.

Meanwhile, the nature of the policies that had been imposed up to that time were notably (although not entirely) supra-national in that they focused upon an EU interpretation of what was necessary to develop and improve the sector rather than having a particularly national dimension that allowed interpretation in different ways by different member states whilst still achieving EU-wide policy ambitions. This move towards what the EU termed subsidiarity in all policy-making (devolving where possible the detailed application of policies to the lowest possible level – for example to member states or even lower) had yet to make itself genuinely felt in the maritime sector.

The continued decline in member state fleets encouraged the Commission to take a rather different view on how the future of maritime policy should look and together with the growth in favour towards subsidiarity within the

EU (and its clear implications for the encouragement of national policy-making within a supra-national framework) led to a distinct revision of policy measures. As Kiriazidis and Tzanidakis (1995) observed, the European shipping industry needed a 'generous programme of fiscal relief' to survive the consequences of unfair, international competition and policies were needed to recognise this. This central issue to the survival of EU flagged vessels was about to be provided in the years to come and reflected a derogation of policy detail and application down to member state level. This in turn was aimed at reducing the conflict between policy levels which at times had been apparent and which had partly been the reason for the failure of EU maritime policy-making with regard to fleet revival up to then. This change in approach and its particular application through maritime state aids will be the focus of a later chapter, but first we will turn to the issue of globalisation and internationalisation in shipping in the context of the EU.

6. The Impact of Globalisation on the European Union Shipping Industry

INTRODUCTION

Since very early times, Europe has been a major force in shipping and in the development of the legal and political regulatory system which surrounds it. However, despite the development of various flags and a multitude of owners within the EU, over the last part of the twentieth century the age of globalisation in terms of both trade and politics has created new challenges of its own which have seen major problems for the survival of this industrial and commercial network (International Association of Independent Tanker Owners, 2001). Nevertheless, by virtue of its geography, history and despite the pressures today of globalisation, the EU is still highly dependent on maritime transport, perhaps more so than ever (Commission of the European Communities, 2001a).

During a variety of significant maritime crises in the period following the 1950s, opportunity was given to less developed countries to enter the maritime industry providing a service that was possibly less sophisticated and certainly cheaper than those of the established EU fleets. In particular, the distribution of world tonnage among the different groups of countries underwent significant changes following the effects of the world economic crisis after 1973. This period also corresponded with increased development in the supply of tonnage worldwide, and which created attractive conditions for the rise of the lower-cost fleets of developing countries which could feed the less financially secure trade markets of the time (Thanopoulou, 1995).

As we have noted in earlier chapters, the Open Registry fleets displayed their sharpest increases in tonnage in the 1970s, following an upward trend through the 1980s and resulting in today's tremendous growth in contrast to the fleets of the traditional maritime countries including those of the EU. Figure 6.1 shows the EU owned fleet in terms of flag choice, a result of a study presented by the European Commission (Commission of the European Communities, 1996). The flags used by the interview sample are a good reflection of the total EU fleet.

The difference in popularity between Open Registries and national fleets certainly does not appear to be diminishing, representing a global, widespread phenomenon of today's shipping (Bergantino and Marlow, 1998). From the EU maritime sector viewpoint it is hard to be optimistic and this inevitably poses some serious questions for the current maritime environment creating more specifically a challenge on its own for European Union maritime policies and initiatives.

In the following sections, the importance of shipping for European Union nations will be presented along with the factors that lie behind the current phase, with the increasing pressure on EU operators to flag-out to Open Registries. This in turn provides the context for the following discussion on the role of state aids in the maritime sector which has been a significant policy initiative of the EU in the late 1990s.

SHIPPING'S CONTRIBUTION TO THE EUROPEAN ECONOMY

The European Economic Area (EEA) registered trading fleet (including the EU plus Iceland and Norway) amounted to over 6,900 vessels with a total of 92m gt as of 1st April 2001 (Figure 6.2). This share represented some 17.2% of the world fleet (Figure 6.3), an increase of almost 6% over the previous year. The importance of shipping to the European Union is demonstrated by the fact that over 90% of its external trade between member states is carried by sea. The recent oil crisis, for example, highlighted the dependence of the EU on ships for the transportation of its oil trade and for the continuity of its energy supply. Moreover, due to its extensive cross-trading activities, European shipping provides valuable resources for sustainable economic development through invisible earnings and therefore presents a substantial contribution to the national product of individual European countries (ECSA, 2002a). The magnitude of these activities has been particularly difficult to estimate for the EU as a whole, since no figures are currently available for several member states and those available are not on a uniform basis. However, older estimates have indicated that, in broad terms, one-third of all income of the EU shipping industry come from cross-trading activities (Lalis, 1999a). Moreover, the maritime transport sector – including shipbuilding, ports and related industries and services – employs around 2.5 million people in the European Union (Commission of the European Communities, 2001a).

As we have noted earlier, the shipping industry is important for the EU as an earner of foreign exchange and as an employer both at sea and ashore. In addition to its strategic value including defence, shipping is an essential provider of transport services for external trade to and from the EU as well as for trade within and between member states (Economic and Social Committee of the European Communities, 1986).

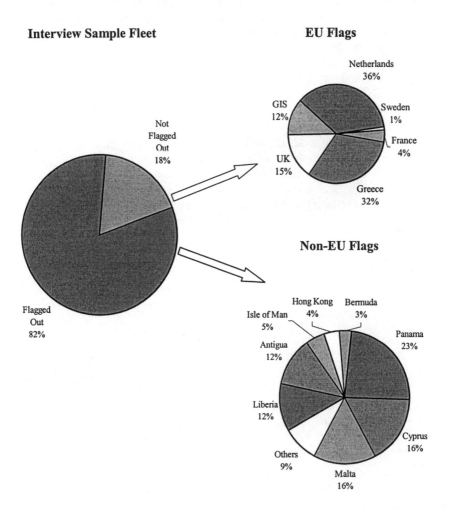

Source: Lloyd's Maritime Information Services, *Vessel Database*, Transport Research, APAS, Maritime Transport VII-38, Structure and Organization of Maritime Transport, European Commission, Directorate General Transport, 1996.

Figure 6.1: EU Flag Choice

The European Union is the leading trading bloc of the world (Figure 6.4) and the shipping sector is important in its own right, primarily because it is the dominant transport mode within the region. Furthermore, maritime transport flows represent almost the entire international trade of some member states, including for example Greece and the United Kingdom (Pallis, 1997).

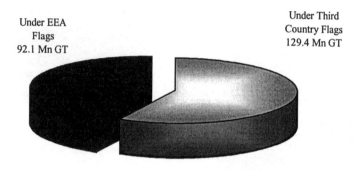

Under EEA
Flags
92.1 Mn GT

Under Third
Country Flags
129.4 Mn GT

Source: ECSA, Annual Report 2000-2001, p.44.

Figure 6.2: European Controlled Shipping Under European and Third Country Flags (1ˢᵗ April, 2001)

The actual contribution of shipping to national economies can be illustrated by the following examples. In Greece, the net receipts from the shipping sector as a whole amounted to €4.2 billion in 2000, representing 38% of the value of total exports of goods. In Denmark, the shipping industry is the second most important export earner with foreign gross earnings of €11.5 billion in 2000. In the UK, the shipping industry had global earnings of €8.3 billion and made a direct contribution to the balance of payments of €2.3 billion and an overall contribution of €5.3 billion (including import savings) (Forum uber Shipping und Logistik, 2001). These examples clearly illustrate the dependency of the EU on world trade and the importance of the international shipping markets for the European maritime interests.

An efficient maritime transport system is also of qualitative importance for the world as a whole and for the EU in particular. Primarily, there is the widespread belief expressed within EU maritime policy that transport is an activity with a negative impact upon the environment and that road congestion in particular is the main cause. These problems cannot be resolved whilst the current split of the modal pie remains – in effect one dominated by the road sector. In addition, whilst sustainable economic development is more crucial than ever, sea transport provides an environmentally attractive alternative to the use of the road mode. Secondly, due to the EU's geographical position, the expansion of maritime trade could enhance its socio-economic cohesion. The qualitative magnitude of sea transport is further emphasised by geopolitical developments in Europe, in particular the changes in East Europe and the accession of 10 countries to the EU in 2004, which have created an important window for the development of short-sea shipping (Pallis, 1997).

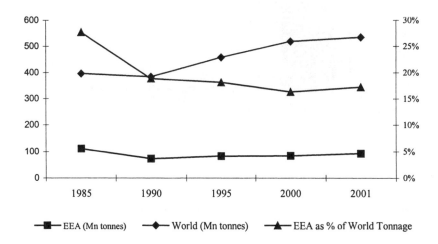

Source: ECSA, Annual Report 2000-2001, p.44.

Figure 6.3: European and World Shipping 1985-2001 (million tonnes)

EU SHIPPING POLICY TRANSITION – ISSUES, TRENDS, CHALLENGES AND CONCERNS

European maritime social, safety and environmental standards have become a crucial factor in the functioning of the single market and the EEA. Furthermore, they also play an important role in supporting a number of vital policy objectives of the EU, including the competitiveness of enterprises, innovation, the protection of health and safety, consumer interests and environmental protection. The need for common standards is thus underlined by the increasing globalisation of trade and the convergence of technologies (Commission of the European Communities, 2001a). However, when it comes to international transport and indeed shipping policy-making, and as rightly expressed by Gwilliam (1993):

'the difficulty lies in the fact that all of the forms of international shipping policy (either through multilateral, bilateral, or self-regulatory agreements) are limited either in spatial or industrial coverage and can only include specific measures which are consistent in each detail with the separate national interests of the parties involved.'

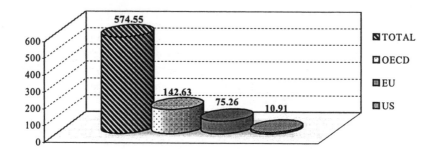

Source: Lloyd's Register of Shipping, *World Fleet Statistics 2001*.

Figure 6.4: Merchant Fleets of the World by Registration (100 gt and above) (million gt)

Meanwhile in recent years, whilst Greece and certain countries in the Far East have seen a rapid increase in their share of the world fleet, the remaining EU countries have seen a continuous and substantial decline.

At 31st December 1994, the world merchant fleet amounted to approximately 480 million tonnes, reflecting a 13% growth over previous years. Various factors have contributed to the increase. The world fleet, which has remained fairly stable between 1980 and 1982 (+1%), underwent a net laying up of 5% from 1983 to 1988 and a 16% growth between 1988 and 1994 (Figure 6.5).

Moreover, on the same date, the European Community merchant fleet (EC12) amounted to 67,775,000 tonnes. At the same date, on the eve of their accession, the merchant fleets of Austria, Finland and Sweden amounted to 4,335,000 tonnes. The combined tonnage therefore totalled 72,110,000 tonnes, equal to around 15% of the world fleet.

Between 1980 and 1994, the Community fleet (EC12), in contrast to the world fleet, declined by 44%. This dramatic fall is the outcome of a reduction of 51% between 1980 and 1990 and a 6% growth after 1991. The latter is an indication of the greater dynamism of the merchant fleets of the new Baltic country members. However, this had not compensated sufficiently for the opposite tendency in the other 12 countries. This figure illustrates a number of trends in the world shipping market over the previous decades. The worldwide recession of the early 1990s did not help this process and led to a further significant slowing down.

This downward trend in the Community/Union fleet is confirmed by the figures dated 1st January, 1995, for tonnage ordered or under construction. This amounted to 10.7 million tonnes compared to a world total of 75.07 million tonnes and corresponded to a share of only 14.2%, thus confirming erosion of the EU's share of the world fleet. It should be noted that Norway's merchant fleet – which accounts for nearly all the non-EU part of the EEA fleet, measured just under 21.5 million tonnes at the end of 1994, which was equal to 30% of the EU fleet and 4.5% of the world fleet (European Parliament, 1997).

The Decline of EU Seafarers

The EU maritime industry today presents a picture of contrasts and contradictions. The movement of goods by sea has shown a constant growth rate (Figure 6.3). However, this has been accompanied by a decline in the size of the flagged EU fleet. At the same time, as the fleet size has been eroded, the number of qualified EU seafarers appears to be in terminal decline and the industry has been unable to respond in any effective way. The trend has been caused largely by the growth of Open Registries, itself the consequence of cost differentials between such flagged ships and those of traditional registries from the EU (BIMCO, 2000).

As was outlined earlier, the world recession of the early 1990s resulted in the significant decrease of world trade growth in general and the EU in particular (Figure 6.5). As a consequence, shipping companies in the European Union (and elsewhere) were forced to react to the economic tension caused by declining freight rates and a resulting over-supply of tonnage in several ways.

The primary reaction was the reduction of manning levels on vessels because this seemed to be the easiest cost factor to make smaller (Dirks, 2001). The total numbers of seafarers employed in the European Union shipping sector in 1995 are indicated in Figure 6.6. However, the size of the national fleets must also be taken into consideration in order to provide a more accurate picture of developments in the European seafarer employment market. In this sense, it could be misleading to present the differences between national and non-national seafarers in the member states without taking into account the different potential of the national fleets for providing jobs. Figure 6.6 is clearly for indicative purposes only. As is clear from the graph, Italy had the highest number of national seafarers, followed by Greece, whereas the Norwegian fleet employed the highest level of non-national seafarers.

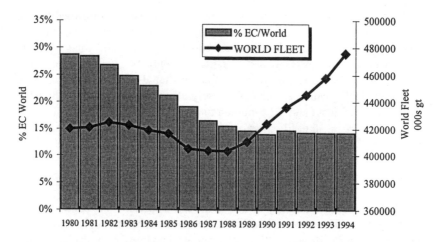

Notes: The graph illustrates fleets by EU flag. These are: Belgium, Denmark, France, Germany, Greece, Italy, Ireland, Luxembourg, Netherlands, Portugal, Spain, UK, Austria, Finland and Sweden.

Source: European Parliament (1997).

Figure 6.5: EU Fleets 1980-1994 (1000 gt and over)

The shortage of seafaring personnel however is not a European issue alone. According to reports from both BIMCO and the ISF, only 12,000-15,000 officers graduate every year, worldwide. This global trend, as already discussed in the earlier chapters, constitutes another consequence of the use of Open Registries with a trend towards substantial recruitment of non-national cheap labour made possible only by flagging-out (Kouri and Naniopoulos, 2000). All in all, it appears that the severe financial pressure caused by an over-supply of tonnage, along with intense and growing international competition from substandard vessels, led ship-owners in the EU (along with other traditional flagged countries) to a second attempt to resolve their crisis. This again meant that they registered their ships under

Open Registry flags, as this would commonly lead to further cost reductions (Dirks, 2001).

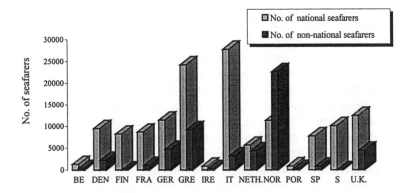

Source: ECSA, Annual Report and ISL Shipping Statistics, 1996.

Figure 6.6: Employment in the EU Shipping Sector, 1995

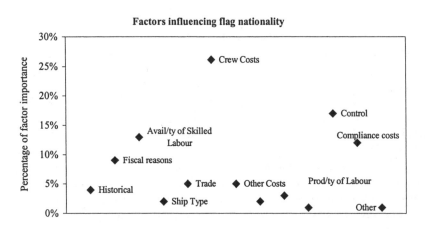

Source: Bergantino, A. and Marlow, P.B. (1998).

Figure 6.7: Factors that Influence Flag Choice

This aspect of flag selection was further examined in a qualitative analysis conducted by Bergantino and Marlow (1998), where it was shown that labour cost was the most significant factor determining flag nationality (Figure 6.7).

This analysis included a list of variables which were considered to be influential in the decision-making process of the ship-owner regarding the choice of the flag flown by his vessels. As shown, it is crew costs that present the central focus of attention from the shipping companies' point of view. However, a number of other factors including the degree of control that can be exercised, fiscal issues and availability of appropriate skills are among the most important aspects of the flag decision. One of the most significant impacts of the importance of labour costs for ship-owners was for a substantial number of third-country flags to develop a systematic source of seafarers, one which would provide relatively low-paid crews, particularly in comparison with those from traditional flag states (including those of the EU). Thus the natural globalised characteristic of shipping – in that it carried freight throughout the world and commonly between a variety of nation-states was made more globalised by the internationalisation of the labour market. This was made even more so by the development of Open Registries to capitalise on the demand for cheap international seafarers, these registries characterised by little true association with their named nation state and more association with the registration of vessels from many countries of the world, again including the EU. International shipping had thus become a globalised industry not only in terms of its labour force but also in terms of its organisation. Issues such as sources of finance, insurance, legal regimes and other ancillary activities (broking, freight forwarding, agencies, etc.) were to emphasise the internationalisation further.

However, it was the crewing costs issue that was perhaps more important than any other in creating a truly international and globalised industry. According to a 1996 ITF survey, the average salary of all categories of vessels was US$1,457. ITF questioned 6,500 seafarers in 93 countries and created a benchmark wage by interpreting the ILO minimum wage of US$385 and equating this to US$893 based on a 40 hour week and 103 hours of overtime. Seafarers on Open Registry vessels made up 44% of those taking part in the survey, approximately the same proportion as the gross tonnage of the world fleet (Kouri and Naniopoulos, 2000). The study showed that the lowest paid seafarers were commonly nationals from Russia, Ukraine and Croatia, with 59%, 48% and 42% of them respectively being paid less than US$699 per month. Other nationals who tended to receive lower wages than average were Filipino, Indonesian, Chinese and those from African and Middle East countries (Kouri and Naniopoulos, 2000). Figure 6.8, with the exception of Greece, clearly illustrates these characteristics. The significance of this pattern of increased globalisation for the EU traditional flags is clear from their decline, but also was highly important for the development of maritime policy with all the difficulties it presented for the relationships between the emergence of co-ordinated and effective policy at international, supra-national and national levels, whereby the desire to impose a national maritime policy might well be in conflict with the characteristics of the industry and with the policy ambitions of a higher authority.

Easier tax standards and lower requirements in terms of nationality and skills of crews were not the only criteria leading to the decision of many traditionally flagged shipping companies to register their vessels under Open Registers. Other factors have also been identified as important in determining these decisions. They include:

- The shipping sector; liner shipping for example, bears higher network costs in terms of infrastructure (that relating to ports, terminals and inter-modal transport), whereas bulk shipping is more labour intensive and therefore more sensitive to labour costs.

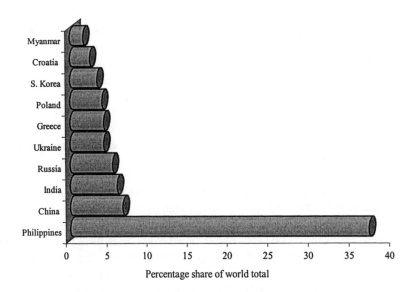

Source: Lloyd's Register of Shipping, *World Fleet Statistics 2001*.

Figure 6.8: Major Crew Nationalities (January 2001)

- The characteristics of the maritime service infrastructure such as communications, ancillary service industries (i.e. insurance, legal services, finance and credit facilities), the need for independent jurisdiction and a stable political environment can also affect the decision upon flag.
- The economic environment; including the ability to maintain high standards in markets where the existence of unprofessional shipping companies may be crucial.
- The expectation of the implementation and enforcement of internationally agreed standards and rules (Dirks, 2001).

However, there is no doubt that ultimately, crewing costs have been the major driving force in the growth of Open Registries, the decline of traditional flagged fleets, the problems faced by the EU maritime nations and subsequently the need for policy initiatives that have recognised the complex interaction between spatial levels that this new environment requires.

Other Reasons for the Decline in Number of EU Seafarers

Along with the reasons for the reduction of European seafarers noted above, there has also been a variety of other factors which have had their impact in reinforcing these trends. Manning levels on board modern ships have generally reduced. This trend has been compounded by a tendency for expansion of vessel size without any increase in crew size to match. In the period from 1986 to 1994, the average size of vessels in the world fleet rose from 17,967 to 19,192 GWT, an annual growth rate of 0.95%. During the same period, the number of ships in the world fleet slightly increased from 34,773 to 35,158.

In 1995, the Bremen Institute of Shipping Economics and Logistics (ISL) carried out a study of on-board communication of multi-lingual crews and concluded that only 120 men are now needed to man eight container vessels in the Asia/Europe trade to have the same transport capacity as in the 1960s. Then, an estimated 4,000 personnel on-board would have been needed on 100 conventional vessels to transport an equivalent amount of cargo. The reasons that have led to such changes include increased vessel speed, increased tonnage capacity and the development of technology on-board and in ports. Though there is still a lack of reliable data regarding the decline of manning levels caused by the modernisation of ships, there is nevertheless strong evidence that technical changes will lead to further reductions in crew sizes and that the effects in the past have been substantial (Dirks, 2001). Clearly these latter impacts have been worldwide and not just affected EU vessels but the more technologically advanced EU fleets (relative to the world in general) and their large presence in the more significant markets (where technological change has been most obvious) has exacerbated the effects of these changes. This is exemplified perhaps most obviously in the containerised liner trades where the EU has a major presence (for example Maersk/Sealand, P&O/Nedlloyd, Hapag Lloyd) in the most important (and technologically advanced) markets (for example the North Atlantic and Far East-Europe trades) (Alderton and Winchester, 2002a).

A Responsive Policy to Flagging-Out: The Formation of International Registers

The decline of nationally owned and registered fleets in recent years has led many European Union countries to establish a new policy approach to attempt to deter the trend of flagging-out, namely through the introduction of international or second registers – a sort of halfway house to Open Registries with the aim of capturing the benefits of both traditional and Open Registration. Examples of such attempts are the UK's Isle of Man, Germany's GIS or ISR (German International Register or International Ship Register) and Denmark's DIS (Danish International Register) (Haralambides and Yang, 2003). These registers aim to allow ship-owners to remain under the national flag while at the same time enjoying many of the benefits of global sourcing, notably of labour (Sletmo and Holste, 1993).

The international registry option became increasingly popular during the late 1980s and it presents a rather misleading term as these registries are normally only identified with traditional maritime countries and are no more or less international than any other type of registry. Subject to certain conditions they are open to citizens of all countries and allow ship-owners to replace elements of their national work force with seafarers from other countries with lower wage costs (and quite often with lower skills) (Sletmo and Holste, 1993; Hammer, 2000; Dirks, 2001). Shipping companies have the opportunity to choose between national and foreign seafarers, who are paid according to pay scales negotiated in their home countries (Hammer, 2000).

The alternative of international or second registers theoretically represents the best of both worlds as it combines the advantages of flags of convenience (i.e. taxation benefits, lower crew costs and more liberalised manning regulations) with those of the traditional maritime countries (i.e. access to capital markets, specialised know-how in shipping matters, high reputation and highly developed infrastructure). As a result, their main attraction is characterised in providing a 'merger' between these features, with the clear aim of retaining some control over the national shipping industry at the same time as fulfilling the need for a more competitive environment on the part of ship-owners (Sletmo and Holste, 1993; Hammer, 2000; Haralambides and Yang, 2003).

The international or second registry system undoubtedly provides an alternative choice of flag registration as a result of which a notable number of traditional maritime state shipping companies (including those from the EU) can manage to maintain their international market position during difficult economic times whilst at the same time retaining the advantages of their national flag. However, the flexibility they represent along with Open Registration, and their ability to allow ship-owners to register their vessels in whatever flag they choose, makes the relationship between the maritime sector and its home country become seriously unspecified along with all the policy implications that result. The definition of a national (or EU) fleet as a result is not straightforward since ships are registered in countries which are not necessarily the domicile of the owner (or in fact the financier, insurer, etc.). The concept of a national (or EU) shipping industry can no longer refer to an homogeneous entity (Marlow et al., 1997).

INTERNATIONALISATION OF THE SHIPPING INDUSTRY

As we have seen so far, the issues that surround the choice of a ship's flag, whether this is for an open, international or second register, have played a significant role in the internationalisation of the shipping industry. In particular, this consequent internationalisation of the industry has distorted the significance of vessel nationality by encouraging the separation of vessel ownership from its management and operation. Low-cost labour, commonly from countries with no vested interest in the vessel, dominates (regardless of flag), where owners have a wide choice in this matter. Examples abound – ships are commonly built most cheaply in the Far East, insurance for the vessels is usually written in London, inspections might take place almost anywhere, crews are more commonly from Third World countries, the flag is often a matter of economics rather than national association. These decisions take place regardless of who owns the vessel or its cargo. As a result it is increasingly difficult and in some ways misleading to discuss nationality when a ship may be built in Japan, owned by a Greek bank, crewed by Indonesians, Chinese and Filipinos, managed by an American company, and underwritten by a British firm.

This hypothetical but in many ways typical example of the modern international shipping industry is made further complicated if we assume that the same vessel may be carrying Saudi Arabian oil to Chile for an Australian dealer and flying the flag of Liberia. Within this context, which states have claim on the vessel? Under international law, it is a vessel of Liberia and thus it is that country which is responsible for codifying and enforcing the legislation under which it operates. However, many states have an interest in it, and there is a similar number of policy-making bodies at a variety of spatial levels that have a role to play or one which they would like to impose (Aspinwall, 1995).

International Regulation

At the international level, various policies, agreements and organisations with interests in safety and environmental conditions have emerged in order to control and regulate the shipping industry (Aspinwall, 1995). The world maritime fleet is currently characterised by systematic ageing and a tendency towards registration patterns with negative characteristics when considering their safety and environmental profiles – typically stemming from growth in flags of convenience and the internationalisation of the industry. Moreover, the economic environment that has typified the late twentieth century has encouraged, at least to a certain extent, the operation of high-risk, 'third-age ships' that may not comply with basic international rules and are manned by less-qualified and low-cost crews (Pallis, 2002).

During these years, various forms of international regulation have prevailed to attempt to control these negative effects of the maritime industry. The most important of these regulations have emerged from the International Maritime Organisation (IMO), the International Labour Organisation (ILO), the World Trade Organisation (WTO) and the United Nations Conference on Trade and Development (UNCTAD) (Aspinwall, 1995). Some characteristics of the work of these organisations are outlined below, reflecting the globalisation and internationalisation of the shipping industry.

UNCTAD, for example, began to address shipping matters in 1964 and its actions have mainly consisted of four maritime conventions. These are: the Convention of Carriage of Goods by Sea (the Hamburg Rules, 1978), the Convention on International Multi-modal Transport of Goods (1980), the Convention on Registration of Ships (1986) and the Code of Conduct for Liner Conferences (1983).

Recognising the need to develop an international agreement on safety at sea, a United Nations conference was held in 1948 which established the International Maritime Organisation (IMO), originally known as IMCO (Intergovernmental Maritime Consultative Organisation). In 1958, the convention came into force and the organisation undertook responsibility for the development of international standards and regulations to ensure safety of life at sea and the protection of the marine environment (OECD, 2002).

The International Labour Organisation (ILO) was established in 1919 in an effort to promote basic human rights regarding employment, such as freedom of association, abolition of forced labour and elimination of employment discrimination. Manning levels, crew skill requirements as well as crew welfare issues in general are also based on conventions made at the ILO. Since 1919, ILO members have reached agreement on over 300 conventions and recommendations. More specifically, within the shipping context, conventions cover areas such as recruitment, repatriation, vocational training, occupational safety and health, crew accommodation, adjustment to technological change, wage levels, working hours and manning holidays, health and welfare facilities and maritime industrial relations (Aspinwall, 1995).

However, the social standards that ILO conventions and agreements cover are not as clear cut as the more technical standards of the IMO, mainly because only a limited number are internationally implemented, and many of these conventions have not been ratified by nations commonly considered to have a greater maritime significance (Aspinwall, 1995; Alderton and Winchester, 2002b; OECD, 2002).

In addition to these organisations, national governments, which were part of both IMO and ILO, have enforced a series of internationally agreed agreements related to matters of ship safety and pollution and the welfare of seafarers respectively. The most important of these are the Safety of Life at Sea convention (SOLAS), the Prevention of Pollution from Ships convention (MARPOL) and the Merchant Shipping Minimum Standards convention with regards to the welfare of seamen. These have been ratified, for example, by all EU maritime states (Aspinwall, 1995).

This international policy-making activity is a reflection of the increased global environment in which shipping works and also the rise in interest in global issues that has taken place throughout populations. This combination of international pressures has encouraged the introduction of international policies for the shipping sector. However, as we have noted a number of times already, there remains a strong thread of national interests in shipping and a growth as well of supra-national involvement (typified by that of the EU) which has the potential for policy conflict if the issues involved are not carefully assessed and incorporated.

We will turn to how attempts have been made to resolve these potential conflicts in the next chapter, but for the moment will concentrate further upon the rise of globalisation in shipping and some examples of how this affects its operation and the policies that surround it.

A More Realistic Representation of the Global Shipping Environment

Shipping is thus an inherently global industry even though strong national interests exist (Heaver et al., 2001a; Heaver et al., 2001b; Notteboom and

Winkelmans, 2001). Its market-place and its regulation and control are directed and emanate from international bodies and interests that may well have national implications and significance but which are vitally inter-linked with globalised activities and organisations. There are many ways that this can be demonstrated and many have been outlined in earlier sections, but to re-emphasise this dimension a number of significant issues are discussed here.

1. *International sourcing.* Whereas, once upon a time, cargoes were locally defined and sourced and there were identifiable constraints upon where such cargoes could be obtained, today the options for a shipper or industrialist are much wider. Thus crude oil can be sourced from the North Sea, the Caspian Sea, the Gulf, Venezuela, etc..; coal can be sourced from Poland, the USA, Australia, etc..; coffee from South America, Africa, the Caribbean, etc. This variety of sources has helped to globalise the shipping industry as it adapts to meet the demands of shippers as markets and prices rise and fall and alternative sources of commodities come and go. Shipping policies have had to adapt to this flexible market-place, where national policies cannot meet all the needs of an industry constantly in flux.

2. *Security issues.* Since 11th September, 2001, the shipping industry has been made more aware of the potential security implications of its activities – in particular those of container shipping. Terrorism and all its associated activities are not constrained by national boundaries and international security policies are essential to meet the threats which may exist. These policies also need to be closely aligned to national security policies for the shipping sector so that implementation is effective at a more local level. In addition, shipping has been used as a vehicle for money laundering, including the profits of terrorism and further international policies implemented at local and national level are essential to combat this.

3. *Information technology.* The significant role that information technology has come to play in the international trade and shipping industries, along with the associated changes in communications, has increased the international nature of shipping dramatically so that national policies are now no longer appropriate on their own for the sector. International policies are more relevant for an activity which is characterised by international and immediate communication and computer networks whereby the location of vessels, the nature of the cargoes they carry, information on their

owners and other significant data can be accessed at all times from almost anywhere.

4. *Global businesses.* Shipping is now an industry with a significant number of global (and supra-national) companies which are heavily involved in all sectors, although perhaps mostly in the liner sector. Companies such as Maersk/Sealand and P&O/Nedlloyd are international organisations with offices and representatives worldwide and with a multi-national view on the markets (Cooper, 1994). In fact, the largest 20 international container carriers are responsible for around 80% of all containers carried and although this is no guarantee of market concentration as the proportion of the market that each of these carriers possesses varies considerably, each certainly only has a tenuous national identity (Lloyd's Shipping Economist, 2003). There remain plenty of nationally based shipping companies, particularly in the bulk sector (e.g. characterised by the classic Greek family firm), but the domination of nationally based companies is now no longer universally the case and policies have had to adapt to accommodate this trend of internationalisation of ownership and management. This trend is also apparent in the ancillary sectors of ship management, ship broking, finance and law as well.

5. *Free trade.* The growth of importance of the World Trade Organisation and its attempts to include the shipping sector in its agreements on free trade from 1997 onwards has widened the policy environment beyond the national forum. International and global free trade principles applied to such issues as liner conferences and subsidies have forced policy-makers to look beyond national issues and ambitions.

6. *Intermodalism.* The concept of seamless transfer of cargoes between the sea-going mode and that of road and rail in particular opens up new international markets and has created some difficult issues that can only be resolved at an international level. Thus the 'through' freight rates that liner conferences might wish to apply to containers moving from Central Europe to inland states of the USA have been subject to considerable debate in the 1980s and 1990s in terms of the applicability of EU Regulation 4056/86, which provides exemption to conferences from Treaty of Rome competition laws. As we saw earlier, such exemption has been denied to the inland parts of such movements but in consequence the relevant policy framework lies far beyond any national boundary – for example it is EU legislation that is impinging on the application of through rates in the USA.

7. *Load centres.* The developments occurring in ports and in particular the rise in the size of growth centres which can serve the biggest vessels has led to a reduction in the number of container ports within many regions, each serving a large number of countries other than the one in which they are located. Notable examples from Europe include Rotterdam (Netherlands – serving much of Western Europe) and Hamburg (Germany – serving Central and Eastern Europe and Scandinavia), but others can also be found in Hong Kong (China – serving the whole of the Far East), Singapore (similar to Hong Kong) and Pusan (Korea – serving China, Japan and the associated region). National shipping policies once again lose much of their relevance in these circumstances.

8. *Port privatisation.* The marked trend towards privatisation of state-owned ports around the world has encouraged the internationalisation of their ownership. Thus Felixstowe and Harwich in the UK are now owned by Hong Kong interests, the ferry and container terminal in Ventspils (Latvia) is owned by Belgian interests and the Port of Gdynia container terminal in Poland is owned by a company based in the Philippines. Although port policy is not the central issue in our discussion, the international dimension in the maritime sector is reinforced by these trends as ports can no longer be seen as domestic extensions to national government ministries.

9. *Capital mobility.* Shipping has long been a prime example of the principle of capital mobility in that the financial structures that enable the shipping industry to function – and in particular the mechanisms that exist to acquire capital for vessel funding – can be found in many different financial market-places around the world. Each of these locations competes with one another in the financial services market and thus globalisation of shipping finance adds another international level to the sector which needs to be reflected in the policies which emerge. The intensity of competition for shipping finance has increased in recent decades and consequently the need for an international policy framework has grown as well. Capital can thus be moved around the world and individual, national shipping policies alone cannot be adequate to provide a framework for the industry.

10. *Physical mobility.* Along with capital mobility, shipping is different from the large majority of other industries in that the physical assets can be moved between markets relatively easily. Thus a container vessel redundant in a declining market in the Far East can be readily deployed to new markets in Europe or South America. Whilst this is

also true of manufacturing plants to a certain extent it is by no means as simple, cheap or easy. Such physical mobility demands international or supra-national policies to be derived (the latter for example the case for Baltic ferries re-deployed in winter to the Mediterranean but remaining within the EU area) rather than simply national policies.

11. *Labour mobility and the issue of flags and crews.* The capital and physical mobility described above manifests itself perhaps more than any other way in terms of labour mobility in that vessels can now be flagged almost anywhere in the world with an Open or Traditional Registry, subject to some sort of financial payment and meeting a set of specific criteria commonly relating to crew nationality. In so doing, vessel owners aim to minimise their costs by operating vessels using national labour from relatively cheap countries whilst commonly serving nations where the profits from shipping are at the level of the developed world. The result is that the registration of a vessel and its consequent crewing arrangements have become intensely international and as we have seen already, provide a prime example of the effects of globalisation and internationalisation in shipping. The question then is what relevance is there for national shipping policies, and it is the conflict between the demands for the latter typically by seafarers' unions, traditional domestic shipping companies and national governments, in the context of international and supra-national policy growth, that we turn to in the next chapter in an examination of EU state-aid policy development and application.

12. *Shipping alliances and conferences.* The marked increase in the number of shipping alliances in the liner sector and the continued existence of conferences (albeit in a rather restrained format) has contributed to the increased internationalisation of the shipping industry. In particular, the growth of shipping alliances has been characterised by coming together of the major operating companies of the liner industry so that industrial players no longer emerge from a single country as in the past but now are a joint activity from a number of countries. National shipping policy is thus ineffective and inappropriate and international policies become necessary to control, encourage and sustain such activities. A good example of such trends in recent years comes from the North Atlantic where TACA (the Trans Atlantic Conference Agreement) formed by the major liner operators between North America and Europe has been subject to the shipping policies of the EU, the Federal Maritime Commission of the USA and the Canadian government. The notable

differences in the policy agendas of these three policy-making bodies has caused some considerable stress and has flagged up the need for policy-making at a level superior to the nation state. Other joint ventures and alliances in the markets of the Far East have revealed similar problems which can only realistically be resolved at an international (or at least supra-national) level.

13. *Vertical integration.* Major liner operators today need to offer an integrated service which meets the demands of modern manufacturers and their logistics needs. This includes the provision of moving containers from their point of origin to the point of final destination – a complete transport service rather than just the sea transport link alone. To do this many of the major liner operators and alliances noted above now offer vertical integration in their portfolios including warehousing, road and rail transport, broking, insurance, freight forwarding services and so on. Given that many (if not most) container movements are actually across a number of international borders, then the individual national shipping policy of any particular country becomes rather less relevant than wider, international transport policies that cover all modes, and all countries that the movement involves. Vertical integration by container operators – typified by that of Maersk/Sealand and P&O/Nedlloyd – demands a policy framework that is wider than that of the nation state and also wider than that of the maritime sector alone.

14. *Growth of hinterlands.* As the process of logistical improvement and sophistication increases so does the size of hinterland and foreland for product sourcing and sales. One effect of modern logistics has been to reduce the economic friction of transport and this in turn has opened up greater areas of the world for each product, reflected in modern consumption patterns in developed countries. The result is inevitable internationalisation and the consequence of this is that maritime policies need to reflect the spatial characteristics of these market changes. Typically, major ports are no longer providers of services for a nation state but commonly for many such nations (for example Rotterdam, Hamburg, Trieste, Pusan and Singapore) and the consequence of this is that maritime policies have to accommodate the variety of hinterlands and forelands involved.

15. *The growth of supra-nationality worldwide.* The increased importance of the EU since its formation in 1957 and the development of other supra-national bodies such as the North American Free Trade Agreement, incorporating the USA, Canada and Mexico, has emphasised the increasing importance of policy-

making at this level and the reduced significance of the national level for maritime policy implementation and initiatives. Both the EU and NAFTA are more than likely to increase their membership in the near future, whilst the role of the IMO in maritime policy-making at an international level continues to increase. This role is further emphasised by the moves of the EU in incorporating IMO approved measures through EU policies and consequently national policies of member states as a result. The increased significance of supra-national and international policy-making for the maritime sector is reflected in these moves.

16. *Safety and the environment.* These two generic issues are fundamental to maritime policies and have been for some years now. They are impossible to sustain and enforce on a national basis alone. International policies are required to produce international standards of safety and the environment, otherwise rogue nations and flags will undermine efforts to maintain acceptable levels. It is quite true that measures such as Port State Control, the ISM Code and Flag Registration ultimately have to be applied at the national level – and thus national application of these international standards is a requirement. However national policies, beyond ensuring that these international standards are maintained, are unnecessary and in the worst cases may conflict with the internationally agreed standards and thus only confuse.

17. *Technical conformity.* It is perhaps stating the obvious, but this issue has been fundamental to the growth of the maritime sector in that the adoption of (for example) the container as a means of transport has required internationalisation of technical standards. Although not directly central to maritime policy, the effect of this technical conformity (which has occurred in the liner, bulk and ferry sectors worldwide) has been to affect markedly the shipping and ports industry as a whole, which in turn has become that much more internationally directed.

18. *Globalisation of industry.* It is not just the shipping industry that has seen globalisation of course, but in practice, it is the majority of industrial activity that has been characterised by increased internationalisation. Thus steel companies, car manufacturing, chemicals and pharmaceutical companies are all now commonly international activities rather than national organisations and their internationalisation has had clear ramifications for the shipping sector. A multi-plant industry located in a variety of countries around the world and selling in a large number of other locations

demands international transport services and thus international shipping policies.

These are just some of the main factors which suggest that national shipping policies have a substantially reduced role to play in the new world of shipping and places seriously into question why any country needs a national shipping policy at all except to enforce international (and at times supra-national) shipping policies. Clearly, international standards and regulations and the activities of international companies have to be regulated at a national level as well, but it is surely only in applying these spatially wider requirements that any national involvement is needed at all. The industry itself has now become thoroughly international from its operation and ownership, finance and employment, through to the markets it serves and the physical environment in which it works. National policies are thus largely irrelevant (and in many cases a hindrance to effective support and control) except to translate international and supra-national policies into effective mechanisms for the industry.

From the preceding discussion it may seem remarkable that there are any national maritime policies at all given that the evidence for the superiority of international and supra-national policy generation is so overwhelming. The reasons for the continued existence of national policies can be summarised as follows:

1. Employment. Despite the fact that shipping creates few jobs directly, the employment argument for a national shipping policy (and in effect national shipping promotion and protectionism) is often used. It is politically appealing if largely incorrect.

2. Politics. This follows in part from the employment argument but also suggests that support to shipping may be a vote winner. In some countries this may well be true (for example to a certain extent Greece and Poland) but in others shipping is a political irrelevance.

3. Prestige. Some governments see a nationally flagged shipping fleet as providing prestige for a country and representing the nation around the world. This is particularly the case in developing countries.

4. Ship-owner pressure. Governments at times are susceptible to pressures from ship-owners for tax concessions, threatening that without them they will flag-out. The numerous tonnage tax regimes in the EU are a part consequence of this sort of action.

5. Expertise. There is a widely used argument that the ancillary sector in shipping (including legal, insurance, freight forwarding, broking, P&I, finance and so on) needs a steady influx of people with sea-

going experience (Gardner and Pettit, 1999a). Hence a national policy is needed to support an ailing fleet – the scenario for the City of London with its large ancillary maritime sector and the UK flagged fleet. This is disputed by some (for example Selkou and Roe, 2002) but remains a common argument.

6. History and tradition. This incentive for a national shipping policy should not be understated. Shipping is a highly traditional industry with a long history in many countries. Clearly there is no economic basis to this argument.

7. Defence. A widely accepted need for a national maritime policy is because a merchant fleet is a necessity in times of war to support naval vessels. Without some sort of national policy (such as that adopted by the USA through the 1920 Jones Act protecting domestic shipping) traditionally flagged merchant fleets would have disappeared.

8. Financial earnings. Merchant shipping does earn money for the country in which it is located although the argument that a fleet has to be flagged in that country to provide financial benefits is weak.

Figure 6.9 is an attempt to present the globalised shipping complex in terms of basic international, national and EU regulation and show how these interact and co-operate with each other within the competitive framework of the shipping industry. First of all, international regulations, as earlier mentioned, provide the framework of international standards and agreements by drawing up the conventions, which are then to be implemented by the countries involved.

The EU takes the responsibility to ensure that both the Flag States and Port States effectively implement safety and environmental protection regulations. In particular, the Commission and ultimately, the European Court of Justice, are accountable for the strict implementation of all safety measures as well as for the certification of marine equipment and the training of crews (Lalis, 1999b). Moreover, the Commission is best qualified to comment on how it concludes that competition would be distorted both in terms of sub-standard shipping and in terms of any other attempt such as improvement of quality in services, employment issues and taxation. Distortion of competition, in any way this may occur, is currently determined by reference to the Commission's State Aid Guidelines reissued in 1997 and further renewed in 2003 (Commission of the European Communities, 2003; Lloyd's List, 2003z). These guidelines provide member states with the framework within which decisions are to be made and they are obliged to notify the Commission on the details of these decisions. After the submission of these measures, the Commission is then to decide whether or not the proposed mechanisms are appropriate.

Finally, national governments, in reality the immediate targets of EU legislation, carry the obligation to enforce the regulations and to ensure that their maritime administration is able to assure an effective implementation. One of the most effective ways that implementation of EU regulations can take place is through Port State Control (PSC) – in that it can effectively decrease the number of sub-standard ships visiting ports through the establishment of common criteria for the control of ships and harmonised procedures for inspections and detentions, as set up by the legal PSC mechanism of the EU and included in the Paris MOU (Posidonia Congress, 2002; Lalis, 1999a).

Nevertheless, the implementation of international rules is not as simple and straightforward a process as it might appear. A series of accidents in the 1980s and 1990s, including the *Scandinavian Star*, *Exxon Valdez* and the more recent *Erika* disaster, highlighted the need for the improvement of maritime safety through stricter and more uniform application of existing regulations (Allan, 2000). As previously mentioned, during its forty years of existence, IMO has produced a significant number of international maritime conventions. However, despite some recent achievements, a major problem IMO is facing is that the process of both implementing and amending most of these conventions can be rather lengthy. As an OECD (2002) study concluded:

'IMO is continually reactive and is playing a 'catch-up' agenda; by the time a convention or amendment comes into force, parts of it may already be out of date' (OECD, 2002).

This constant and long process of amendments can become extremely complex but the important issue is that of IMO criticism from countries or regions, including the EU. Moreover, regarding the maritime accidents mentioned above, the industry appeared to have inadequate control procedures whether these stem from the flag states, port states, classification societies or the industry itself (De Palacio, 2002).

As a result, two types of actions were taken in recent years. One is the introduction of an IMO sub-committee, namely the FSI (Flag State Implementation) sub-committee. FSI was introduced on the basis that the effectiveness of IMO safety and pollution instruments depends primarily on the effective and consistent application and enforcement of their requirements by national governments. This is reflected in the discussion above where it was shown that national policy now largely undertakes the role of effectively implementing international rules. As a result, its primary objective is to identify the necessary measures to ensure effective and consistent global implementation of IMO rules, paying attention to the particular difficulties faced by countries in this respect (Allan, 2000).

The Globalised Shipping Complex

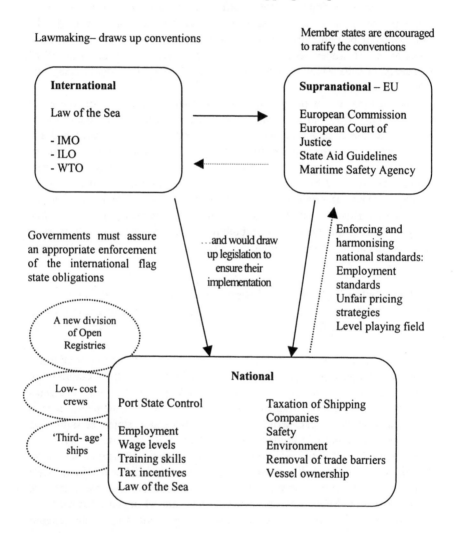

Figure 6.9: Globalisation and National Shipping Policy

The second attempt was the effort by the European Commission for the establishment of a European Maritime Safety Agency (Commission of the European Communities, 2000b), one that could monitor the performance and effectiveness of EU member states on issues of maritime safety and would make the necessary recommendations to ensure that adequate standards have been maintained. Moreover, the agency is set up to provide the member states and the Commission with technical and scientific assistance in line with the development of international legislation in this field. The Agency, to be located in Lisbon in Portugal, will act as an EU body and have a 'legal personality'. However, national governments have the right to appeal to the Commission when their interests are affected either directly or indirectly (Environment News Service, 2002).

The creation of the European Maritime Safety Agency has proved to be controversial, with some member states and industry groups already expressing their dislike for the idea. The criticisms are many and varied and include the charge that the EU is 'dismissive of the international consensus necessary for a global shipping industry' (Lloyd's List, 2001dddd). However, in its defence, the Commission would argue that proposals are only made after considering the democratic support that exists for the proposal and the maritime industry's viewpoint and after judging whether or not the majority of all fifteen EU member states will support the measures in negotiations on the issue concerned (Lalis, 2001a).

GENERAL CONCLUSIONS

What can be concluded by the preceding analysis is that international regulation in the maritime industry is enacted on a national basis by:

'Transforming the universally accepted goals and rules into a binding legal obligation in each state's sovereign privilege' (ILO, 2001).

Although it is the case that many IMO Conventions apply to more than 98% of the world's merchant shipping tonnage, the capacity of ship registration in Open Registries is also increasing. It has been argued (Alderton and Winchester, 2002b) that the reason for this situation is the appearance of new entrants in the Open Registry market, marketing themselves as suppliers of commercial services of ship registration only. For these states, such registration carries only minimal regulatory burden, whereas for the unscrupulous ship-owners it represents an escape from such burdens. While the PSC system of vessel inspection becomes more effective, so the older, larger and more established Open Registries have sought to conform to internationally agreed standards. This increase in standards has left a gap in the market for both ships that have been deleted from more established Open Registries, and ship-owners who do not wish to, or cannot, incur the cost implications of increased regulation. It is this very space at the bottom of the market for which these registers enter and fight amongst themselves (Figure 6.9). Paradoxically, perhaps even ironically, the attempts at international regulation have created a new division of Open Registry that is even less regulated than the previous one (Alderton and Winchester, 2002a).

The EU decision to introduce (as an example) a European Maritime Safety Agency might then prove to be a well-thought-out initiative to safeguard the safety-related interests of its member states, yet that remains to be seen within the years to come. What is nevertheless true is that where legislation relies on the state only, the context itself remains inherently global. As some observers have correctly implied:

'in this global environment, there will always be a gap, a gap that, due to its sovereign principle can create an unregulated environment where capital is free to act as it pleases, and the voice of labour is excised at its very source' (Alderton and Winchester, 2002a).

The Prisoner's Dilemma and the EU Market Approach

The globalisation of shipping and the maritime safety and environmental problems caused by the use of sub-standard ships, crews and flags may be recognised as a case of the 'prisoner's dilemma'. For example, if all ships of all flags pollute, they will all suffer. If none pollute, none will suffer. If most do not pollute, that is, if most ship-owners agree on the long-term benefits of maintaining high standards on board their vessels, they may still be forced by those who do accept lower standards, to switch to non-traditional (and therefore non-EU) registers to receive the advantages of short-term cost savings resulting from lower levels of taxation and safety obligations which commonly characterise Open Registries (Gwilliam, 1993; Dirks, 2001).

Recent EU maritime policy, however, has focused on the importance of a 'market' approach, that is, an approach concentrated not only on the outcomes, but also on determining the context in which the shipping market is to be allowed to produce an outcome. This however does not mean to imply the lack of regulation or social objectives. On the contrary, EU shipping policy includes economic and social aspects of support and attempts to provide a framework, the so-called 'level playing field', and along with the EU dimension in safety and environmental issues one which tries to guarantee the assurance of EU interests both internally and externally. In this sense, if the EU can have free movement outside its boundaries but can control the ability of foreigners to move within its boundaries, while at the same time promoting the common and commercial interests of its member states, it can secure a differential advantage at the expense of sub-standard, foreign operators (Gwilliam, 1993).

The main attempt to establish a level playing field within EU states has been the Commission's State Aid Guidelines. The Commission's initial effort on this issue dates back to 1989, where financial and fiscal measures were defined, under which state aid to shipping would be considered compatible with the common EU market. The 1989 guidelines however proved insufficient to stop the further decline of the European-registered fleet (Figure 6.5).

The EU Response of 1996: Towards a New Maritime Strategy

In 1996, however, a review of these guidelines covering any aid granted by member states or through state resources was presented. At the same time, the EU response to the decline of European shipping, in the face of international structural developments in the industry, was set out in the Commission's Paper, 'Towards a New Maritime Strategy' (Haralambides and Yang, 2003). The 1996 Paper highlighted the importance of an optimum future maritime policy against flagging-out and considered the benefits and the drawbacks of global open market policy and competition (Commission of the European Communities, 1996; Lloyd's List, 1996). As a result, the Commission considered a two-fold strategy for the reverse of EU shipping decline:

- action to ensure safety and fair competition in international open markets; and
- a Community framework for enhancing the competitiveness of the shipping sector.

Some of the main objectives for the proposed strategy were generally, the promotion of EU employment (both on-board and on-shore), preservation of maritime know-how in the EU and the development of maritime skills, safety improvements and state aid. As stated above, the 1989 state-aid guidelines – which recognised that the major part of competition comes from countries outside the EU with low tax and poor working and social conditions – were subsequently reviewed in 1997 and again in 2003, and the new guidelines came into force, creating a more liberal framework of decisions and recognising the transparent and non-discriminatory character of the EU (Haralambides and Yang, 2003; Dirks, 2001; Commission of the European Communities, 1996; Milne, 1996).

The 1989 guidelines for state aid to shipping (Commission of the European Communities, 1989) were published as a response to the proliferation of state aids in the European Community which in turn had emerged as a reaction to the desire to sustain traditional fleets which were increasingly suffering from the trend of flagging-out. In addition, the issues of decreasing safety and the rise of environmental problems stemming from the rush to Open Registries had conspired to increase the significance of state aid to ship operators in the EU.

The main feature of these Guidelines focused upon the concept of a ceiling acting as a maximum for permissible state aid within the EU. Calculation of the ceiling was based upon the identification of a cost handicap which ships operating under an EC flag would suffer in comparison with an Open Registry. The hypothetical costs of registering under the lowest cost EC flag (at that time Portugal) were to be compared with those of a typical Open Registry (in this case Cyprus) with the costs weighted according to the vessel composition of the flag involved. State aids were allowable to redress the additional costs faced by the EC flag.

Revision of these state-aid guidelines was undertaken in 1997 and followed experience with their application and various developments in general maritime policy. They were published in a Commission Communication, 'Community Guidelines on State Aid to Maritime Transport' (Commission of the European Communities, 1997). The main principle of the guidelines – compensation for any additional costs that might be incurred by a member state flagged vessel in comparison with an Open Registry – was retained but the costs used now reflected true costs rather than some theoretical ones. This change was introduced because the ceiling was difficult to calculate meaningfully. Recognition was given to the fact that cost differentials between flags were largely due to fiscal costs in shipping – primarily wage costs and corporate taxation – rather than capital costs which were largely the same whatever the flag.

The EU was insistent that aid should be exceptional (in that it should only apply where needed), temporary (in that it should be withdrawn as soon as it was unnecessary) and progressive. However, it was accepted that the issue was not short-term and so state aid would be required for some time. The impact of the World Trade Organisation through GATS in restricting and removing state aids in the maritime sector was only a very long-term process.

The scope and objectives of the revised guidelines were made clear:

1. State aid must not distort competition between member states. Hence subsidies for shipping in one member state should not provide an advantage over shipping in another.
2. It must be transparent – open to inspection and clear where it goes.

3. It must be directed towards specific activities and not a blanket payment.
4. The provision of other state aid to the sector must be included in the calculation.
5. All types of maritime aid had to be included – cash, credit, taxation, cargo preference, etc.
6. Beneficiaries could include state and private operators, individuals, companies, etc.
7. Shipbuilding and fisheries were excluded.
8. Infrastructure aid was only allowed if it was for the sole use of that beneficiary.

State aid was normally to be allowed only for ships registered under member state registries. Its broad objectives were to improve safety, preserve knowledge, develop skills and safeguard on-shore and on-board employment.
The following categories were outlined:

1. *Fiscal treatment for ship-owning companies.* Undoubtedly this has been the most significant area and caused the most contention. EU member states had already applied a variety of preferential tax measures for their flagged fleets to reduce flagging-out. These incentives have included accelerated depreciation on investment in ships and (as we shall discuss in depth in a later chapter) the initial stages of introducing an industry specific tonnage tax whereby in general terms, corporate profit taxation would be replaced by one on vessels reducing the tax burden for ship operators. These measures were endorsed by the EU in the revised guidelines as they undoubtedly help to safeguard employment in ancillary sectors. However, they have to have a distinct link with a member state flag. Only exceptionally, and if it encouraged ships back to EU flags and if their owners paid any corporation tax due to a member state, then non-EU flagged operations might fiscally benefit. In all cases they had to be subject to EU safety and environmental standards and the operation to benefit had to be essentially shipping.
2. *Labour-related costs.* Unlike all other industrial sectors in the EU, labour issues are considered a special case. Consequently, aid in the field of social security and seafarers' income tax, which reduces the burden on employers without reducing the level of social security for seafarers, was allowed. It could only relate to employment on-board ships. A reduction to zero was permissible where it brought employment costs towards those of Open Registries. There could be

no state aid to pay wage costs. As a result, those EU flags which had lower wage costs would retain that advantage.

3. *Crew relief.* Costs related to repatriation were previously limited to 50% but were now extended to 100%.

4. *Investment aid.* The EU expressed its general dislike of investment aid as it tends to encourage over-capacity in the market. Shipbuilding subsidies were allowed to continue, however, as they can also encourage improvements in the industry and restructuring of markets (Commission of the European Communities, 1998). In addition, aid might also be allowed where it contributed to the EU Safe Seas Policy. Regional aid, for example from the European Investment Bank to support port facilities, would only be permitted in the sector where there were clear local benefits and they were limited to a confined time period.

5. *Training.* The Commission demanded that they must be notified of specific aid to training schemes in the maritime sector. It would be allowed where it was transparent, non-discriminatory and proportional and only where directly related to EU flagged vessels. If it involved work on-board vessels, the trainee must be an extra worker.

6. *Restructuring and privatisation.* Aid to encourage sector restructuring (commonly meaning contraction) and privatisation would continue to be allowed under existing EU policies.

7. *Public sector obligations and contracts.* No aid would normally be allowed for direct operating costs unless a Public Sector Obligation (PSO) approved by the EU was in existence. Here the carrier concerned would be obliged to provide a service satisfying fixed standards of continuity, regularity, capacity and pricing which could not be assumed if true market forces applied. The main shipping markets in the EU centred upon the peripheral island trades. There were conditions – open, public tenders must be provided; aid could be directed only towards the losses that would be made; the aid must be specific to an identifiable service; it would be normally limited to five years at most; it could be awarded to one operator if only one tendered; the lowest cost tender (within the constraints of safety and other legislation) must be awarded the aid.

The EU was well aware of the potential of a tax race between member states and as a result the total maritime aid provided to a member state was limited to tax concessions and zero seafarer social security charges. If any other aid was provided this had to be taken off this total. All proposed aid had to be notified to the Commission at the draft stage and the Commission had the right to investigate, fine and demand the return of state aid if any of the rules were broken.

CONCLUSIONS

The latest Guidelines on State Aid to Maritime Transport were adopted through a Communication of the European Commission on 29th October, 2003 and they generally followed the same approach as those of 1997 but reinforcing many of the main principles (Commission of the European Communities, 2003). The main aim was to further ensure a favourable tax environment for ship-owners to counter international competition by Open Registers. They emphasised the role that tonnage tax could play in this process and also the contribution of reduced fiscal and social security contributions by seafarers and an increase in training aid. Four main provisions were included:

1. New and clearer provisions on seafarers' tax exemptions. Such cost alleviation is allowable for all seafarers, irrespective of nationality or domicile with the exception of ferry services whereby the provision would only apply to EU/EEA citizens.
2. A flexible but effective flag link principle for tax arrangements. To qualify for state aid a vessel must fly an EU flag. Although some tonnage tax systems are 'flag-blind', (for example the UK), shipping companies operating less than 60% of their tonnage under an EU flag will now have to maintain under an EU flag, at least the same tonnage that they have when the new Communication comes into force. If not, they will not be able to benefit from any of the measures for any non-EU flagged vessel added to their fleet. Member states may only derogate from this measure if their nationally flagged fleet is not declining and only then, subject to Commission approval.
3. A variety of new aids for new services in short-sea shipping, particularly where road traffic is reduced as a result. These would be time limited to three years and operated in a transparent and non-discriminatory manner.
4. A number of small amendments to taxation regulations.

These changes were significant if relatively minor, in that they emphasised the importance of state aid and also the commitment of the Commission to tonnage taxation in particular. It is in the context of these new arrangements that the discussion in the next chapter on tonnage tax will be undertaken.

Meanwhile, perhaps the most important conclusion to be drawn on globalisation and EU shipping policy development at this stage is the recognition that the efficiency and effectiveness of such policy was through their national implementation. Thus nation states remained important in policy terms but only as vehicles for operationalising supra-national policy. One of the proposed policies that received attention by member states in the late 1990s, whilst at the same time serving different interests for each of them, was the much discussed tonnage tax which emerged from the various revisions of state aid to shipping discussed earlier. The significance of tonnage tax within an EU policy supra-national and member state national context is presented in the following chapter.

7. Cohesion in European Shipping Policy: The Case of Tonnage Tax

INTRODUCTION

The preceding chapters attempted to provide a clear and in-depth demonstration of the internationalisation of the shipping industry, along with its importance to global economic activities with a particular emphasis upon the interests of Europe as a leading trading bloc. An important feature of the maritime sector in Europe, which has been particularly highlighted, is the constant decline of European flagged shipping activities, predominantly stemming from the increased globalisation that characterises the industry and has grown to dominate the market within which it has to operate.

As stated in the concluding part of the previous chapter, the European Commission's response to this clear decline in European flagged shipping and in the face of international structural changes in the industry was set out in a major paper, entitled 'Towards a New Maritime Strategy', published in March 1996. The main objective of this revised policy paper was to stress the importance of global competition and together with the Commission's State Aid Guidelines of 1997, there was proposed a series of measures which it was hoped would lead to a more competitive maritime environment for European flagged shipping and one in which vessels registered with a member state would have the potential to succeed (UK Department of the Environment, Transport and the Regions, 1999).

The Commission's proposals for a far more market-orientated and liberal shipping policy, but one which provided conditions for a competitive EU flagged sector, was discussed by the member states and quite quickly formed the basis for the Commission's programme for new legislation. By then it was clear enough that the proposals would help to promote the EU flagged maritime industry, strengthen it in terms of safety and the environment, help to develop third-country relations, and improve overall its competitiveness and general conditions.

In some ways these proposals, and in particular the Commission's new attitude towards state aid for the shipping sector within the EU, provide an excellent example of the position of shipping within the spatial policy frameworks we have discussed earlier and the tensions that clearly exist between those of the supra-national and national policy-making levels. The emergence of tonnage tax as a method of providing support to member state flagged vessels in itself was simple enough, but the interest lies in how the Commission itself has allowed this financial incentive to be picked up and adapted by member states as they see fit to promote their own flagged vessels whilst retaining a supra-national control over the process as a whole. EU maritime policy has thus attempted to resolve the spatial dilemma that exists in reconciling the wider demands of the Treaty of Rome for full competitiveness, harmonisation and liberalisation and the narrower needs of member states' shipping fleets which have to compete in the international environment with its multitude of shipping subsidies that exist outside the EU region. We shall examine the concept of tonnage tax and its application in EU member states to assess the attempts made by the Commission to reconcile spatial policy conflicts.

Clearly, an essential competitive element of the new shipping policy that emerged at the end of the 1990s was the introduction of a tonnage tax scheme for shipping. Essentially, a shipping tonnage tax is a form of taxation based not on shipping companies' profits (the common approach for commercial taxation in other sectors), but on the size of shipping company fleets (UK Inland Revenue, 2000c). Tonnage tax provides an alternative scheme to traditional corporation tax and ignores company profits, instead computing a notional profit on the basis of the number and size of ships operated, and then taxes this profit at the normal corporation tax rate. Tonnage tax rate is set so that notional profits, and thus tax liability, are minimal (and hence it forms an indirect subsidy to the industry), whilst at the same time being compatible with international tax treaty obligations (Brownrigg et al., 2001).

The first signs of the introduction of a tonnage tax regime by EU member states as a measure to improve the fiscal policy for shipping, was found in the Commission's 1997 State Aids Guidelines and more specifically in the general conditions contained therein. The Commission emphasised the importance of:

'Supportive measures, which largely remove the financial disadvantages of conducting shipping from the EU' (Commission of the European Communities, 1997).

Under European law, a shipping tonnage tax is a state-aid and as such, clearance has to be obtained from the European Commission that it is not contrary to the interests of the common market before it can be implemented. This type of tax regime, by 2003 had been successfully put into practice by the majority of European member states. In all cases, the Commission has made it clear that whilst permitting tonnage taxation regimes to exist within the guidelines, policies and laws of the EU, they are also happy to allow individual member states to adapt the principles applied to their own specific circumstances – although these circumstances and the tonnage tax rules used in each member state are subject to Commission scrutiny and permission. The tonnage tax system thus represents an example of policy integration at the spatial level in the maritime sector where the conflicts that might exist between different levels have been recognised and potentially reconciled (Lloyd's List, 2001b).

Table 7.1: Tonnage Tax in EU Member States: End 2003

Member State	Date Introduced
Greece	1975
The Netherlands	1996
Germany	1999
United Kingdom	1999
Finland	2001
Denmark	2002
Spain	2003 backdated to 2002
The Republic of Ireland	2003
Belgium	2003
France	2004 backdated to 2003
Sweden	Under consideration
Italy	Delayed to 2004 at least

Source: *Authors.*

The different regimes that exist and the debate that has surrounded them is outlined in some detail in the following sections for all the member states where in late 2003, a tonnage tax system had either been introduced or was seriously proposed (Table 7.1). Table 7.2 attempts to summarise the main characteristics of the regime. Notable omissions are thus Portugal (with no proposals), Luxembourg (which acted as a substitute home for Belgian flagged ships until the introduction of a tonnage tax by the latter in 2003) and Austria (with effectively no fleet). The approach adopted here has been to use topical information sources and in particular Lloyd's List – the London based shipping newspaper – which would provide an immediate information source and commentary on what was going on. The following sections are thus developed mainly (but not exclusively) from newspaper sources, recognising issues of questionable reliability which are compensated by those of immediacy and topicality in a constantly changing framework.

Greece

Greece has the longest history of all EU countries in applying a tonnage tax regime, although the current system dates in the main from the revisions adopted in 1975 (Law 27/1975). This system has been widely criticised in recent years by the ship-owning community with the result being the proposals currently under consideration for its redevelopment. This has stemmed in part at least from its age and from the multitude of new schemes which have emerged in the EU over the past 10 years that have proved increasingly competitive.

The system applied between 1975 and 2003 can be summarised as follows. Taxation is based upon the income realised from ships owned by Greek interests according to their tonnage and age. Profits derived from shipping business are ignored. It is different in two main ways from all other EU tonnage tax regimes; its status is protected for the future (apart from changes in tax rate) under the Greek Constitution and its provisions on commercial ships; and in addition, it is not an elective, in that it applies to all Greek flagged ships.

Table 7.2: Tonnage Tax Characteristics in the EU, 2003

Member State	Companies	Window and Limitations	Income Subject	Other Issues
Belgium	Partly approved in 2003. Subject to further European Commission investigation.	Optional but binding for 10 years.	Lump sum profit taxation based on tonnage. 50% reduction for vessels under 5 years; 25% vessels 5-10 years old.	Particularly low taxation rates on vessels over 40,000 gt. Further tax deductions linked to losses from other (non-transport) divisions of shipping companies.

Member State	Companies	Window and Limitations	Income Subject	Other Issues
Denmark	Introduced from 2002. Limited shipping companies registered in Denmark; EU shipping companies with a permanent base in Denmark; any shipping company where the management is located in Denmark and subject to company taxation in Denmark.	Optional but binding for 10 years. Qualified companies are obliged to choose either corporate or tonnage taxation before filing for income tax. All qualifying shipping companies within a group have to select the same option.	Transport of goods and passengers and related activities are shipping business and only this can be subject to tonnage tax. Also associated business – terminals, dockyards, containers tickets, etc. Stand-by vessels, cable-laying ships included. Fishing and dredging excluded. Income taxed derived from own fleet, and vessels on bareboat and time charter of 20 gt or more. Time chartered vessels can be included on 4:1 ratio to own tonnage.	National seafarers are granted a special standard deduction from taxable income.

Member State	Companies	Window and Limitations	Income Subject	Other Issues
Finland	Introduced from 2002. Ferries and passenger ships excluded from crew subsidies.	Ship-owners to choose between corporation and tonnage tax. 10-year period.	Duty-free sales excluded.	Company dividends taxed at normal rates.
France	Available to companies drawing 75% of their revenue from merchant shipping.	Owners must opt by end 2004. Rates will reflect those of other North European states.	Flat rate taxation scheme. Duty-free sales and revenues earned from overland transport are to be resolved.	Tugs, fishing boats and fixed vessels excluded.
Germany	Introduced in January 1999. Restricted to German ship-owners with merchant vessels in international operations. Management of the company must be in Germany.	Vessels must be German registered. 10-year commitment.	Includes chartering of ships as well as operation and incidental, related activities.	Profits include sale of ships and closing down of shipping businesses. No depreciation allowances under tonnage tax.

Member State	Companies	Window and Limitations	Income Subject	Other Issues
Greece	Introduced in April 1975. Applies to all Greek flagged ships – no options.	Non-shipping activities are excluded. No taxation on capital gains from ship sales. Ships built and registered in Greece pay no tax for 6 years; those repaired in Greece and under 20 years old pay a reduction; ferries and cruise vessels pay 50%.	Taxation based on vessel type, gross tonnage and age. Specific definition of ship types.	Status guaranteed under Greek Constitution.
Ireland	Introduced in 2001. The company must be subject to corporation tax, operate qualifying ships, and be strategically and commercially managed from Ireland. Companies part of a group must enter as a group.	10-year option; cannot return for 10 years. Maximum 75% of net tonnage of fleet can be chartered in.	Taxation rate reduces as vessel size increases.	Vessels must have a certificate of navigation and be over 100 nrt. Excluded – fishing, sports, recreation vessels; offshore installations; dredgers, tugs and coastal/river ferries.

Member State	Companies	Window and Limitations	Income Subject	Other Issues
Italy	Earliest attempts detected in 1996 in parallel to proposals for a second register.	Minimum 5 year option.	Based on vessel weight; variable according to trade and age of vessel.	Proposals finally introduced in January 2004.
Netherlands	Introduced in 1996. Must have a significant presence in the Netherlands.	Binding for 10 years.	Based on net registered tonnage.	Flag blind. Combined with significant seafarer tax concessions on wages and social security payments.
Spain	Introduced in 2003, backdated to 1st January, 2002. Must be registered as ship operators and be managed from the EU.	Sole activity must be ship operation. Ships had to be capable of sailing on the high seas. Voluntary. Ten year option but can leave at any time. Cannot return within 5 years.	Subject to approval of taxation authorities. Chartered in vessels must not exceed 75% of the total net tonnage of the fleet. Taxable base was the net tonnage, on a reducing scale.	Basque regional tonnage tax as well. Awaits implementation.
Sweden	Under negotiation	–	–	–

Member State	Companies	Window and Limitations	Income Subject	Other Issues
UK	First established 2001. Can opt for the existing capital allowances system or tonnage tax. Company must be registered in UK and a substantial commercial base must take place there.	Minimum 10-year option. Can leave but at a cost of £500 per month per vessel. Companies entering shipping have one year to opt in. Renewal of tonnage tax for a further 10 years can be at any time.	Profits from shipping ring-fenced. Only shipping related activities allowable.	Training commitment or training levy payable. Flag blind.

Source: *Authors.*

It is applied to any registered owner of a Greek flagged ship on the first day of the calendar year regardless of whether that person operates or charters the ship and of their nationality or residence. Any person who operates that ship or is appointed as agent and is in effect the owner, is liable for tonnage tax and if the vessel is sold or transferred then the new owner is responsible for any tax owing at that stage. However, a person operating a ship for someone else is not liable – including manager or time charterer.

Unusually, there is no definition of a ship in the legislation, but there is an indication that it should cover small vessels and that they must be used for commercial purposes. Definition of contentious cases is agreed on an 'ad hoc' basis. Any income not subject to tonnage tax is subject to general income tax.

The tax calculation methods are divided into two types dependent upon ship characteristics (Norton Rose, 2002). The first category consists of vessels noted in the Greek Constitution and as such, the provisions of the tonnage tax are protected. These vessels include bulk carriers, tankers and reefers of at least 3,000 grt; similar vessels of between 500 and 3,000 grt that trade internationally; passenger ships trading internationally (from Greece to foreign ports or between foreign ports); passenger ships of at least 500 gt that have undertaken exclusively and regular leisure trips for the previous six months and are publicly advertised; floating rigs and refineries used for exploration, drilling, pumping, refining or storage. The resulting tonnage tax for these ship types is payable in US$.

The second category consists of all motor, sailing and small vessels which do not meet the criteria of the first category. They are not protected from the point of view of tonnage tax by the Greek Constitution. This category of vessels must pay tonnage tax in euros (Yannopoulos, 2003). Tonnage tax applied to both categories is reduced if the ship is unable to trade for at least two months.

Other, non-shipping activities are excluded from the tonnage tax regime and no taxation is liable on capital gains from ship sales. Other exemptions also apply – these include ships built and registered in Greece which pay nothing for the first six years; ships trading regularly (i.e. ferries) internationally and all cruise vessels are given a 50% reduction; ships repaired in Greece and under 20 years old are subject to reductions in tonnage tax, increasing as the amount spent on repairs increases.

The Greek tonnage tax system is in many ways the most complicated of all within the EU and this is largely a consequence of its age which is considerably greater than any other. It is the only tonnage tax within the region that is not a direct consequence of the measures adopted by the EU towards state aid and the complex policy inter-action that exists between member states and the EU. Despite these rather different origins it remains of interest in the context of policy conflict as it attempts to adapt to the competition that has arisen and also because it is a regime designed to facilitate and encourage the Greek shipping, ship-building and ship repair markets in the concessions offered. It thus presents obvious conflicts with a broad EU tonnage tax and state-aid policy that looks for some consistency across member states and competitiveness as a regional body against flag states elsewhere in the world. The EU has been sensitive to Greece in its dealings over shipping, flags and state involvement and has (for example) allowed the Greeks to protect their ferry industry for much longer than other countries against competition and also to retain some measures of protection for the foreseeable future. Tonnage tax in the EU is thus not always the same beast in all countries and the Greek example is perhaps one of the best of the variety that exists within nation directed policies, and yet operates within a supra-national context.

The wide concessions on taxation that the application of tonnage tax in Greece seems to imply, have still been subject to serious criticism from within the country. For example in November 1999, Greek ship-owners were complaining that a system which was once the envy of Europe had become one of comparative, and as we have seen, compulsory disadvantage. The

Greek fleet was dominated by older ships and these were seriously penalised by the Greek tonnage tax system which, it was estimated, was five times more expensive for old ships than the new tonnage taxes introduced by the Netherlands and the UK (Lloyd's List, 1999e, 1999f). In addition, manning requirements remained relatively high for the Greek flag (membership of which was compulsory for tonnage tax).

Promises emerged of a proposed cut in tonnage tax in April 2001 in reports from the Minister for Mercantile Marine at the time. The Greek government, it was reported, had wide plans to support the Greek seafarer and their education and training as well as the ship-owner through taxation changes (Lloyd's List, 2001uu). The models of the UK and the Netherlands were put forward as ideals that the industry needed to follow and as the Union of Greek Shipowners emphasised, tonnage tax needed to be reduced drastically if it was 'to be of any use'.

However, things moved slowly. It was not until September the same year that the government finally announced a package of economic reforms that included reduction in tonnage tax rates by half along with income tax reform for seafarers (Lloyd's List, 2001vv). Whilst owners reacted positively and the measures were supported by the Prime Minister, the delay in progress was still notable and it was agreed that the resulting tonnage tax rates would still be more than those of the UK or the Netherlands. However, other benefits were expected to make up the difference.

Progress towards reductions were encouraged by the activities of the Greek Shipping Co-operative Committee and the Union of Greek Ship-owners but by late November there remained no tangible progress (Lloyd's List, 2001ww). Some dispute also emerged over the comparative benefits with the UK flag which was quoted by the representative of the Greek Shipping Co-operation Committee as being still half the cost and offering a much wider range of national insurance and pension benefits. As such it was under consideration by a number of Greek owners.

Changes in tonnage tax finally occurred in January 2002 with a 70% reduction accompanied by other reductions in income tax for seafarers and officers (Lloyd's List, 2002q). Further (unspecified) measures were planned. However, it was widely recognised that the Greek flag would remain the most expensive in Europe as employment of EU officers remained obligatory (Lloyd's List, 2003y).

The Netherlands

The developments in the Netherlands have assumed particular importance as the authorities introduced a tonnage tax system on 1st January, 1996 before the publication of the EU's 1997 Guidelines for state-aid to the maritime sector. The arrangement is so-called 'flag-blind', in that it applies to all ship-owners operating from a company located in the Netherlands irrespective of the flag flown by the ships.

Initially, and until the end of 1996, the Netherlands was given approval from the European Commission, which at that time was preparing to issue the new guidelines for shipping which were to emerge the next year (Norwegian Shipowners Association, 1996).

At the time, the Netherlands shipping sector was much troubled by economic difficulties. Owners were on the verge of deserting the national flag in substantial numbers and what was a once highly significant shipping nation was close to having no merchant fleet at all. The first in a broader series of maritime cluster studies changed all that, emphasising the importance of a Netherlands national fleet to the nation's economy and heralding a new era of fiscal provisions and significant improvements to aid the economic well-being of Netherlands-based ship-owners.

In practice, the measures had a broader effect, even attracting new, non-Netherlands shipping companies to relocate their operations and re-flag their vessels to the Netherlands. Until that time, the ship-owning activities of the country were disappearing, owners were flagging-out and the sector was in decline. From a Netherlands ship-owner's view, the only reason against flagging-out was that they considered the national flag to still be a hallmark of quality (Dickey, 1999). From an economic point of view it had no role to play.

As a result, on 1st January, 1996, Netherlands tax legislation was amended to encourage shipping companies to locate in the Netherlands (Lloyd's List, 1996a). In so doing, liability for corporation and income tax could be assessed on the basis of the net registered tonnage of their ships, rather than the company's actual operating profits although ship-owners could still opt for the latter approach (Lloyd's List, 1996b). The scheme applies irrespective of the flag flown by the vessels, but companies must have a significant presence in the Netherlands. Because profit may be determined on net registered tonnage, profits per day from ocean-going shipping companies are determined as the net tonnage per ship multiplied by a fixed amount per 100 net tons (Ernst and Young, 2002).

In addition, another advantage was offered to ship-owners in order to attract them to the Netherlands flag. For seafarers resident in the Netherlands, employers receive tax relief equivalent to 40% of gross wages and 10% for non-residents subject to social security payments. For ship-owners, this typically results in an attractive 30% reduction in wage costs (Lloyd's List, 1997a).

The reforms have been highly successful in tonnage terms, although it is admitted that this success has not so far extended to making seafaring sufficiently attractive to young people. An almost immediate effect noted in 1996 was the re-flagging of 50 vessels to the Netherlands register (Lloyd's List, 1996b). One notable feature of the scheme is that owners have to commit themselves to the tonnage tax system for a 10-year period. As we shall see later in this chapter, the Netherlands approach in general has been used as a model for the UK tonnage tax regime (Lloyd's Ship Manager, 2000).

As we have noted, the success of this approach to maritime policy was almost immediate. During 1997, van Ommeren Shipping, the Netherlands based dry cargo and bulk shipping group announced it was re-flagging three of its owned ships back to the Netherlands registry (Lloyd's List, 1997a). In June 1998 it was announced by the Netherlands Ministry of Transport that the tonnage tax policy had resulted in a growth of the Netherlands fleet from 386 to 489 vessels which included ships from 20 foreign shipping companies and a considerable number previously flagged under Open Registries (Lloyd's List, 1998a). Meanwhile, by the end of 1999, the Dutch merchant fleet had grown by 42.6% in relation to the previous four years and a further 13.8% by the end of 2001 (Figure 7.1).

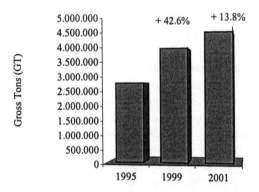

Source: Data for 2001: Lloyd's Register of Shipping (2001). Data for 1995-1999: Maritima Conference (2000) *Strengthening the National Fleet*, Paris.

Figure 7.1: Netherlands Registered Vessels 1995-2001

This policy success was not missed by a European Commission looking to stimulate the EU registered fleet within the boundaries laid down by the Treaty of Rome. The result was the widespread acceptance of tonnage tax regimes by the European Commission and its overt inclusion within the state-aid guidelines adopted in 1997 (Lloyd's List, 1997b).

Not all went smoothly however. In February 2001, German based tugboat operator Bugsier challenged the Netherlands tonnage tax system suggesting that it was being offered to Netherlands registered tugboats despite the fact that they were not ocean-going vessels and that the state-aid guidelines expressly forbade this (Lloyd's List, 2001d, 2001e). The European Commission launched an enquiry into this practice, the existence of which interestingly had not been denied by the Netherlands Ministry of Transport.

A second problem (and one mirrored by later developments in the United Kingdom) was outlined by the Netherlands Minister of Transport in October 2001. This centred on the increasing shortage of Netherlands masters and officers exacerbated by the success of the tonnage tax system in attracting vessels back to the Netherlands flag. This in time could lead to a loss of vessels to other flags and also a shortage of expertise for the ancillary (land-based) maritime sector.

The central aim of the Netherlands maritime policy which was now focused around tonnage tax, was to improve the business development and investment climate for maritime companies. Shipping companies were thus permitted to opt for the new tax where the taxable profit is based on the ship's tonnage rather than on commercial results. This has a major advantage in that ship-owners know in advance how much tax they will be required to pay in addition to a tax regime that included concessions in the amount payable compared with the previously existing regime.

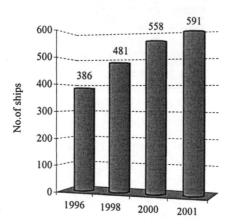

Source: Lloyd's List (2002a).

Figure 7.2: Growth of the Netherlands Merchant Fleets 1996-2001

Also worth noting was not only the growth of the number of vessels registered under the Netherlands flag, but also the severe competition which the Netherlands had been experiencing from the Netherlands Antilles register (Dickey, 2000). The register of the crown dependency and the register of the Netherlands have competed for vessels in recent years although ships on both registers fly the same flag. For statistical purposes, the information provided for the Netherlands Shipping Register concerns only the Netherlands and does not include Netherlands Antilles vessels. The introduction of the tonnage tax reversed the trend towards flagging-out to the Netherlands Antilles and presented an example of how to achieve this which was later to be copied by the United Kingdom (amongst others).

Apart from the growth of the Netherlands register, the most notable result for the country's maritime sector was the stimulation to enterprises giving service to the shipping industry. Measures aimed at creating an improved tax environment for shipping companies along with a substantial package of related policy legislation, resulted in a direct added value to the shipping industry, from €656m in 1995, to €918m in 2001 (Lloyd's List, 2002a). This tremendous increase stemmed partly from the fact that within the above-mentioned period, approximately 40 companies were either established in the Netherlands or reduced their branch offices abroad in favour of increasing the responsibilities of their headquarters in the Netherlands (Seatrade, 2002).

A consequence of the success of the new maritime policy of 1996 and the improvement in competitiveness of shipping investment in the Netherlands, is that the demand for seafaring personnel since then could not be met by the outflow from national nautical schools. The main problem, and one that has affected not only the country in question but also a number of European countries since the widespread application of tonnage tax regimes and the growth in re-flagging with national registers – is that both the education and the profession itself seem to be perceived as unattractive by young people (Veenstra, 2002). The Netherlands government's action to increase the number of students entering maritime education is currently a prime area of concern. As a result, and in co-operation with the Dutch Maritime Network, a series of projects has begun in order to promote the industry's profile as a modern, attractive and important economic sector.

In summary, it appears that the main characteristic of this new and successful state shipping policy was the implementation of the fixed tonnage tax for shipping companies instead of the traditional tax on profit. In addition, the government has decreased company expenditure on manpower through subsidising up to 30% of income tax of all mariners working on Netherlands registered vessels. However, there are no limitations applied to the work of foreigners on-board vessels flying the Netherlands flag but clearly, non-nationals do not benefit from the income tax subsidy. The requirement that the master is a citizen of the Netherlands is not applied either (Lloyd's Ship Manager, 1995; Lloyd's List, 2000b; Kuiper and Loyens, 2001).

The Netherlands tonnage tax scheme, although successful, was not expected to be extended in the 2003 Budget of September despite pressure from ship-owners to include survey, drilling and crane vessels similar to many other EU countries (Lloyd's List, 2003aa). In addition it was hoped that new shipping companies could delay opting for the tax until they were sure of their financial situation. At present an immediate choice has to be made with a commitment for 10 years. As expected, the Budget introduced no new measures for shipping in any form – although tonnage tax was at least retained despite financial pressures from elsewhere (Lloyd's List, 2003bb).

The strategy for the Netherlands shipping policy was to maintain and expand the level of maritime activities. For those reasons, the Netherlands had to become an internationally competitive economic domicile again with an attractive ship register. Nevertheless, it was imperative that safety and environmental standards were to remain at the prevailing high level. These ambitions were achieved by adopting a company tax for shipping in the form of the tonnage tax.

Germany

First indications of an interest in developing a tonnage tax scheme in Germany emerged in February 1997 when the German Shipowners' Federation ('Verband Deutscher Reeder' – VDR) warned of a loss of vessels from the German Register unless something was done (Lloyd's List, 1997l). Existing financial support to German owners had been cut and combined with competition from the new tonnage tax regime introduced in the Netherlands, this was expected to have a detrimental effect upon ship registration.

The effect was fairly quick in that the German Minister of Transport announced in July 1997 that a tonnage tax based around a 10-year commitment by ship-owners, would be introduced with other tax reforms from 1st January, 1999 (Lloyd's List, 1997m). The proposals were warmly welcomed by the Bremen Ship-owner's Federation ('Bremer Rhederverein') who claimed that the total package would be worth about the same as the concessions lost recently to ship-owners (Lloyd's List, 1997n, 1997o). The measures were introduced with the 1997 Tax Reform Bill (Lloyd's List, 1997p, 1997s).

Delays to the proposals were encountered in October 1997 when although agreed by the two houses of the German Parliament, they were held up by a dispute between the two over other issues (Lloyd's List, 1997q). Meanwhile the major German transport trades union OETV ('Offentlicher Dienste Transport und Verkehr'), whilst welcoming the tonnage tax proposals, was critical of the government and its relationship with VDR who it claimed represented an industry where almost all vessels were flagged-out and where German seafarer employment was minimised (Lloyd's List, 1997r).

By March 1998, the Budget and Transport Committees of the German lower house, the Bundestag, had agreed a resolution which incorporated the concept of a tonnage tax. The proposals included:

- Ship-owners would be able to choose between a tonnage tax and income tax on profits. There would be a 10-year commitment. Owners could retain the 40% seafarers' income tax deducted at source. This only applied where the seafarer was employed for more than 183 days a year.
- New manning rules would apply, variable according to vessel type and its trade. Nationality rules would also become more flexible.

Although welcomed by the VDR, the OETV was less favourable towards the manning changes seeing them as weakening the position of seafarers on German registered vessels and made attempts to gather together opposition to the Reform Bill in the German Upper House (Lloyd's List, 1998g, 1998h, 1998i). Despite some delays, the result was a clear success for the government in that the Bill passed easily in late May and made way for all of the tax changes proposed including the introduction of a tonnage tax (Lloyd's List 1998j, 1998k, 1998l).

The new tax was to take effect from January 1999 with ship-owners based in Germany able to choose between a tonnage tax (based upon net tonnage and days of operation) and income taxation for internationally trading vessels. It was widely welcomed by the ship-owners association (VDR) who saw the main benefits arising from the return of older vessels to Germany which had been flagged-out to other registries, rather than more modern vessels financed under the KG (limited partnerships) tax regime which benefited ship construction through depreciation concessions. The German registry was expected as a result to exhibit an increasingly ageing profile (even though opting for the tonnage tax did not require German flag registration) but the industry as a whole would gain around 170m DM a year from the range of tax concessions now available (Lloyd's List, 1998m, 1998n).

One further interruption to the plans for the introduction of a tonnage tax followed the election of a new German government in October 1998 which saw the Social Democrats and Greens come to power for the first time in 16 years. Inevitably the proposed tax reforms came under renewed scrutiny before it was agreed to put the reforms into effect as soon as possible (Lloyd's List, 1998o, 1998p, 1998q). One expected effect was to reduce container ship over-capacity which had developed on the back of the depreciation concessions available through the KG scheme and which bore little relation to market demand. The new tonnage tax would be much more market orientated and thus would distort the economics of the industry much less – a characteristic highly favoured by the European Commission which had to agree to the scheme before it could be introduced (Lloyd's List, 1998r).

Some reaction to the new scheme began to emerge in November 1999 with comments about the restrictions placed on ship-owners in that the decision to enter the scheme had to take place within three years of ordering a new vessel or for existing vessels by the end of 2001. German ship-owners were generally happy with the arrangements which they saw as aiding the operation of vessels rather than encouraging new-buildings (Lloyd's List, 1999a, 1999b). However, there remained some doubts about the taxation of shipping companies in general stemming from the tax authorities and the possibility that tonnage tax savings could not be combined with other shipping investment tax relief (Lloyd's List, 1999c; Lloyd's Shipping Economist, 2000).

Despite these initial issues, the success of the tonnage tax scheme was indicated by the transfer of a number of ships to the German register in December 1999. These included vessels managed in Cyprus which under the new scheme now had to be managed from Germany instead (Lloyd's List, 1999d). At the same time, one effect of tonnage taxation was to reduce the appeal of German shipping funds which had previously been highly successful due to the substantial tax concessions which had been available. These now had been largely removed and replaced by the tonnage tax on operations thus reducing the incentive to build new vessels (Lloyd's List, 2000k, 2000w). Germany's leading investment fund – 'Norddeutsche Vermogen' – was included amongst those reducing or even ceasing ship financing as a consequence of the new scheme, the effects of which were compounded by the continuing dispute over tax concessions for investment (Lloyd's List, 2000l).

Criticism of the new tonnage tax regime came from the German transport workers' trades union OETV which claimed that the German registered fleet (and therefore employment for German seafarers) had shrunk dramatically since the introduction of the tonnage tax on 1st January 1999 (Lloyd's List, 2000m, 2000o). This was a result of the fact that Open Registry vessels could benefit from the new taxation regime, a situation confirmed by the German Ship-owners Association (VDR), and the union claimed this could only be countered by making German registration a condition. Further criticism came from the German shipyard 'Peterswerft Wewelsfleth' which faced bankruptcy following the tax changes which saw investors taking their money away from German new-buildings (Lloyd's List, 2000n).

By June 2000, the new tonnage tax was being proclaimed a success (Lloyd's List, 2000p). The VDR indicated that some 500 vessels had been placed under its regime out of a total of 1,600 operating in international trades, and that owners had until the end of December 2001 to opt for the scheme and so the final total was likely to be higher still. The effect was also being felt in the ancillary sector in that the tonnage tax regulations required that the vessels were to be managed from Germany and that vessel masters and officers must be employed by German companies and as a consequence a number of ship management companies were returning particularly from Cyprus. Others were establishing subsidiary companies in Germany whilst retaining their company headquarters elsewhere. An early example of these moves featured Christian F. Ahrenkiel and the move of 15 vessels it managed back from Limassol in Cyprus to Hamburg. These included chemical tankers, gas carriers, car carriers and reefer vessels (Lloyd's List, 2000q).

Meanwhile, the expectation that the changes in tax laws would result in less expenditure on German new-buildings with the loss of some of the previous financial benefits, was not apparent with the order for two new container ships from a shipyard in Rostock by a German ship-owner (Lloyd's List, 2000r, 2000s). The success of the tonnage tax element of the tax reform was also emphasised by the annual results from Hapag Lloyd, the major German container shipping company which announced tax relief for their vessels of around 10-15 million DM per year (Lloyd's List, 2000t).

Despite these successes there was also news of problems in the industry and inadequacies of the tax regime. The number of vessels flying the German flag had declined by 133 during 1999 despite the introduction of the tonnage tax, which had attracted 500 vessels back to the flag but at the same time even more had continued to leave. Manning costs remained the most serious issue (Lloyd's List, 2000u). However, by October 2000 the position looked much better with early announcements that the number of vessels flagging-out during 2000 was only about 12 compared with over 100 in 1999 (Lloyd's List, 2000v, 2000y). It was claimed by the VDR that ship-owners were not only bringing the management of these vessels back to Germany (as required) but also the manning and registration. The problem remained of ensuring that these vessels remained under German registration for the future. However, the VDR estimated that many more vessels would return to the German flag before the deadline of 2001 eventually rising to 75% of the German controlled fleet (Lloyd's List, 2000x). It was estimated that around 7,700 of 12,000 seafarers on German flagged vessels were by then of German nationality.

The progress of tonnage tax in Germany and its impacts upon the German maritime sector was then steadily noted for some time before more dramatic issues once more intervened (Lloyd's List, 2001v, 2001w, 2001x, 2001y, 2001z). In May 2001 comment was made upon the success of the scheme and the problems this was causing in a shortage of German crews (Lloyd's List, 2001aa). In addition, the effects of the new tax were also noted in the second-hand market where the removal of many incentives to build new vessels was encouraging ship-owners to maintain their existing fleet instead (Lloyd's List, 2001bb). In June the same year, the tonnage tax was further bolstered by announcement of the first direct subsidies to ship-owners by the German government since 1999. Some 86m DM was approved and allocated to non-labour costs including training. Meanwhile, the ship-owning arm of the major German ship financiers 'Norddeutsche Vermogen', announced plans to expand their fleet by between 22 and 27 more ships partly as a consequence of the benefits from tonnage tax (Lloyd's List, 2001cc, 2001dd, 2001ee, 2001ff).

By late 2001 it was clear that one indirect effect of tonnage tax was that some German owners were returning to their domestic register. The German tax only required owners to operate and manage their vessels from Germany, not register them there, but this requirement was also encouraging owners to re-flag to Germany at the same time despite relatively strict manning rules (Lloyd's List, 2001gg, 2003i). New-buildings were allowed to remain within a foreign registry for three years after the contract for construction was signed after which the tonnage tax had to be opted for or foregone.

However, at the same time vessels were still being flagged-out at an increasing rate and as a result the German government announced a second package of aid for ship-owners which was aimed at training provision for young seafarers and lowering the non-wage costs of labour. Although not a requirement, the government hoped that German ship-owners would respond by reducing the trend towards flagging out (Lloyd's List, 2001hh). Despite welcoming the financial support, the German Ship-owners Association (VDR) claimed it was insufficient to reverse the trends in registration.

Another year passed without great incident in terms of tonnage tax until the surprise announcement in October 2002 that the newly re-elected government of Social Democrats and Greens were to scrap the tonnage tax and all other shipping subsidies (including income tax relief to seafarers) as part of a plan to reduce overall public expenditure (Lloyd's List, 2002d, 2002e, 2002f). No detail was given as to what would happen to vessels already registered for tonnage taxation. The impacts were expected to be enormous in that it would lead to a return to flagging-out and a withdrawal from Germany of all the ship management companies that had located there to take advantage of the tonnage tax regulations – these included Cosco and

P&O/Nedlloyd. By this time around 1,500 vessels had been registered under the scheme and nearly 850 shore-based jobs had followed. VDR expected to reverse the policy, which they claimed had been introduced hurriedly and without discussion with the Ministry of Transport or the industry itself.

Resistance to the move quickly grew in the form of the Christian Democrat opposition in the German Parliament which attempted to co-ordinate action against the move from the coastal states of Germany (Lloyd's List, 2002g). The effect was rapid in that indications that the policy would be dropped emerged only a week after and the proposal quietly disappeared by the end of the year following recognition that tax revenue would be less without it (Lloyd's List, 2002h, 2002i, 2003h).

In one of the latest twists in the German tonnage tax story, ship financiers began discussions on the formation of a lobby group to protect their interests following the threats to the tonnage tax at the end of the previous year (Lloyd's List, 2003j). Almost immediately, there emerged stories of proposed changes to the tonnage tax which would prevent the practice of off-setting losses from shipping against other income for tax purposes under the KG system (Lloyd's List, 2003k). Operators would then be encouraged to focus solely on profits from shipping rather than investment. At that time, the tonnage tax law allowed German owners to operate under a foreign registry for up to three years during which time specific losses could be partly off-set against income tax. After three years the ship would be placed under the German registry and tonnage tax. The proposal would be to abolish the off-setting concession and to demand immediate registration under the German flag to enjoy the benefits of the tonnage tax scheme.

Concerns about the German flagged fleet continued throughout 2003 with the Secretary of State for the Federal Transport Ministry commenting that she was '…deeply concerned…' (Lloyd's List, 2003q). Despite the existence of the tonnage tax, German ships were continuing to be flagged-out including 66 more vessels in the first three months of the year. Ongoing discussions about the tonnage tax were not helping and although the German Chancellor had promised its retention, this did not preclude its revision.

Re-affirmation of retention of the tax followed in late May but there also emerged a disagreement between the Chancellor and the Finance Ministry who saw it as a drain on tax revenues at times of low income. From a ship-owner's point of view, vessels were long-term investments and therefore needed long-term tax strategies (Lloyd's List, 2003m). The German tonnage tax, allowing owners to flag-out vessels on a bare-boat charter, had attracted many ship management operations back to Germany with consequent employment benefits in ancillary industries. It was expected that the tax would continue under pressure to attract vessels back to the flag and would have at most two years to prove its value from this viewpoint.

Discussions on tonnage tax continued through the summer accompanied by attempts from the wider industry to lobby government for its retention (Lloyd's List, 2003dd). The significance of the tax in attracting management companies particularly from Cyprus was emphasised (Lloyd's List, 2003ee) and by October there was renewed hope that the threat had declined as the benefits of the KG scheme and its close relationship to the tax had been recognised (Lloyd's List, 2003ff).

The United Kingdom

Tonnage tax in the UK has been extensively discussed and the aim here is not to provide further analysis in depth of the reasons why it emerged as a preferred government option. Instead, this section aims to outline the developments from 1997 and then to go on to assess the implications for the regime since its full introduction in 2000. Much of the argument here is based upon Selkou and Roe (2001; 2002), with additional commentary where appropriate.

As McConville (1999) commented, until around 30 years ago the presumption within the maritime sector was that governments universally:

' . . . were concerned and vigilant regarding their national flag fleets – further, that they would provide the necessary legislation and resources to ensure their progress; simply, that there was a community of interest between national registered merchant fleets and the states.'

However, this presumption clearly no longer holds universally true in a number of traditional maritime nations, evidenced by the:

' . . . plethora of inquiries and restructuring of policies engendered during the 1990s. Such readjustments have in general addressed or attempted to rectify apprehension about the ability of the registered fleet to be available or capable of fulfilling the country's commercial, economic, strategic and international obligations. Despite the wide brief, the central focus has invariably been on the importance of the national seafaring labour force.'

It is widely agreed that the success of these attempts at supporting national fleets is partly dependent upon state intervention, and this normally can be interpreted as some form of fiscal support. As McConville went on to say:

'This is the key variable on whether a government wishes to maintain or increase the industry's share in volume terms of world shipping. Norway and The Netherlands are prime examples of such policies, which have secured for them increases in the size of their fleets. The United Kingdom on the other hand has in the past viewed such intervention as an anathema.'

UK governments between 1970 and 1997 largely ignored the country's shipping decline, being willing for the most part to rely on foreign ships and seafarers for the carriage of trade. As a result, overwhelming economic distortions caused by substandard operators and foreign subsidies and the decline of the UK merchant fleet and associated UK seafaring employment, were accepted as the inevitable outcome of market forces (UK House of Commons, 1988).

In 1997, a newly constituted UK Government Shipping Working Group attempted to suggest ways in which the seemingly inevitable UK shipping industry's decline might be reversed (Lloyd's List, 1997u; Lloyd's Ship Manager, 1997; Roe, 1997; UK Department of Environment, Transport and the Regions, 1998). With the later publication of the Alexander report in August 1999 of the 'Independent Inquiry into a Tonnage Tax', the fiscal areas of UK shipping were covered in more detail. Subject to EU and UK Parliamentary Approvals, the principles were announced and appropriate legislation implemented.

The implementation of the new legislation regarding the procedures for registration under the UK flag and tonnage tax was not solely for fiscal reasons, but also an attempt to reverse the decline in ship registration in the UK and in the employment of UK seafarers both at sea and in the various maritime industries ashore. The UK government was committed to the strategy for 10 years in terms of the tonnage tax and to continue to review its registration procedures.

Some features of the United Kingdom shipping industry had lost their comparative supremacy in recent decades – in particular in terms of ship registration and the consequential impacts upon seafarer and officer employment. This continuous decline in the UK fleet is well documented (for example Brownrigg, 1993; Goss, 1987, 1991; Ledger and Roe, 1992) and will not be analysed further here. The implications of this decline for the employment prospects of UK seafarers and officers and the subsequent effects upon shore-based institutions particularly in the City of London have also been considered in recent years (Gardner et al., 1996; Gardner and Pettit, 1999a, 1999b). McConville and Glen (1997) for example, have stressed the sizeable decline in skills base within the UK industry, reflected in the decline in numbers of UK seafarers and officers matching that of the flagged fleet.

The Shipping Working Group noted earlier brought together all sides of industry, together with officials from six government departments. Their proposals formed the basis of the government's shipping policy paper 'British Shipping: Charting a New Course', published in December 1998 which set out in detail a long-term and integrated strategy to secure the future of British shipping, involving a partnership between the industry, the unions and the government (UK Chamber of Shipping, 1999). The Shipping Working Group's terms of reference were more ambitious than those of the last UK government/industry review in 1990 (Gardner et al., 2001). They were to:

1. Enable the maximum economic and environmental benefit to be obtained from the UK shipping industry.
2. Reverse the decline in the UK Merchant fleet which had been on-going since at least the 1970s and which had not been addressed in any serious form up until then.
3. Increase the employed and training numbers of UK seafarers.
4. Encourage ship-owners and the wider maritime industry to commit more resources to seafarer training.

The Group reported in March 1998 with a range of proposals on seafarer training, employment, the fiscal environment and opportunities for UK shipping. Meanwhile, a government White Paper published in July 1998, set out four broad aims of an integrated shipping policy:

1. To facilitate shipping as an efficient and environmentally friendly means of carrying (UK) trade.
2. To foster the growth of an efficient UK-owned merchant fleet.
3. To promote the employment and training of British seafarers in order to keep open a wide range of job opportunities for young people and to maintain the supply of skills and experience vital to the economy.
4. To encourage UK ship registration, to increase ship-owners' identification with the UK, to improve regulatory control of shipping using UK ports and waters and to maintain the availability of assets and personnel that may be needed in time of war.

This White Paper set out, for the first time, a long-term and integrated strategy for Britain's shipping industry – integrated not only with wider economic and industrial aims but also in the way the measures involve the industry, the unions and the government and the support amongst them in creating 'a virtuous circle' of growth in order to break the historic pattern of UK's shipping decline (Jaques, 1999).

The UK Department of Environment Transport and the Regions paper 'British Shipping; Charting a new Course' (UK Department of Environment Transport and the Regions, 1999) contained 33 recommendations to support the UK shipping sector. Although there was nothing specifically about tonnage tax, fiscal means of supporting the industry were noted and following the subsequent Report by Lord Alexander of Weedon, a tonnage tax approach for the UK shipping sector was adopted (Gardner, 1999; ImarE Bulletin, 1999).

Under the Finance Bill for 2000, the government introduced a new form of corporation tax for shipping companies based on a tonnage tax system. Linked to this provision, the government required shipping companies to raise their training procedures through an increase in the number of places at sea for prospective cadets. British shipping companies will thus be required to recruit one cadet for every 15 serving officers over a three-year period until the ratio between cadets and officers reaches 1:5. Such a ratio is deemed to be sufficient to cover natural wastage. There is a clear linkage between the tonnage tax and training as the training obligation is a key condition for entry into the scheme.

Each company's training initiative and the consequent subjection to the new tax regime was backdated from the introduction of a new Finance Bill in 2000, to the start of the individual year.

Tonnage tax for the UK operates on the following criteria:

1. Shipping lines will be given the option of either opting for the new tax, or remaining with the old-style capital allowances system. Importantly, if the decision is made to use the new system, the company will be obliged to remain with that system for a minimum period of 10 years or make payment in lieu estimated at around £500 per month.

2. Profits from UK shipping are ring-fenced. This is to prevent the abuse of the tonnage tax system by companies 'transferring' non-maritime related activities into the maritime sector to take advantage of the lower tax regime.

3. Unlimited 25% capital allowances are inappropriate to the tax-exempt system, and there are significant restrictions on capital allowances leased to companies within the tonnage tax system.

4. There is a provision for foreign profits from UK shipping to qualify for tonnage tax. However, this will be subject to the ring-fencing and anti-avoidance provisions.

The European Commission gave the go-ahead to the tonnage tax scheme in July 2000 and following UK Parliamentary approval, the new tax regime was made available for accounting periods from 1st January, 2000 (Fairplay, 2000).

The aid intensity proposed by the UK authorities is virtually identical to that approved for the German and Netherlands tonnage tax schemes, whilst the net tonnage steps specified are identical with the German scheme and comparable with the Netherlands. The annual cost of the scheme to the UK Treasury is anticipated to be in the region of £40 million a year in tax foregone.

A company enters the tonnage tax scheme by electing for an initial period of 10 years. For existing UK operators the election had to be within one year of Royal Assent of the UK Finance Act, in July 2001. Businesses newly liable to UK tax have one year from commencing the operation of ships in the UK. The regime applies to the accounting period in which election is made, commencing no earlier than 1st January, 2000 but entry must be backdated, or postponed for up to two years, in certain circumstances. A tonnage tax election may be renewed for a further 10 years at any time prior to its expiry.

The UK Inland Revenue has indicated three areas where there will be exit charges:

1. On ceasing to be a qualifying company: for reasons relating wholly or mainly to tax.
2. Where more than 75% of the tonnage is time chartered in.
3. Where the qualifying company has entered into a transaction that is an abuse of the tonnage tax regime which gives a third party a tax advantage to itself in respect of its non tonnage tax activities or it reduces its tonnage tax profits artificially (this excludes UK tax leasing).

The tonnage tax regime has no requirement that ships need to be registered under the UK flag, only that the company is registered in the UK and that a substantial part of its activities are based there. Linked to the expected future increase in tonnage, are the numbers of new trainee seafarers. It was hoped that the expansion of the skills base would have a dynamic effect in the medium term on Britain's maritime industries ashore, both in manufacturing and in maritime London (UK Inland Revenue, 2000b).

In principle, electing into the tonnage tax regime should prove attractive to many UK operators for whom it will result in a lower tax burden. Entry into the scheme would lead to a phased reduction of existing deferred taxation liabilities, and the timing of acquisition of ships will no longer be tax critical.

In most cases, entry into the regime will produce certainty and reduce the tax compliance burden, provided that non-qualifying activities can be identified and suitably ring fenced, perhaps in a separate company outside the regime (Watkin, 2000).

More specifically, the advantages of the tonnage-based corporation tax for the UK shipping industry are (Lloyd's List, 1999g):

1. Certainty. The tonnage tax scheme offers ship-owners the certainty of knowing exactly how their tax bills will be calculated, and at the same time, should reduce the deferred tax provision in their accounts.
2. Flexibility. Companies have more freedom to choose when to buy ships and how to finance them. Their decisions are not driven by tax considerations. Also, in terms of protection by the UK's double tax treaties, a shipping company should be able to operate branches in foreign countries without a significant exposure to overseas tax while still operating in an effective low tax environment (the tax charge will be based on the net tonnage of ships operated).
3. Clarity. A shipping company's tax position will be more easily understood by observers e.g. shareholders, analysts and potential business partners.
4. Compatibility. Finally, the new tax regime offers compatibility and competitiveness with other countries' regimes, particularly relevant for companies in international partnerships.

Initial reaction by ship-owners to the UK tonnage tax was cautious and even by September 2000, many were saying that it was too early to make a decision (Brownrigg, 2000). New guidance from the UK government was still emerging and issues such as the vessels to which it applied, the training commitment and tax obligations were still being clarified (Lloyd's List, 2000jj). In particular, worries were emerging over the cost of training even with government help, and the shortage of training places that might be available both at colleges and on-board ships.

Meanwhile, labour representatives at the annual UK Trades Union Congress emphasised their commitment to the tonnage tax and welcomed the collaboration with employers that had resulted in its introduction (Lloyd's List, 2000kk). Employers were quick to agree, with tanker shipping company James Fisher noting the immediate contribution to profits it had made in its first six months. However, they also noted that the training commitment was met before the tax was introduced and consequently would have no effect on their training scheme, an issue that was to raise its head increasingly over time (Lloyd's List, 2000ll).

The response of ship management companies was largely negative. Northern Marine's Managing Director indicated that he did not see that tonnage tax would give a boost to ship management and that ship-owners would contrive to avoid training commitments (Lloyd's List, 2000mm).

However, in October 2000 the Shipping Minister Keith Hill stressed that although the tonnage tax was 'flag-blind', it would help to continue the recent growth in UK flagged vessels, up 17% since 1998 (Lloyd's List, 2000nn).

Training worries were to continue as tonnage tax became increasingly popular. A joint study by the UK Officers' Trades Union and London Guildhall University in 2000 suggested that there would be insufficient places available on ships for trainees as the popularity of the UK flag – encouraged by the tonnage tax – increased (Lloyd's List, 2000oo) whilst further exhortations to ensure that the framework for training was in place, followed from the marine insurance sector in October 2000 (Lloyd's List, 2000a, 2000pp).

Overseas interest in the UK regime was quickly generated with Greek ship-owners the first to express an interest followed quickly by brokers and freight forwarders looking to invest in vessel acquisition which would be managed from London and under the tonnage tax scheme (Lloyd's List, 2000qq, 2000rr). Meanwhile the growth in cadets was confirmed by the UK Maritime and Coastguard Agency in November 2000 (MCA, 2000). Some 118 new cadets had been generated by 14 of the 16 shipping companies opting for the tax since its introduction in August 2000. The other two companies had chosen to pay the training levy instead (Lloyd's List, 2000ss, 2000tt).

By the end of the year a number of companies were still assessing the benefits of tonnage tax. P&O had re-flagged 20 vessels with a promise of 30 more and had signed on to the scheme and the number of vessels under the UK flag as a whole had increased by 30% over the year, but as tonnage tax was 'flag-blind' this was not wholly a consequence of the new tax scheme. It was increasingly agreed that each company would have to judge the tax on merit and for some it would not be worthwhile. The increase in training places was particularly encouraging as this was a major theme of the tax but there were a number of complaints about the complexity of the UK approach mirrored in the 150 pages of legal and tax documents it had generated. The equivalent in Germany was four and the Netherlands two (Lloyd's List, 2000uu).

The year 2001 saw considerable activity as the new tax began to take effect. Trades union criticism of the tonnage tax emerged in their condemnation of the places offered by shipping companies. In particular the places offered for ratings had actually declined (although for officers it had increased) and a number of well-known UK shipping companies who had opted for tonnage tax had recently replaced many UK crews by overseas seafarers. One union official was quoted 'There's not been one extra job from tonnage tax' (Lloyd's List, 2001c, 2001xx, 2001ooo).

Despite this, the larger UK shipping lines continued to promote the scheme. P&O emphasised the training commitment which would benefit UK seafarers and officers throughout the world and open them up to new employment markets (Lloyd's List, 2001yy). However, the difficulties in the market – and in particular in finding employment on UK flagged vessels – continued to rumble on in February 2001. The UK Chamber of Shipping commented that the additional skills gained from UK training would make them more employable elsewhere but they refused to be drawn on the tonnage tax as it was too early to see the true impacts yet (Lloyd's List, 2001zz; UK Chamber of Shipping, 2001).

Encouragement for the new scheme came the same month as CP Ships announced that they were studying the UK tonnage tax with a view to re-flagging following company restructuring (Lloyd's List, 2001aaa). In the UK the government was also expected to make few if any changes to the tonnage tax scheme in the forthcoming Budget as it was too soon yet to pass judgement (Lloyd's List, 2001bbb). Meanwhile the European Commission was reported as considering introducing a European-wide tonnage tax to help to attract ships back to member states. To be modelled on the UK approach, it would also include a training element and would focus on attracting only safer and cleaner ships (Lloyd's List, 2001ccc). Its relationship to national registers remained unclear.

By late March 2001, 38 companies representing over 600 vessels had made enquiries of the UK Treasury regarding the tonnage tax. Around 75% of these were UK companies. Some 18 had had their training schemes approved by the UK Transport Ministry. However, the final number of existing shipping companies opting for the tax would not be known until after the deadline at the end of July (Lloyd's List, 2001ddd). Meanwhile, the eligibility of dredgers and North Sea supply vessels remained unclear. However, the number of shipping companies taking up tonnage tax was lower than had originally been expected and the problems surrounding the training commitment remained, particularly where the vessels placed within the tonnage tax remit were entirely manned by overseas seafarers and officers – a possibility given the 'flag-blind' nature of the scheme (Lloyd's List, 2001eee). Additionally, questions were being asked by trades unions about whether new roll on/roll off vessels for the UK Ministry of Defence would be placed under the scheme, and the implications for training places this implied (Lloyd's List, 2001cccc).

Further doubts emerged in May concerning recruitment of the 1,200 cadets a year envisaged by the government. A number of training colleges expressed doubts that this could be achieved despite recent increases (Lloyd's List, 2001fff). In addition, union representatives continued to be concerned about the devaluation of the UK flag to one of a flag of convenience with tonnage tax forming part of the package. The prospect of UK flagged ships manned by crews outside of ITF agreements was especially unacceptable and there were threats that such vessels would be classed as flying a flag of convenience (Lloyd's List, 2001iii). The continued failure to attract large numbers of training placements was also a disappointment to the unions who had seen it as the most attractive aspect of tonnage tax (Lloyd's List, 2001ggg, 2001kkk, 2001ppp).

Further negative news came with the announcement by UK coastal ship-owners FT Everard that they would not be opting for the tonnage tax. The decision was largely based on the depreciation allowances enjoyed from other activities (including ports and electronics) that would be lost if the tax was chosen (Lloyd's List, 2001jjj).

More positive news came from an International Financial Markets Survey which indicated that the UK was by nearly all measures, the top maritime centre in the world. The only drawback was that skills shortages were emerging which although addressed by the tonnage tax, this would take some years to be effective (Lloyd's List, 2001hhh, 2001nnn). Meanwhile, Belgian towing and salvage specialists URS announced the re-flagging of a number of vessels to the UK flag whilst taking advantage of tonnage tax benefits (Lloyd's List, 2001lll) whilst P&O Princess Cruises indicated that tonnage tax had helped to support profits (Lloyd's List, 2001qqq).

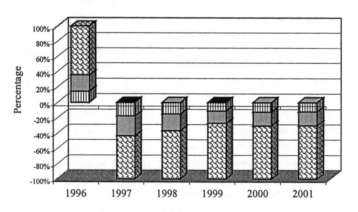

� Deck Officers ▨ Engineer Officers ☐ Dual Purpose Officers ▨ Ratings

Source: Improving Employment Opportunities for European Seafarers, *An Investigation to Identify Training and Education Priorities in the UK*, University of Bremen, 2001.

Figure 7.3: Employment of UK Officers 1996-2001

The deadline for existing UK shipping companies to opt for the scheme was towards the end of July 2001 but because training schemes or payments in lieu of £550 per seafarer per month were taking a month to gain approval, the deadline was effectively the end of June. Rather worryingly, over £17,000 had been received in payments in the first few weeks suggesting that companies were taking advantage of the scheme but avoiding the more complex issue of training and thus the contribution to UK seafarer employment was potentially insignificant, as illustrated by the trend in numbers of UK officers during the same period (Figure 7.3). Given its central role and also the requirement of the EU that the UK scheme should have a training link if it was to meet state-aid rules on flag association, this was an even greater concern (Lloyd's List, 2001mmm). It also formed a major justification in providing a tax subsidy for the industry in political terms.

The success of the tonnage tax in attracting existing operators into its regime was announced on 1st August, by the UK Shipping Minister. Some 47 companies had opted to join representing 586 ships in total. The UK flag incidentally, had been boosted by the tax with numbers registered increasing by 37% in the past year. The Minister expected continued growth (Lloyd's List, 2001rrr).

Further criticism of the training and UK job creation element of the tonnage tax was received in September with trade unionists again questioning the value of the scheme from an employment viewpoint (Lloyd's List, 2001sss). Reinforcing such worries, the UK Maritime and Coastguard Agency (MCA) were noting a large increase in the demand for Certificates of Equivalent Competency, issued to maintain consistency across EU member registries and to ensure that international seafarers met the demands of STCW95. The increase was felt to be a consequence of the introduction of tonnage tax which had increased the number of foreign seafarers employed on UK registered ships (Lloyd's List, 2001ttt). Further to this, by October 2001 it was clear that the intake of cadets was less than half those needed. Some 550 had registered for entry in 2001, up from 470 in 2000, but substantially below the number of 1,450 needed to avoid future skills shortages (Lloyd's List, 2001uuu).

Better news came in October, however not in terms of training but in signs of vessel registration from overseas. Container carrier Lloyd Triestino announced that it was considering adopting the UK flag because of its association with the tonnage tax regime. This was partly at least a reaction to the continuing delay in Italy's adoption of a scheme. Meanwhile, Evergreen, the independent Taiwanese container operator that owns Lloyd Triestino, made it clear that it was to flag two new 6,200 TEU vessels with the UK flag. The ships were due for almost immediate delivery and would be UK flagged as a UK lease vehicle was being used to finance them (Lloyd's List, 2001vvv,

2001www). It was thought that the number of vessels attracted to the UK flag, in part at least by the tonnage tax system, was by then over 150 including container vessels operated by CMA/CGM and Maersk/Sealand (Lloyd's List, 2001xxx, 2001yyy, 2001zzz). At the same time plans were announced by Evergreen for three further post-panamax containerships to be subject to tonnage tax although in this case the flag was undecided. Training places were to be made available on the vessels above the number required. Negotiations with the UK Treasury were long and complex because Taiwan was not recognised by the UN (Lloyd's List, 2001aaaa).

However, the good news could not last and the issue of training raised its head again with the announcement that P&O/Nedlloyd was to axe the last remaining British ratings employed on their deep-sea containerships. Union representatives expressed anger at the decision to replace the 67 ratings at the same time as the company was taking advantage of the tonnage tax scheme (Lloyd's List, 2001bbbb).

Despite this, a series of successes were to follow through 2002 but again centring upon overseas operators and contributing little to the cadet situation or training facilities. It began with suggestions that Evergreen would transfer up to 40 more vessels from the Panamanian to the UK flag because of a combination of advantages of taxation, prestige and the ability to use Taiwanese officers with UK certificates (Lloyd's List, 2002r, 2002s). A new subsidiary, Hatsu Marine Limited was established specifically to act as an operational base in the EU for the five containerships that the company had pledged to UK flag (Lloyd's List, 2002u, 2002v). This was followed rapidly by Maersk announcing the re-flagging of six more vessels to the UK flag within the year, largely because of benefits from tonnage tax (Lloyd's List, 2002s, 2002w).

Further overseas acquisitions for the UK flag followed in November 2002 with Italian based Cafiero Mattioli Finanziaria announcing that its eight new bulk carriers would all be flagged with the UK because of the advantages of the tonnage tax. Blenheim Shipping, the company's agent in London, was to act as the managers (Lloyd's List, 2002x). Meanwhile Confitarma was losing patience with the Italian government and was beginning to organise a mass exodus of the Italian registered fleet to the UK. In particular this was to focus on the coastal trading fleet of over 400 vessels with a cost to the Italian government of over 50 million euro a year and therefore more than the sum which the state had refused to pledge to the industry in the next Budget (Lloyd's List, 2002t, 2002y). The migration, if it occurred, was expected to take over a year to complete.

Despite these successes, the issue of training would not go away. UK Seafarer Trades Union Numast expressed annoyance that the UK government would not reveal which shipping companies had opted for the tonnage tax. As a result, the trades union could not check on which had met training requirements and which had paid the levy instead. The UK Treasury refused to comment as they never provided details of tax-related matters due to the needs of commercial confidentiality. The UK Chamber of Shipping sided with the trades union in wanting more information although it was known that 620 vessels were registered under the scheme (UK Chamber of Shipping, 2002; Lloyd's List, 2002z; Osler, 2002).

Meanwhile, changes to the scheme were under discussion by early 2003, leading to criticism from many in the sector that the costs to lessees adopting tonnage tax would increase substantially (Lloyd's List, 2003ii). Unlike many other tonnage taxes, the UK version had special benefits in terms of capital allowances for lessees, and these were now likely to be removed. New anti-avoidance legislation related to this issue was introduced in December 2002 which was expected to hit those leasing expensive ships such as gas carriers and cruise ships in particular (Lloyd's List, 2003kk).

Encouraging words for the regime continued as well however, including the UK Maritime and Coastguard Agency (MCA), which confirmed the growth in sea cadet numbers whilst recognising that more were needed (Lloyd's List, 2003jj). In contrast, reports also emerged that the planned number of trainees (1,200) was too many for UK flagged vessels to accommodate and some shipping companies were already unable to offer posts when training was completed (Lloyd's List, 2003ll). Clearly some further management of the scheme was needed as ship-owners were complaining that they were expected to train and employ more personnel than they needed for the eventual benefit of sustaining the City of London maritime cluster of agents, brokers and the like some time in the future (Lloyd's List, 2003mm).

Further good news followed in February when Abbey Shipping, a new UK shipping company, was launched under a government sponsored Enterprise Investment Scheme, and aimed to place its new vessel under the UK tonnage tax (Lloyd's List, 2003nn, 2003oo). Meanwhile, James Fisher extolled the financial benefits of the tonnage tax in March and Carnival Cruises announced that the new Queen Mary II, under construction in France, would be registered with the UK flag because of the UK tonnage tax (Lloyd's List, 2003pp, 2003qq). Finally, in July 2003, Zodiac Maritime Agencies (the London office of the Israeli based Ofer Brothers Group) announced it was to place half of the 140 vessels it managed onto the UK register, moving them from a variety of Open Registers. These ships included containerships, car carriers, reefers, chemical tankers, LPG tankers and bulkers (Lloyd's List, 2003rr, 2003ss, 2003ww). Zodiac intended to take up its entire training commitment with an anticipated 380 cadetships, although this was no change in policy for the company as all officers had progressed through the existing training scheme.

Debate about the value of the scheme continued through August 2003 (Lloyd's List, 2003tt). The issue of leasing remained at the top of the list although despite the introduction of new legislation by the UK Treasury, few problems seemed to have emerged (Lloyd's List, 2003uu). The benefits of the new regime were still emerging through the growth of the flagged fleet, helped by the new 'user-friendly' approach of the UK MCA. An increase in tonnage of around 38% had been registered between 2002 and 2003, from 6.53m gt to 9.02m gt, and of over 170% since the scheme's introduction (Lloyd's List, 2003vv). Tonnage under the flag was now the highest since 1986 and due to increase further as Cosco announced plans to transfer vessels to the UK (Lloyd's List, 2003yy).

Meanwhile, increased concerns were expressed by the Chamber of Shipping over other moves by the UK government which would detract from the UK flag and thus work against the tonnage tax – these included changes in national insurance and the removal of the ability to pay foreign seafarers at their local rates of pay (UK Chamber of Shipping, 2003 Lloyd's List, 2003xx). In addition, proposals to revise UK corporation tax laws related to leasing raised their head again and were seen to pose a direct threat to the scheme (Lloyd's List, 2003zz).

The UK tonnage tax system represents a complex application of the approach to the issues facing ship registration, manpower training and competitiveness in the EU. It borrowed heavily in style from earlier incarnations of tonnage tax, in particular the Netherlands, whilst introducing novel features, in particular the links forged with compulsory training programmes. In terms of national and supra-national relationships its specific features reflect the policy needs of both the EU and the nation state, with the advantage of satisfying demands from each jurisdiction.

Finland

The initial moves towards the introduction of a tonnage tax in Finland began in August 1997 soon after the EU publication of its latest state-aid guidelines with Finnish ship-owners urging their government to introduce such a regime to prevent an exodus from the flag (Lloyd's List, 1997t). The Finnish Shipowners Association (FSA) had opened discussions with the Ministry of Transport in the context of the substantial decline in domestically flagged vessels which was occurring in neighbouring Sweden.

As a result, a special committee was set up consisting of representatives from the Finance and Transport Ministries and the Finnish Maritime Administration which would report in May 1998 back to the Finance

Ministry (Lloyd's List, 1998s). Opinion was apparently divided with the Finance Ministry in particular concerned about subsidising a specific industry. This division in opinion was to be reflected in the eventual scheme produced which was also influenced by the presence of the second Finnish registry with its existing concessions.

Calls for a tonnage tax system came from Finland's largest shipping company Finnlines in May 1998 and in early June of that year, a new tonnage based regime was announced by the Ministry of Transport to be presented to the government's Economic Policy Committee in August (Lloyd's List, 1998t, 1998u). The plan was that the new measures would be introduced in 2000 and would centre around the substitution of corporation tax by a tonnage tax, increased employment of non-EU crews and refunds of 9.5% of seafarer pension rights to employers (Lloyd's List, 1998v).

However, surprisingly the measures were excluded from the 1999 Budget proposals largely because of doubts expressed by the Finance Ministry and also the impact of a looming national election (Lloyd's List, 1998w). Instead, a joint review was set up to report back by mid-September 1998. In theory, the proposals could still then be incorporated into the Budget and come into effect in 2000 but as was to become clear, this was not to happen (Lloyd's List, 1998x).

There was no progress during 1999 and the issue remained a sore point within the maritime community of Finland which watched as registered vessels continued to leave the flag. In February 2000, this reached a highly political climax with the announcement by Finnlines that it was to out-flag 11 of its 14 ferries to other tonnage tax flagged regimes because the shipping sector appeared to have neither economic nor political influence (Lloyd's List, 2000z, 2000aa). By April 2000, the first two vessels were moved to the Danish register (Lloyd's List, 2000bb, 2000cc).

However, by June 2000 there were the first signs that the government was going to move on this issue (Lloyd's List, 2000dd) and although there had been no good news for ship-owners in the supplementary Budget presented in May, the government had promised in March that at an unspecified time in the future, tax concessions would be introduced (Lloyd's List, 2000ee). On 26th June, after three years of industry pressure, these concessions were finally announced.

The new tonnage tax would take effect from 1st January, 2001 but full details were not immediately available. The only thing confirmed was that ferries and passenger ships would be excluded from the associated crew subsidies. Ship-owners would have the right to choose between conventional corporation and tonnage tax and would have to opt for a 10-year period. The issues which remained of concern to the FSA centred upon the definition of ship-related activities and the regulations concerning the proportion of a company's fleet that could sail under a foreign flag (Lloyd's List, 2000ff).

The immediate impact was two-fold; ferry operator Viking Line was unimpressed and commented that they would not be returning their vessels to the Finnish flag. Meanwhile Finnish energy group Fortum Oil and Gas confirmed that two new Aframax tankers under construction would be registered under the Finnish tonnage tax regime (Lloyd's List, 2000gg).

Progress on the tonnage tax bill was far from speedy however, and there was still no sign of implementing the measure by Spring 2001 (Lloyd's List, 2000hh, 2000ii, Navigator, 2001). By June the proposals were still in embryonic form except that detail had emerged that duty-free sales would be excluded much to the annoyance of ferry operators although passenger vessels in general were now included (Lloyd's List, 2001ii, 2001jj).

In fact it was not until January 2002 that the tonnage tax proposals were introduced but within a few months there was a storm of protest from the FSA. The Finnish government had long had a policy of not subsidising any industry unless there were very pressing reasons and the tonnage tax regime that was implemented reflected this reluctance. The FSA predicted that not one ship-owner, small or large, would choose the new system, described as a 'disaster' and one that if selected by a ship-owner, could lead to a 'quintupling of taxes' (Lloyd's List, 2002j, 2002k). Existing tax debts stemming from depreciation of vessels were not accommodated adequately and the 10-year commitment was viewed as too long (despite being common elsewhere). Meanwhile duty-free sales were not included in the system and yet represented the biggest source of profits for Finnish ferry owners, whilst passenger ships remained excluded from concessions on crew taxes and social costs. These latter were restricted to cargo ships as a result of strong opposition by seafarers unions.

Further criticism from the industry continued during late 2002 with Antii Lageroos, Group President of Finnlines quoted as saying:

'In the long term I see no reason why new ships should be flagged in. The tonnage tax structure is worthless . . . Even the five or six ships we still have under national flag may leave' (Lloyd's List, 2002l).

The Finnish tonnage tax system has been the longest in gestation of all those adopted so far with the FSA one of the first ship-owner associations to demand its introduction in 1997 (Lloyd's List, 2002m). The Finnish government prevaricated for so long because it retained a fundamental policy of reducing and eliminating subsidies to industry and only changed their mind when threatened by a strike by the Finnish Seamen's Union which would have paralysed international trade. The tonnage tax was introduced as a concession to ship-owners to give them the room to pay seafarers more and thus end the strike. Introduced in this way, there were always question marks about whether the Finnish government was really serious about it as a policy (Lloyd's List, 2002k).

By September 2003, the Finnish financial regime for shipping was condemned by one of the biggest law firms in Finland as 'the most expensive in Europe' (Lloyd's List, 2003cc). In particular, although the Finnish government had introduced measures to support the fleet after the EU had clarified state support in 1997, the measures taken had been far less beneficial to shipping than in other member countries. The tonnage tax was described as a 'total disaster' and had been rejected by all Finnish ship-owners. Amongst other things, it was severely complex, dividends were taxed at the normal rate and on-board sales to passengers were excluded.

Denmark

Following the publication of the EU State-Aid Guidelines for the Maritime Sector in 1997, Denmark moved relatively rapidly to introduce a tonnage tax system with the initial developments in 1998 and the new tax regime introduced in 2002. There were difficulties and delays on the way but Denmark in some ways represents a clear example of a national policy-making body developing strategies within the overall framework of the EU and its supra-national presence.

Moves were first reported in May 1998 that Danish ship-owners were looking towards the introduction of a tonnage tax system to replace the existing taxation of financial earnings and more specifically on 19th May, the Danish Shipowners' Association (DSA) called for a full review of shipping taxation in their annual review (Lloyd's List, 1998b). At the time, both the Netherlands and Norway had recently successfully introduced a tonnage tax whilst Germany had announced firm plans (Lloyd's List Focus, 1997, 2000).

The Danish plan was to develop a tonnage tax system that would encourage owners to base their investment decisions upon market needs rather than tax considerations which distorted supply and demand pressures. Consideration of proposals by the DSA and the government was announced on 22nd May (Lloyd's List, 1998c).

However, some severe delays followed and it was not until early 2000 that any details of these discussions and the proposals were made public (Lloyd's List, 2000c). Clearly based upon the Netherlands approach to tonnage taxation, although there were no details at this time of rates, it was announced that there would be restrictions to prevent speculators switching in and out of the system for short-term gain. The DSA expected the new system, which would include binding those that opted for it to a 10-year period, to be introduced from 2001, but that this was dependent entirely upon political progress in the Danish Parliament.

Overall, the tax concessions were not expected to be large in financial terms as Danish ship-owners already benefited from extensive new-building subsidies; however the aim was to level the playing field with other tonnage tax regimes in the EU and Norway.

Further problems emerged in September 2000 when the DSA criticised the government tax proposals which were now part of a wider plan incorporating improved depreciation allowances as well (Lloyd's List, 2000d). The DSA saw the proposals as being both confusing and an encouragement to ship-owners to register their vessels under foreign flags. Instead of the tonnage tax being a clear and single approach to shipping taxation, it would run in parallel to the new depreciation allowances with the danger that neither would be particularly successful. In addition, the existing subsidies to shipbuilding would cease from 2001 leaving the new dual approach the only financial support to shipping.

Little was heard again except for continued lobbying in 2001 by the Danish ship-owners A.P. Moller and D/S Torm for a tonnage tax to be introduced quickly (Lloyd's List, 2001f, 2001g, 2001k). At the same time, the Engineers and Navigation Trades Unions in Denmark pressurised the Danish government to speed up the introduction of tonnage tax but the DSA remained pessimistic about progress as no talks were taking place. The DSA remained opposed to the proposed depreciation allowances or the suggestion that a taxation regime should exist for those ship-owners who reduced their activities to unacceptably low levels (Lloyd's List, 2001h).

The unions planned to meet with the government Shipping Policy Committee if they received no satisfaction from the Ministry itself. Failing this, plans were afoot to attempt to make the issue central to the general election due in March 2002. Further ship-owner pressure on the government followed in June 2001 as time passed and the stalemate continued (Lloyd's List, 2001i, 2001j).

However, late August brought news of a new government tonnage proposal that was largely acceptable to the DSA. This was expected to be along the lines of the UK tonnage tax regime and it was hoped would be presented to the Danish Parliament in Autumn of 2001 (Lloyd's List, 2001l). Some negotiation between the government and ship-owners was still expected especially over the considerable amount of chartered tonnage operated but the signs were generally positive particularly since there was support for the measures from all political parties.

By January 2002, firm proposals were put forward by the newly elected Danish government which although they failed to address all the issues raised by the DSA, were still warmly welcomed by ship-owners (Lloyd's List,

2002b). The voluntary tax was to be based on tonnage alone and not earnings, whereas the proposals of the former government retained an element of earnings-related taxation. The European Commission's approval was awaited with some expectation, as the proposal resembled those already agreed in the UK, the Netherlands and Germany. The Danish parliament was expected to approve the concept without delay. The proposals would be backdated to January 2001.

The tonnage tax system eventually agreed, was passed by the Danish parliament on 18th April, 2002 and its introduction was widely welcomed over the next year by a number of Danish ship-owners (Lloyd's List 2003a, 2003b, 2003c). These included the Danish Shipowners' Association for Smaller Vessels and dry bulk and tanker operators D/S Torm and Norden.

The Danish tonnage tax system was a direct result of the EU's revised state-aid guidelines for shipping and was designed to place Denmark on an equal footing with the other member states that had already introduced or were planning to introduce a tonnage tax system – in particular the Netherlands, the UK and Germany. As such it represented along with them a good example of a supra-national policy adapted to fit domestic needs so that the demands of the Treaty of Rome (in this case the origins of supra-national policy) were met whilst still recognising the need for national interpretation. Here we see not conflict but policy integration across spatial levels and as such, its impact and effectiveness are likely to be enhanced. This contrasts with for example, EU Regulation 4056/86 which exempts liner shipping from the requirements of the competition rules of the Treaty of Rome but which has been subject to considerable debate and argument between the supra-national and national authorities. Other areas of spatial disagreement include shipbuilding subsidies and port investment support.

Spain

Spain has come late to the idea of a tonnage tax to support their merchant fleet and measures were only introduced in 2003, although back-dated to the 1st January 2002. The initial suggestions emerged from the ship-owners' association Anave in the period up to June 2001, at which time it was announced that agreement on the structure was now close (Lloyd's List, 2001rr). Subject to agreement of the European Commission, necessary in all such cases, it was hoped to introduce the new regime with almost immediate effect through the 'Accompanying Law of the General State Budget' for 2002. Approval of this was expected in December 2001.

By March 2002, Anave was happily forecasting the growth of the Spanish fleet following the anticipated introduction of a tonnage tax from 31st March of that year (Calhoon MEBA Engineering School, 2002) and mid the same month, the European Commission announced that it was happy to approve its introduction by the Spanish government under the 1997 Guidelines.

A related incident occurred in February 2003 with the announcement that the European Commission had also approved the introduction of a regional tonnage tax to cover the autonomous district of the Basque Country which followed the same principles as that agreed for the country as a whole (Lloyd's List, 2003l). The new tonnage regime would have effect only for those companies with a fiscal base in the Biscay District and would directly benefit the employment of seafarers in that area.

The tonnage tax proposed both regionally and nationally had the following characteristics. The companies concerned had to be registered as ship-operators and managed from Spain or another EU member country; the sole activity had to be the operation of ships; the ships had to be capable of sailing on the high seas; and qualification was always subject to the agreement of the taxation authorities. Chartered in vessels must not exceed 75% of the total net tonnage of the fleet. Tonnage tax was voluntary and companies could leave the regime before the normal 10-year period expires. A five-year gap before re-registration would be allowed must then follow. The taxable base for the vessels was to be determined by the net tonnage of the vessels and not their operating results; and the scale applied was to be between €0.20 and 0.90 depending on vessel size, reducing as tonnage increased.

However, by June 2003 the national implementation of a tonnage tax in Spain was still in doubt and there remained an ominous silence (Lloyd's List, 2003e).

Ireland

Ireland was another country which came relatively late to tonnage tax as a national policy initiative for the shipping sector but despite this has incorporated it into its maritime sector with enthusiasm and some specific characteristics not found elsewhere. The initial moves were reported in February 2001, when the Irish Maritime Development Office (IMDO), an advisory group to government, noted a 'continuous and catastrophic' decline in the Irish shipping industry (Lloyd's List, 2001kk). The Irish Chamber of Shipping had long been campaigning in the background for the introduction of a tonnage tax regime but the Budget for 2001 had failed to include any such measures. The decline was exemplified by the reduction in number of vessels registered in Ireland from over 80 in 1981 to only 42 by 2001.

The difficulties facing the industry were further emphasised in April of the same year when it became clear that the tonnage tax proposal had been passed around between the Ministries of Marine and Finance, the

Departments of the same name and also the Marine Institute and the Cabinet, none of which was willing to make a decision (Lloyd's List, 2001ii).

By June of the same year, the Irish Ferries owner Irish Continental Group (ICG), were threatening to flag all their vessels out to the UK registry unless a tonnage tax was introduced, as they were currently uncompetitive in Europe as a result. The Chairman of the Group Tom Toner, summarised the issue that has stimulated the development of national tonnage tax regimes through most of the European Union:

'We will not be able to continue to fly the Irish flag indefinitely if our tax regime is more onerous than that of our competitors who are free to trade into Irish ports while enjoying the benefits of other EU countries' tonnage tax regimes' (Lloyd's List, 2001mm).

The ICG demands essentially were looking for a tax regime that would equate to zero corporation tax and as such were largely in line with the ambitions of the IMDO. Although the latter had no power or influence directly in taxation matters, it was able to work closely with the Irish Finance Ministry and Irish ship-owners. Initial indications of the type of tonnage tax system preferred seemed to suggest one that was simple to operate and was wholly transparent (Lloyd's List, 2001nn, 2001oo). This in turn implied a model of the German or Netherlands type rather than that of the UK.

However, it was not until December of 2001 that the government finally announced the introduction of a tonnage tax in the annual Budget much to the relief of a number of Irish shipping companies (Lloyd's List, 2001pp). In addition to the warnings from ICG, Arklow Shipping had threatened to re-flag all 27 remaining Irish flagged vessels to the Netherlands unless a tonnage tax was introduced, but now withdrew the threat and announced that two new-buildings for 2002 would also be flagged in Ireland. It was estimated that the new tax would secure the future for 2,800 employed in shipping and related industries in addition to the 1,100 employed at sea. The details of the scheme are as follows:

1. Companies opting in, do so for a 10 year period and if leaving, cannot return for another 10 years.
2. A qualifying company is one that is subject to corporation tax, operates qualifying ships and carries on their strategic and commercial management in Ireland.
3. No more than 75% of the net tonnage of the company's fleet can be chartered into the tonnage tax regime.
4. Companies part of a group, must elect as a group to enter the scheme.

5. Ships must obtain a certificate of navigation and be over 100 nrt.
6. Vessels excluded include those used for fishing, sports and relaxation, offshore installations, dredgers, tugs and coastal/river ferries. Also excluded is any vessel where the primary purpose is that normally carried out on land.
7. Taxation rates were set to reduce markedly as vessel size increases – for example, up to 1,000 nrt – €1.00 per 100 net tons; over 25,000 nrt – €0.25.

Generally, the announcement of the introduction of a tonnage tax regime in Ireland was welcomed (Auchiney, 2002; Banks, 2002). The aim was to have the scheme in place by the end of 2002 and it would incorporate the best practices already in place around Europe (Lloyd's List, 2002n). In line with tonnage tax elsewhere across the European Union, the European Commission approved the scheme on 11th December 2002 emphasising the benefits in terms of employment of EU seafarers and competitiveness of the Irish fleet (Commission of the European Communities, 2002c; Lloyd's List, 2002o). Ireland thus became the eighth EU country to take steps to introduce a tonnage tax regime along with Greece, the Netherlands, Denmark, the UK, Germany, Spain and Finland although not all of these were yet in place. Of these, all had been introduced after 1997 except the Netherlands and Greece (Commission for the European Communities, 2002b).

The IMDO was charged by the Irish government to market the scheme and it was hoped by all those concerned that a number of international shipping subsidiaries would be established in the country to take advantage of the tax benefits it would bring, thus extending its value beyond that of the dominant national carriers of Arlow and Irish Ferries (Lloyd's List, 2003s).

This need for international expansion was further emphasised in July 2003 and the favourable overall tax environment in Ireland that had been developed for all sectors in the 1990s, was cited as further encouraging ancillary maritime sectors as well as ship operators, to locate in the country (Lloyd's List, 2003t). One specific advantage also identified in the Irish approach was that the tonnage tax regime does not require an ownership interest in vessels to qualify and as a result, ship management companies might well be attracted to Ireland as well.

Ireland was also different in that the tonnage tax was an inherent part of its maritime cluster approach with in addition, a new €58 million National Maritime College to open in 2004 and complete overhaul of the maritime legislation covering the Irish Ship Register (Lloyd's List, 2003u, 2003v).

Belgium

Belgium was relatively late on the scene in terms of progress towards adopting a tonnage tax system but since reaching agreement between the government and national ship-owners, they have then moved quickly. This has to be considered in the light of the fact that by 1991, the entire commercial Belgian registered fleet had been flagged-out (Lloyd's List, 2003g).

The first indications that discussions were actually reaching some sort of conclusion was the announcement in May 2000 by the Belgian tug operators Unie van Redding en Sleepdienst (URS) that they expected agreement on the issue in the coming weeks (Lloyd's List, 2000g). They announced at the same time that, in anticipation of such a move, they would remain with the Belgian flag. The company expected to reduce personnel costs as a result by as much as 70% each year and would be able to depreciate vessels over a much shorter time. As a consequence they would be able to compete with German and Netherlands flagged tug operators who, within the open market of the EU were serious competitors in Belgian ports.

The expectations of URS were not realised immediately however, as by October of the same year the same tug operator was still considering whether to place two new vessels under the Belgian flag in anticipation of the introduction of a tonnage tax in the near future (Lloyd's List, 2001n). By then the Belgian government was seriously considering a change in taxation for shipping. The proposals were outlined in the Belgian Shipowners' Annual Report for 2001. These proposals had been developed by the government in consultation with Anderson Consulting and were designed to meet the guidelines issued by the EU in 1997 on state aid to the maritime sector (Belgian Shipowners' Association, 2002). They consisted of two main measures:

- An optional lump-sum profit taxation based on tonnage. This would be designed to encourage a young fleet benefiting safety and the environment. Those opting for this approach would have to commit themselves for a 10 year period.
- An alternative option based upon the amortisation levels for new and used ships.

These measures were then sent to the European Commission and the Belgian Parliament for their approval. By mid-October, the Shipowners' Association was very optimistic that progress could be made by the end of the year especially since an economic report by private consultants was expected to give a strong positive message. Commenting on the general proposal, they indicated that by late 2001, only France, Sweden and Belgium of all EU maritime states had not implemented any measures under the state-aid guidelines of the EU and that its implementation would lead to a considerable growth in income from shipping to the Belgian state. Additional reasons included a number that were noted in Chapter 2 that are commonly claimed as reasons for supporting the maritime industry – prestige as modern shipping could provide an 'ambassadorial role' for Belgium; it would encourage young people to enter the industry; and it would attract the large number of vessels currently registered in neighbouring Luxembourg (a register designed to accommodate these vessels) back to their home port of Antwerp.

The proposals were expected to recommend a level of taxation similar to that applied in the Netherlands but with lower levels of taxation for younger vessels. It was also hoped that encouraging the largest Belgian ship-owner CMB to re-flag its vessels to the Belgian registry would also help the company in attracting the carriage of Belgian based cargoes, particularly those related to the LNG, gas and oil markets. Relative taxation rates are indicated in Table 7.3. The plan was that the government would propose the tax in the autumn of 2001 and that the legislation would be ready by the summer of 2002 (Lloyd's List, 2001o).

Delays followed however, largely caused by the slow speed the European Commission moved in granting approval. And when it came it was only partial (Lloyd's List, 2003e). The Commission was happy to allow the taxation regime to go ahead in principle but refused to permit the entire proposal to be introduced without further investigation. This was aimed especially at the low taxation rates applicable to ships of over 40,000 gt, but also the reduced rates for ships under 5 years old and the 25% relief aimed at those between 5 and 20 years old. The Commission would also look at the suggestions of tax relief for divisions other than directly related to shipping including those relating to the sale of luxury goods on ships and others aimed at the ship management industry (Lloyd's List, 2003e).

Under the new partially approved regime, it was expected that 20-30 CMB vessels would re-flag immediately, and Safmarine (the former South African liner shipping operator, now owned by A.P. Moller of Denmark) would place eight new-buildings under the Belgian register as well. At one stage Safmarine were owned by CMB. The Belgian owned fleet was not inconsiderable in May 2003, totalling some 117 vessels with a capacity of 5.8m dwt and consequently bigger in capacity than that of the Netherlands or Spain (Lloyd's List, 2003g). The main attraction to ship-owners was expected to be not only the level of tax concession but also the transparency and simplicity of the scheme. Attracting Luxembourg registered vessels back was hoped to lead eventually to a 'Benelux' register in time. However a telling comment of the Belgian Shipowners' Association was that they were disappointed that such a variety of taxation schemes had emerged in EU member states following the 1997 guidelines meaning that a level playing field in shipping taxation was still a very long way off. We will return to this issue later.

In fact the figure for CMB vessels returning in the first phase of re-flagging was soon revised to only 15-20 (generally Exmar vessels – part of the CMB Group) and this would occur only after the new regime was installed and a further administrative period of three months had passed (Lloyd's List, 2003r, 2003x). The CMB fleet was largely flagged at this stage with Liberia or Luxembourg, and the latter was expected to be the source of the majority of vessels returning to Belgium. In fact Luxembourg had really only gained serious status as a flag because it had inherited so many ships from the Belgian register on its demise in the 1980s.

This trend was confirmed in May 2003 when it was announced that the Luxembourg flag was set to lose up to 50% of its registered vessels simply through moves made by CMB (Lloyd's List, 2003n). Luxembourg's response was expected to be a revision of their register in an attempt to attract vessels from elsewhere and this might include the introduction of a tonnage tax, which had never in the past formed part of the flag's attraction. In addition, Luxembourg was proposing the formation of a joint register across Benelux which would help to promote the idea of consistency within the EU – something that is a concern of the Commission as the multiplicity of regimes increases and diversifies resulting in an increasingly 'unlevel' playing field. Initial moves envisaged detailed talks and intense administrative co-operation (Lloyd's List, 2003o, 2003p).

Table 7.3: Some Comparisons of Tonnage Taxation Costs: 35,000 nrt Tanker (US$)

Member State	< 5 Years Old	10+ Years Old
Belgium	11,261	22,522
Netherlands	19,622	19,622
UK	17,720	17,720
Liberia	11,550	11,550

Note: If a ship-owner wishes to enter the Netherlands or UK tonnage tax system but his vessels fly the flag of (say) Liberia, he has to pay a double tax.

Source: Lloyd's List (2001o), Kellett and Robinson (2000a, 2000b).

The success of the Belgian policy and its associated tonnage tax was re-affirmed in October 2003 by the Managing Director of the Belgian Shipowners' Association (Lloyd's List, 2003gg). Following the European Commission approval of the Belgian scheme in the summer of 2003, the first ships returned almost immediately and by the end of the year some 35% of Belgian owned vessels were expected to have returned. The tonnage tax was deliberately designed to encourage the repatriation of ships rather than to attract vessels from other countries which was planned to be a later venture. This situation was a marked recovery from the early 1990s when all Belgian owned vessels had flagged-out, some 50% to the Luxembourg registry. The knock-on effects in training, recruitment and the ancillary sector had led to the adoption of the tonnage tax which in turn had produced quick results. It was hoped that around 4,000 Belgian jobs in the maritime cluster would be saved by the measure.

By November there was more good news with Safmarine – part of the AP Moller Group – announcing transfer of eight vessels back to the flag. In addition, five new container ships to be delivered in 2004 were also likely to be registered in Belgium (Lloyd's List, 2003hh).

France

French moves towards adopting a tonnage tax for shipping were made very late although progress eventually has been relatively rapid. There was only limited sign of any government interest in the maritime sector with the introduction of a restricted package of tax concessions for new ship investment in April 1998. However, in late February 2000, the first indications emerged of a further package of measures aimed at operating costs to make the French flag more attractive to ship-owners (Lloyd's List, 2000h).

The promises of support came as part of a US$751m package announced by the French government stimulated by the Erika disaster and the severe storms that had affected the country that winter. The precise details were to be made clear at a meeting of the Inter-Ministerial Committee for the Sea which would meet in May that year and would be based upon the conclusions of a Report commissioned by the French Transport Minister which had just been completed. In addition the Central Committee of French Shipowners (Armateurs de France) had recently called for a series of measures to make the French flag more competitive internationally. The measures requested included the abolition of social charges for seafarers, the removal of income tax on seafarers' salaries and a tonnage tax (Lloyd's List, 2000j).

However, the report when published, although containing the first two proposals relating to seafarers, failed to address the issue of tonnage tax and was widely criticised by the Shipowners' Association in that it appeared to directly link aid to the shipping industry to guarantees of jobs for French seafarers and was also directed more towards the French international Kerguelen Register rather than the national register (Lloyd's List, 2000i). In addition, the Report stressed that the introduction of a tonnage tax might not bring the benefits to the French fleet that were expected by the ship-owners and which had emerged in other member states where a tonnage tax regime had been introduced – including the UK, Greece, the Netherlands and Germany.

By February 2001, little further progress had been made. The Shipowners' Association was continuing to place pressure on the government for a tonnage tax to be introduced but with seemingly little effect. Even the more concrete proposals relating to seafarers' wages and social costs remained unclear (Lloyd's List, 2001p). The approaching French government Budget was hoped to bring some clarity to the situation with the warning from the Shipowners' Association that if it did not, then France risked becoming the exception in the EU (Lloyd's List, 2001q). This was backed by a report produced for the Central Committee of French Shipowners which showed that France had the least favourable tax and social security regimes for the shipping industry in the entire EU with the lease-purchase ship financing scheme introduced in 1998 acting as no competitor to the tonnage tax schemes introduced in other member states largely since then (Lloyd's List, 2001r). The situation as a whole was confused by the parliamentary and presidential elections taking place the next year whereby both major political movements in contention had indicated that they saw no votes in aiding the maritime sector.

The French national Budget of September 2001 brought the news largely expected in that the Finance Bill contained no mention of the tax – although it remained possible that an amendment could be introduced towards the end of the year which would include provisions for it (Lloyd's List, 2001s). A further possibility would follow the presidential and parliamentary elections due in 2001 when the new incoming government could be expected to modify the Budget provisions of its predecessor. There were signs of some hope in that discussions were continuing between the Finance Ministry and the French Shipowners' Association on the issue and claims that the ministry at least now recognised the need to do something given that around 80% of the world's fleet was registered under flags with a tonnage tax in operation.

However by November of 2001 the Shipowners' Association admitted that there was little hope of seeing a tonnage tax included in the 2002 National Budget (Lloyd's List, 2001t). It was not impossible that progress could be made as both deputies and senators sympathetic to the cause had tabled a series of amendments which could lead to eventual inclusion but these would need general government support which was unlikely to be forthcoming. The Shipowners' Association claimed that:

'The non-introduction in France of this measure will add to the marginalisation of the French fleet and could bring companies to relocate their development poles for fiscal reasons to the detriment of the fleet and employment.'

Meanwhile indications were growing that the only hope for the adoption of tonnage tax proposals would come with the election of an employer-friendly right-wing victory in the national presidency and parliamentary elections due in Spring 2002. Apparently the basis of an agreement had been reached between a prospective right-wing government and ship-owners but clearly this would require their success at the next elections (Lloyd's List, 2001u).

By spring the prospects improved greatly as a right-wing government had gained power although despite agreeing to consider this issue, it was not until December of 2002 that any real progress was made (Lloyd's List, 2002c). Parliamentary approval of legislation for the creation of a tonnage tax had just been achieved but no detailed regulations were yet available whilst any measures would be subject to approval by the European Commission. The Shipowners' Association expressed hope that the legislation and regulations of the Ministry of Finance would be agreed by March or April of that year. Even if agreed, it was unlikely that any impact upon ship registration or repatriation would be noted for at least some months since the regulations would not be in force until 2004 although applicable to the fiscal year 2003. Owners would be given until the end of 2004 to make their choice.

Armateurs de France were quoted as finding the proposals 'entirely satisfactory' but that owners would naturally wait for the details of the scheme before committing themselves to the new system. It was anticipated that the majority of French owners would do so given the experience in other member states. Issues still to be resolved centred upon duty-free sales and revenue from overland transport included in door-to-door services offered to clients by owners.

The measures would be made available only to companies which earned at least 75% of their revenue from merchant shipping. Tugs, fishing boats and fixed vessels were to be excluded. The limited detail available at that stage was that rates would mirror those of other North European states – including the UK.

Sweden

By late 2003 Sweden still had no tonnage tax scheme adopted despite lengthy negotiations between the government and industry and also despite the introduction of a number of other tax concessions in particular relating to seafarers' wages. Initial moves in the form of subtle pressure by the industry on the Swedish government had followed the revised state-aid guidelines of the EU in 1997 and comparisons were made with the scheme recently introduced in the Netherlands and also their near neighbours Norway (Lloyd's List, 1997c, 1997d, 1997e).

The Swedish Shipowners' Association (SSA) pointed out the continuing decline in vessels under the Swedish flag from 256 to 249 vessels during the first six months of 1997 (Lloyd's List, 1997f). They followed this up by lobbying the government directly with a request for the immediate introduction of a tonnage tax system which they hoped would result from an on-going review of the industry by the Swedish government (Lloyd's List, 1997g). Interestingly, the SSA emphasised at this time that they were looking for a 'Swedish solution' to the tonnage tax issue and not necessarily a direct copy of the regime introduced in the Netherlands. Leading tanker owners including Argonaut emphasised this further, claiming that by the year 2000 there would be no Swedish flagged vessels left (Lloyd's List, 1997h, 1997i). Further pressure followed from Swedish owners in November of 1997 to which the government responded by indicating that the review of the shipping industry would be completed by the end of the year (Lloyd's List, 1997j, 1997k).

Little progress followed. By May 1998, and with a general election planned, prospects for the introduction of a tonnage tax were described by Lloyd's List as 'bleak' (Lloyd's List, 1998d). This was not helped by the comments of the representative of the Swedish Maritime Forum that a tonnage tax would only be helpful in times of high profit – something unlikely at that time. The situation deteriorated further for Swedish ship-owners in November 1998 with the announcement by Swedish Orient Line of the flagging-out of four roll on/roll off vessels with the loss of around 60 jobs but the saving of about US$650,000 a year (Lloyd's List, 1998f). This was a direct result of the uncompetitiveness of Swedish shipping and the failure to introduce a tonnage tax (Lloyd's List, 1998c). The company threatened to out-flag all its remaining ships unless the political situation changed soon.

The effect was negligible. By March 2000, the only impact seemed to have been the setting up of a new Working Group under the supervision of the Swedish Maritime Administration which would consider a tonnage tax amongst many other aspects of Swedish shipping policy. In fact, the expiry of the existing policy in December 2001 was the stimulus behind this move rather than pressure from the industry to act (Lloyd's List, 2000e).

Meanwhile by November 2000, the Working Group was expected soon to announce a new net-wage based system for Swedish shipping whereby foreign seafarers would receive no social benefits paid for by shipping companies and those paid to national seafarers would be simplified. At that time, the social benefits paid to foreign seafarers were reclaimable by ship-owners but the latter estimated that they received only 62-69% of the costs returned. EU guidelines from 1997 indicated that full costs could be covered by subsidies, a system that was in operation in the Netherlands as well as a tonnage tax regime. However, there was no indication that the Working Group would suggest a tonnage tax for Sweden (Lloyd's List, 2000f). This was confirmed when the Working Group reported in December 2000 that although a net-wage system was to be introduced, there was to be no tonnage tax (Lloyd's List, 2001m). Some commentators remained hopeful that despite this, the government would still bring forward measures in Spring 2001.

Further pressure from the SSA continued in January 2002 in anticipation of the government's annual Budget proposals due in April (Lomas, 2002a, 2002b). Noting the fact that Swedish owners had spent the past seven years pressing for a tonnage tax with no success, Hakan Friberg of the SSA commented:

'We feel quite lonely within the European Union. [However t]here is a big possibility to get tonnage tax this spring, and we are preparing a proposal to that effect.'

By January 2003, there were clear indications that the net-wage policy was having some positive effect with an increase of vessels under the Swedish flag for the first time in many years, growing from 220 in January 2001 to 226 in July 2002. Negotiations were continuing between the SSA and the Swedish government over tonnage tax proposals although doubts were being expressed by parts of the industry over the effectiveness of a tonnage tax when the industry was already benefiting sufficiently from a depreciation and net-wage scheme (Lloyd's List, 2003d). In that sense the success of the net-wage scheme in particular could have ended any prospect of a tonnage tax regime for Sweden.

Italy

Italy has made slow progress towards the implementation of a tonnage tax regime and by late 2003 there had been no tangible progress despite a lot of words and a number of promises.

The earliest signs could be detected in June 1996 – early compared to many other countries – when the (then) Minister of Transport told the Italian Association of Independent Ship-owners (Confitarma) that he intended to set up a second register and introduce a tonnage tax regime similar to that proposed elsewhere in the European Union (Lloyd's List, 1996c).

By January 1997, the Transport Minister was expected to present legislation within the next month to the Italian Parliament containing fiscal reforms including a tonnage tax (Lloyd's List, 1997v). It was anticipated that the proposals would be voted upon in March or April of that year and then introduced the next. The package was aimed at halting the severe decline in Italian seafarers from around 40,000 to 23,000 between 1992 and 1997 which was mirrored by a similar decline in flagged fleet from 11.7m dwt to 8.2m dwt.

However, by February 1998, although the proposals existed, there had been no parliamentary vote and ship-owners were beginning to warn that a large proportion of the Italian registered fleet would soon leave the register for international flags as a consequence (Lloyd's List, 1998y). In fact, there was some doubt whether the tonnage tax had survived at all even as a proposal and that any parliamentary approval would only be for a revision of company tax and a second register.

By later the same month confidence was growing and reports suggested that a second register and a range of other measures had been agreed and that although the tonnage tax proposals seemed to have disappeared, lower company taxation would be equally as popular (Lloyd's List, 1998z).

Some time later in June 2001, it became clear that little had in fact been achieved apart from the creation of a second international Italian register and lobbying for a tonnage taxation system was growing once more. A new Minister of Shipping spoke once again to Confitarma, emphasising the progress being made towards a new tonnage tax regime and a series of other stimulating measures (Lloyd's List, 2001rr). However, news broke in October 2001 that tonnage taxation was not included in the state Budget submitted to the Italian Parliament for 2002-2004 (Lloyd's List, 2001ss). The cost of the proposed taxation if included, would have been the major part of US$182 million to be allocated each year to help the Italian register. Comments suggested that the failure to include a tonnage tax at this stage would bring about an end to the Italian flagged fleet and especially in cabotage trades where competition from other flags was growing quickly and costs of using Italian flagged ships were very high.

Paolo Clerici, Chairman of Confitarma, was quoted as saying:

'The Italian government is . . . acting in contrast with European policy and with its own programmes . . . the budget could indeed force many cabotage ship-owners to move their fleets to other European countries with lower cost flags' (Lloyd's List, 2001ss).

Despite the depressing scenario for Italian flagged shipping, the government continued to suggest that a tonnage tax might be introduced as an amendment to the Budget (Lloyd's List, 2001qq, 2001tt). This was further backed up by suggestions from the government in January of 2002 that within the next year, tonnage tax proposals would be put forward and some evidence of this was a series of amendments to the Finance Act 2002 which were supposed to include tonnage tax provisions but which were subject to Confitarma considerations (Lloyd's List, 2002p; European Tax Newsletter, 2003).

The proposals were eventually outlined in May 2003 and although detail was limited, the following principles were to be adopted (European Tax Newsletter, 2003). Shipping companies would be able to opt for a tonnage tax system based on vessel weight, making income generated by the vessel irrelevant. The option would last for a minimum of a five-year period and the rate applied would vary according to vessel trade and age.

However, further disappointment for Confitarma was to follow when in October 2003, the proposals were left out of the annual state Budget so that the earliest they could be introduced would be after the end of 2004 and more likely 2006 (Lloyd's List, 2003w). In fact, detailed plans were only put forward at the very end of December 2003 (Lloyd's List, 2003www).

CONCLUSIONS

What can be concluded from this analysis is that the early results from the introduction of the European Commission's 1996 Paper and the State Aid Guidelines of 1997 appear to be positive for the shipping industry. European Union member states have indicated by their action or inaction that each is able to adapt the guidelines to meet their own national and commercial interests, while at the same time improve their safety and environmental standards. At the same time they continue to work within the policy initiatives of the supra-national authority of the European Union. Without doubt, tonnage tax has become the central focus of attention for all the member states examined albeit some have yet to introduce measures which have been proposed. At times, this is in addition to a series of employment and training policies for seafarers which are used to back up the tax measures.

The European Commission and the majority of member states seem to have accepted that shipping can be a national asset. The willingness on the part of the majority of member states to implement a tonnage tax regime is based upon their recognition that they derive no tax from shipping services which are beneficially owned by their nationals but operated under other flags. Therefore a tonnage tax system does not deprive them of traditional profit-related tax which they were not receiving anyway. A number of member states including the Netherlands and the UK, have concluded that their interests in the maritime sector are wider than just the domestic register and therefore the tonnage tax regimes they have adopted are 'flag-blind'. The hope is that there will be spin-offs for the domestic flag even though it is not a requirement to enter the tax regime, and that the wider maritime clusters in London and Rotterdam, will benefit more from this liberal approach.

The policy motivation behind the facilitation by the European Commission of tonnage tax regimes is to provide a level playing field in terms of taxation both within the EU and against other regimes, particularly those of Open Registries. Tonnage tax is not a European concept only. Similar tax regimes can be found in countries such as Singapore, India and Hong Kong, as well as in Open Registry flags such as those of Cyprus, Liberia and Vanuatu. In this respect, the tonnage tax system can provide a valuable solution for ship-owners in terms of combining the advantages of a quality flag whilst being competitive, and at the same time allowing national variation whilst maintaining supra-national policy objectives.

In the final chapter we shall look in some more detail as to how tonnage tax regimes within the EU have presented some policy conflicts between national, supra-national and international levels and how some of these are being resolved. However before that, in the next chapter we turn attention to policy models which help to interpret the process of maritime policy-making and in particular to the concepts of neo and post-Fordism.

8. Globalisation Conflicts and Dimensions: Neo and Post-Fordist Developments in Shipping Policy

INTRODUCTION

The analysis so far has attempted to illustrate the main features of the globalisation processes that have affected the shipping sector worldwide and their interaction with the European Union shipping market in the context of the range of policy levels and influences that exist. We have seen how the objectives, methods and influence of policies vary between the national, supra-national and international level and how one particular application – that of tonnage tax in the European Union – has presented specific problems and opportunities within the sector for the development of the shipping industry. In the final chapter we will examine how these inter-relationships between policy level work and attempt to derive some overall conclusions. In this chapter, we shall take some widely adopted policy models – those derived from Fordism, neo and post-Fordism, and see how they can help us understand the sector, the derivation of policies and the changes occurring between the contrasting spatial levels of policy-making in shipping.

It appears that the shipping industry, although unique in many ways, can also be seen to present an indicative portrait of the broader globalised world economy. In doing this, the adoption of the Fordist range of models can help to understand the processes going on and the inter-relationship between globalisation and the sector. On the one hand, we can identify the neo-Fordist model, characterised by the principle of *comparative advantage* of lowest possible input costs with the example of the advent of flags of convenience particularly emerging during the 1970s (Asheim, 2001). On the other hand, we have also identified a newer era that has been characterised as post-Fordism, typified by the far more dynamic principle of *competitive advantage,* where the rapidity and scale of capital flows in shipping make it more difficult for the national governments to secure stable policy strategies and the modes of regulation shift to quality objectives and the inevitable rise of international and supra-national policy standards in an attempt to control and develop the sector (Asheim, 2001; Allen, 1996). Here, the Open

Registries which emerged during the 1970s have continued to pressurise the traditional registries characterised by those of the EU member states to the extent that EU policy-making has had to allow the development of policies such as the tonnage tax, which in many ways is a violation of the principles of the Treaty of Rome and which has been applied in many different ways across the EU to facilitate local needs and demands.

Thus, the post-Fordism situation is one where the complex relationships between policy-making levels have been allowed to vary at different spatial levels, whilst accommodating the broader over-arching aims of each authority. In classic post-Fordist style, the individual needs, desires and demands of the market-place are being met whilst the advantages of international and supra-national co-ordination and collaboration are retained. Internal diversity is achieved within the beneficial confines of economies of scale; specific industrial needs are met within broader global perspectives. Further discussion will follow at a later stage.

It should be noted however, that the issues of post and neo-Fordism have taken on a wider set of meanings by various analysts. Our approach is primarily concerned with the economic, social and regulatory environment of the shipping industry today and its gradual shift from the neo to the post-Fordist phase. Within this context, the EU as a supra-national policy-making body is due to play a central role in its relationships with member states and one that mirrors many of the problems that the development of the shipping industry in an international and continuously globalising market presents for international bodies such as the IMO. The Fordist range of models provides a means of clarifying the issues and structuring an interpretation of the relationships between the levels of policy-making identified in earlier chapters.

The Nature of Fordism

We must begin by making the basic framework clear as the concepts of neo and post-Fordism are widely regarded as a movement from the original model of Fordism (Jessop, 1994). This will help in going on to see how these models can be applied to the maritime sector and in the interpretation of policy initiatives and structures. There is a considerable body of reference material on the development and nature of Fordism as a generic approach towards understanding industrial relationships and market structures and we can only refer to a little of it here. It is also a highly contentious area with little agreement on precise definitions. The contributions by Amin (1994), Bonefeld and Holloway (1991), Lipietz (1987) and Roobeck (1987) are important, along with the work by Allen (1996) and Womack et al. (1990).

However, for our purposes Jessop (1994) provides the most rigorous and suitable basis for the following discussion.

Jessop in particular identified four fundamental themes that lie behind all definitions of the Fordist movement including those relevant to shipping.

1. *Labour or production process.* This feature stems from the 'mass-production of complex, consumer durables based on moving assembly line techniques operated with semi-skilled labour of the mass worker' (Jessop, 1994). The original Fordist concept was associated with car production but is extendable across other sectors including shipping. Thus shipping developed from a traditional and fragmented background in the early twentieth century to one characterised by ever more organised and generic services with a labour force characterised by semi-skilled seafarers of uniform character and vessels with similar characteristics. The very nature of the Fordist market for durable goods encouraged the growth of regular liner shipping services with features that themselves were Fordist in nature. Clearly not all shipping services were the same, but the mass production characteristics of the industry and of its markets gave it its 'dynamism' (Jessop, 1994).

2. *Accumulation regime.* Fordism was seen as a stable mode of macro-economic growth characterised by a 'virtuous circle of growth in relatively closed economies' (Jessop, 1994). This was based on mass production creating economies of scale, rising incomes stemming from this, resulting in turn in greater demand and more economies of scale. The shipping sector mirrored this growth with increasing vessel and port facility size and provides an indicative paradigm, leading to lower overall costs through economies of scale and also reducing labour costs through the tendency towards standardisation and automation which came with it. Shipping also benefited from the move towards increased international trade involving mass production of exports to finance mass imports.

3. *Social mode of economic regulation.* There are a number of key features of Fordism here. Firstly, the separation of ownership and control in large corporations. Classic Fordism sees this as the emergence of multi-divisional, decentralised organisations subject to central controls – mirrored again in the growth of the large liner shipping company such as Maersk/Sealand or P&O/Nedlloyd. The growth of overseas investment in the shipping industry, marked by the increase of foreign direct investment with its distant but significant controlling hand at a local level, and the move to Open Registries (where ownership and control are distinctly separated and

characterised by the remoteness of flag from national policy-making), present indications of this process occurring. Secondly, monopoly pricing strategies. In liner shipping, cartel arrangements, especially emerging during the 1970s by means of conference agreements among contracting operators (designed to achieve an agreed frequency and allocation of sailings through loyalty arrangements and deferred discounts after exclusive use of conference services) are examples of the growth of monopoly arrangements. This was achievable only through the growth of large industrial powers in all sectors but not least shipping. Thirdly, union recognition and state involvement in managing the conflicts between capital and labour. Here, Fordism was characterised by the close involvement of the state in manipulating industrial relations, wage bargaining, conditions of service, etc. The appearance and growth of Open Registry flags during the Fordist period has been criticised by national governments (for example leading to the protection of US coastal shipping under the Jones Act), and through international organisations (such as UNCTAD). However, the most substantial pressure upon Open Registries has come from organised labour, notably the ITF. Whereas the ITF first brought the issue to ILO attention in 1933, it was not until after 1945 that a fully organised campaign was introduced in a way reminiscent of Fordist structures (Aspinwall, 1995). Meanwhile, growth of state involvement in shipping is apparent in many ways during this period, including tax incentives for inward investment, the promotion of national shipping industries and employment, protection of domestic cargoes, etc. In this way, the state actively intervened in the market to reconcile conflicts between traditional capital and labour to sustain the virtuous circle of demand identified earlier.

4.   *Societalisation.* Fordism was also characterised by the consumption of standardised, mass produced consumer durables by what were described as 'nuclear households' and the provision of standardised services by a bureaucratic state. Shipping reflected this pattern with its increasing dominance by standardised commodities, vessels and equipment typified by the process of containerisation. The sector was heavily regulated by national governments.

The Crisis in Fordism

Fordism as an industrial period was at its peak from 1950 and it was not until the 1970s when the first attempts at a systematic construction of a history of the concept appeared. The term was used to describe industry structures on the basis of evidence drawn from the US economy and was actually only first introduced by Michel Aglietta (Aglietta, 1976). At that time, a state of economic uncertainty was evident across the western economies as a slow-down in productivity and decreasing profitability (Allen, 1996). At the same period, shipping was experiencing significant changes. As already mentioned, it was during the 1970s when the last major maritime crisis occurred and greater opportunity was given to less-developed countries to enter the maritime industry. Compounded by the oil crisis of 1973, which led to a dramatic increase in energy costs in the western nations and followed by an over-supply of tonnage for shipping and the rise and establishment of lower cost fleets in developing countries, the long post-war boom which had lent credibility to the notion of Fordism as an identifiable industrial era appeared to be at its end (Thanopoulou, 1995; Allen, 1996).

The reasons for the crisis of the Fordist era at the end of the 1970s will not be discussed here. However, one important consequence of the crisis was that international capital together with neo-liberal governments developed a strategy of global restructuring, apparent within the EU policy-making and industrial contexts amongst many others. International deregulation of capital flows and increased flexibility of labour relations proved to be the means to re-establish capital profitability – a process variously known as post and neo-Fordism. The main objective for the shipping industry thereafter was the enforcement of a systematic rationalisation process on a global level, based on fundamentally changed economic, social and political structures (Hirsch, 1995). These structures developed parallel to and in close association with the movements that emerged from the Fordist era – those of neo and post-Fordism and so it is to these we now turn to provide a structural interpretation of the current characteristics of the international shipping industry, its policy-making framework and in particular, within its EU context.

The Nature of Neo-Fordism

Neo-Fordism represents an extension to the Fordist era (in the sense of a new version of Fordism) and can be seen as the immediate successor to Fordism, originally characterised by the new international division of labour and reflected in the growth of worldwide sourcing in the 1970s, based upon the principle of comparative advantage (Jessop, 1994; Allen, 1996). Aglietta (1982) provides a strong defence of the extension of Fordist principles of state interference and regulation to support an understanding of what came after Fordism. Within this new era, the following two main principles can be observed:

1.   The first characteristic centres upon the transformation of the labour
     process and the introduction of a new, *international division of
     labour*. Thus the new market-place was seen as one with definite
     labour specialisations. As we have already noted, foreign direct
     investment and the search for a new spatial context for shipping was
     based on a quest for mass markets and concomitant economies of
     scale and attempts to maintain profitability levels by tapping pools
     of cheaper labour. Ship-owners had the opportunity to re-flag their
     vessels in order to take advantage not only of lower taxation, but
     more importantly, lower labour costs in order to increase their ability
     to compete in the world markets (Aspinwall, 1995; Allen, 1996;
     Lammont, 2000). Inevitably, this was only possible through a
     process of international division of labour whereby certain countries
     (and flags) specialised in cheap labour supply – for example the
     Philippines, Poland, India, China, etc. The result was a decline in the
     demand for traditional seafarers which has been both clear and
     dramatic.

2.   The second characteristic of the neo-Fordist structure concerns
     technological development that requires the introduction of new
     working practices and adds greater flexibility in operations without
     incurring further substantial costs (Allen, 1996; Lammont, 2000). As
     mentioned earlier, one of the reasons for the decline in the number
     of European seafarers is the changed manning levels on-board
     modern ships. In 1995, the Bremen Institute of Shipping Economics
     and Logistics (ISL) carried out a study of on-board communication
     of multi-lingual crews and concluded that only 120 men are now
     needed to man eight container vessels in the Asia/Europe trade to
     maintain the same transport capacity as in the 1960s. Then, an
     estimated 4,000 personnel on-board would have been needed on 100
     conventional vessels to transport an equal amount of cargo. Some of
     the reasons that have contributed to such changes include increased
     speed and tonnage capacity and the increased use of technology on-
     board and in ports (Dirks, 2001). Neo-Fordism requires that these
     technological developments take place to achieve the progress that
     results.

However, neo-Fordism remains a continuation of Fordist principles and
retains the interference of the state, the role of labour pressure and other
Fordist elements. It is widely agreed that this essentially Fordist model cannot
sufficiently represent the processes now going on within industry generally
and the shipping industry in particular, and in our attempt to understand the
policy-making relationships in shipping, a post-Fordist approach –

representing a policy model developed after Fordism rather than a variant of it – is needed.

The Nature of Post-Fordism

Whereas neo-Fordism represents an extension to the Fordist era, post-Fordism signifies a break with Fordism, according to which, global competition is based on the far more dynamic principle of competitive advantage regarding *innovation* as the prime objective of competition. At the same time, particular attention is given to the historical roots of the industry concerned and the challenge of 'localising global tendencies in an aim to achieve a flexible and permanently innovative pattern of accumulation' (Jessop, 1994; Asheim, 2001).

Movement from Fordism to post-Fordism involves a complex and inter-related series of changes in the labour process and the overall dynamic of macro-economic growth, particularly characterised by long-term policies and objectives (Jessop, 1994). Using the structure of analysis adopted to assess Fordism earlier, the post-Fordist economy is one where the following trends can be seen to feature:

1. *Labour or production process.* Here the production process is characterised by flexibility – something which was inherently missing from the Fordist model where the achievement of management control, state interference and economies of scale dictated a rigid and limited approach to the provision of goods and services. Fundamental to the development of flexibility has been the introduction of micro-electronic technologies and communication systems coupled with a work force which is both willing and able to accommodate change. The latter commonly means that traditional employment pools are abandoned for new arrangements, whilst the former demands extensive and expensive investment. The materials intensive nature of Fordism is relieved by the introduction of more sophisticated products and production processes. Within this context, it is possible to note a number of features which post-Fordism shares with neo-Fordism. However, whereas neo-Fordism tends to associate technology advances with job de-skilling and an increased centralisation of management control, post-Fordism, points to a more positive side of technology. This is distinctly post-Fordism because the flexibility that is necessary is introduced, built onto the existing Fordist framework. It is not neo-Fordism which suggests merely an adaptation of the existing Fordist situation (Jessop, 1994). This post-Fordist flexibility in production and

product overcomes the disenchantment with mass-production, limited choices in goods and the desire for individuality that increasing wealth reignites. Meanwhile, alongside job de-skilling, advanced technology is seen as creating new opportunities for 'en-skilling and re-skilling'. Further, a post-Fordist structure is said to promote the prospect of a multi-skilled labour force, operating in a less hierarchical work environment (Allen, 1996).

In the shipping sector, technology and innovation have created a global shift in the development of labour skills. Therefore, these technical changes are meant to create a greater demand for highly educated on-board and land-based personnel who are able to handle this new technical equipment. Moreover, there is evidence (BIMCO, 2000) that due to technical developments and the increasing employment of non-European crews, there will be fewer European ratings employed in the future, but the ones on-board will need to be highly skilled in order to handle the necessary equipment and understand the functioning of the ships (Dirks, 2001; Alderton and Winchester, 2002a). In addition, changes in the skills required by seafarers, notably advanced computer competence and greater interdepartmental flexibility, will probably lead to a future breakdown in the difference between officers and ratings. Flexibility in production has meant that the variety of goods being shipped has increased dramatically towards the end of the twentieth century, with a resultant increase in demand for flexibility by the industry in handling techniques and supply chain management. In addition, the industry itself and its hardware have become increasingly flexible in their approach to markets, with considerable changes in vessels used, port equipment, employee characteristics and management tools applied. The increase in the number of registries adopted by ship-owners, the range of insurance markets and vehicles used, the variability in crew nationality, the variation in financial packages which are now applied and many other examples of flexibility and variety in the sector, combined with the attributes of economies of scale achieved through mass production of vessels, joint ventures in shipping companies and the development of 'super ports' with supra-national hinterlands (such as Singapore and Rotterdam), represents a distinct move of the shipping industry into new post-Fordist territory.

2. *Accumulation regime.* Here the idea of a permanently innovative form of accumulation is envisaged. The model is characterised by flexibility, allowing adaptation to market demands to facilitate continued accumulation. A new form of virtuous circle would

develop based upon Jessop's (1994) view of 'economies of scope' with diversified production (resulting in a wider range of available products) accompanied by process innovation (represented by a wider range of approaches to production). This is accompanied by rising incomes for the flexible skilled work force, continued increasing demand for diversified goods and services, growing profits stemming from technological sophistication leading back into innovation, diversification and flexibility. Fordism envisaged that the prosperity emerging from economies of scale and technical concentration would be spread widely through communities. Post-Fordism is more likely to increase prosperity differentiation with those acquiring skills and flexibility benefiting sharply at the expense of those not. In shipping terms, this pattern of accumulation can already be seen to be occurring. Open Registries facilitate wealth accumulation by the developed world at the expense of the less developed. The biggest liner shipping companies are all based in the technologically sophisticated Far East, Western Europe or North America, and the less-developed world increasingly lags behind, relying upon these services to serve markets. New forms of vessels and skills within the industry are increasingly demanded to meet the ever-changing requirements of the market-place and characteristics of products. Flexibility in supply-chain management is now the most significant driving force in logistics as markets become increasingly sophisticated in their demands.

3. *Social mode of economic regulation.* Here there is an increasing need for innovation and flexibility in labour supply. Thus work-force differentiation between those skilled and paid more, and those less skilled and paid less would grow as we have noted above. Organisations would have to become more flexible and freer to adapt to market variability. Improved quality and service becomes the key to success rather than just the ability to produce a limited product range in large quantities at low cost and price. More sophisticated and demanding customers require products and services that are tailored to their particular needs which themselves would vary more quickly than ever before. Success in the market-place begins to rely upon the ability to adapt to this inherent flexibility that continues to grow as technological characteristics improve. The state's role will also change as it withdraws from the market and leaves the demands of the consumer to increasingly drive producers to become more sensitive. Privatisation is one manifestation of this but also the increased evidence of deregulation which allows industry to adapt to market needs more quickly and

with greater sensitivity. Product innovation races ahead as a result – but only in those sectors and regions where there is the opportunity to do so – increasingly designed and controlled from the developed world but operationalised in the less developed world, using the advantages (to the former) of cheap labour. Thus the divide is exacerbated. In terms of shipping, there is much evidence of this process going on. Privatisation in shipping and ports has been rampant and there is little left to achieve in many markets. Deregulation – apart from a few obvious examples from the FMC and the EU – is also a major trend. The shipping companies have become less traditionally structured and more involved in sectors to which historically they paid little interest – warehousing, trucking, freight forwarding, broking and the like. This vertical integration is a manifestation of flexibility and the need to serve consumers more fully and more sensitively. Issues of quality – both in terms of safety and the environment, and in terms of commercial considerations (delivery times and accuracy, condition of goods, access to real-time information) are now central to the shipping industry, particularly the liner and ferry sector but increasingly so for bulk shipping.

4.   *Societalisation.* It is widely agreed that at this time it is still impossible to see what effect upon society post-Fordism will have. The specific pattern of consumption remains unclear and as a result its impact upon the shipping industry is unclear as well. It is certain that there will be a reduction in state interference in the markets – although it may just be that the interference that exists has been redesigned and now is rather more subtle – a move from state ownership to one of private control but an increase in international and supra-national regulation through the IMO and the EU for example, helping to influence domestic, national policy and thus the shipping industry and its commercial, administrative and fiscal environment. The 'nuclear family' has moved on from its highly predictable focus and demands, to a seemingly more flexible unit which the maritime sector now has to serve, accommodating variation in demand combined with the potential benefits of economies of scale.

This discussion on Fordism and neo and post-Fordism models and their application to the shipping sector has been aimed at helping to understand the processes going on and further to illustrate the nature of the relationships between the international, supra-national and national policy-making frameworks that have been underlined earlier. Thus, it is clear that the domination of international policy-making through the work of (for example) the IMO combined with the activities of national policy-makers, has been reflected in a Fordist model of the shipping sector where economies of scale, limited choice of economically priced goods available to mass markets, combined with the use of cheap labour from developing countries on Open Registry vessels was typical. That in turn, has been at least partially replaced by the growth of variability and flexibility in the market with the increased role of supra-national governments (such as the EU) acting as intermediaries between the international policy-makers typified by the IMO and national policy-makers. Thus the EU takes international policies developed by the IMO for safety and the OECD for competition in liner shipping, and re-interprets them for their member states, diluting the administrative control by facilitating the development of individual domestic policies which reinforce the international message whilst allowing national interpretation and flexibility. This is reflected in the use of tonnage tax which is an excellent example of the decline of international policy domination on the one hand as policies were applied locally in a more sensitive manner, whilst on the other this flexibility actually makes the core themes of such policies of competition enhancement and safety regulation, more effectively applied. Thus, an IMO policy to ensure safer bulk carrier operation is enforced by EU application along with domestic interpretation through encouraging ship-owners to register their vessels with an EU flag, made domestically attractive through a locally designed tonnage tax which meets supra-national desires for a level playing field of competition. In this way, the post-Fordist model meets the needs of everyone (except the Open Registry and dubious ship-owner) in that international rules are applied, supra-national ambitions are met, national member state needs are incorporated in flexible policies, and the commercial and safety ambitions of all parties are registered.

So where does this leave national policy-making? We would argue, enhanced under a post-Fordist model which allows a member state of any supra-national organisation to apply international regulations (a necessity in the international shipping industry) to adapt policies to meet local desires and needs and thus deliver real competition to Open Registries and overseas (cheaper and commonly less safe) competitors. However, even with the rise of post-Fordism (and through the development of neo-Fordism), national governments continue to have retained an element of the Fordist model as they are still significantly involved in the maritime economy (rather more than in other sectors commonly) through the use of Keynesian fiscal and monetary policies which serve in redistributing wealth and reinvestment in the domestic economy. In the Keynesian welfare state, national governments manage the wage relation and labour market policies. The main goal of the Keynesian welfare state is to achieve full employment – and this aim appears both in the Fordist and the post-Fordist period (Jessop, 1994). With reference to European shipping policies and their application, economic incentives given to ship-owners (such as the tonnage tax schemes discussed in Chapter 7) have assisted in promoting the national shipping industry of the countries involved with substantial results. However, as we have hinted above, this continuation of a Fordist tradition has been applied in a distinctly post-Fordist way, allowing interpretation and flexibility between member states. This policy flexibility can be seen both from a national perspective (for example the Netherlands initiative for tonnage tax in 1996) and an EU measure (the 1997 State Aid Guidelines for Shipping, introducing the framework that continues to dominate existing and potential future shipping policies). The EU approach signifies the establishment of supra-national, regional regimes which inevitably result in some experience of weakening national policy initiatives since these are now organised on supra-national or regional levels (Jessop, 1994).

The ways through which national (characterised by EU member states) and supra-national policy-makers (characterised by the European Commission) interact as well as co-operate with each other have already been discussed earlier. The EU has been active in promoting a market philosophy by ensuring a level playing field for the shipping sector in particular. One way in which this has been achieved is through the adoption of the State Aid Guidelines of 1997, which aim to ensure that all member states have similar objectives in the formation of their shipping policies. These centre upon ensuring the same commercial freedom and permitting the same terms for supporting sub-standard shipping activities regardless of location or activity (Commission of the European Communities, 1997; Gwilliam, 1993).

As mentioned earlier, post-Fordism signals a movement beyond Fordism. It signifies a qualitative shift in the organisation of production and consumption, as well as a break in the mode of regulation (Allen, 1996). With regards to the EU maritime sector, this can be viewed as a clear policy shift towards the achievement of quality shipping. In other words, the elimination of cost advantages enjoyed by unscrupulous operators who do not comply with agreed safety and pollution-prevention standards (Gwilliam, 1993; Knoop, 2002). Compliance with international regulation and effective enforcement of Port State Control requirements are both a means to establish an effective policy regime that recognises the post-Fordist tendencies that currently exist and are central to quality promotion in the shipping industry. They may well be, in addition, a conscious attempt on behalf of the EU and national governments to discourage outward investment – and thus to protect domestic shipping activity. Whatever the core purpose, the trend towards quality shipping goes beyond purely economic objectives and aims to create the appropriate conditions both for shipping competition and quality performance. The way it is now achieved, through in particular the tonnage tax approach in the EU (and increasingly elsewhere), is undoubtedly a post-Fordist interpretation of the policy-making framework for the sector.

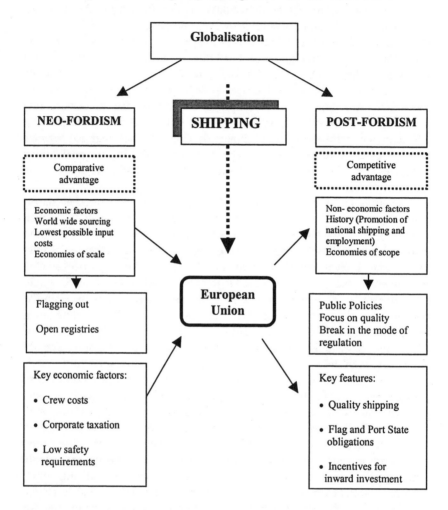

Figure 8.1: Globalisation Dimensions; Changes in Shipping's Competitive Nature and the EU Role

Figure 8.1 presents a visual interpretation of this analysis and illustrates the main impact of neo and post-Fordism upon the EU shipping industry. Both neo-Fordist and post-Fordist policy developments have developed from the trend towards globalisation in shipping. The EU shipping experience, until fairly recently, has been characterised by aggressive competition and a tradition of extensive flagging-out to Open Registry flags in order for the industry to take advantage of the low-cost benefits offered by these regimes. The neo-Fordist principles are thus seen to have an impact on EU shipping until the subsequent rise of the post-Fordist paradigm.

On the other hand, post-Fordist policy developments can be regarded as an EU response to neo-Fordism, emphasised by the promotion of national policy initiatives and the focus on quality objectives. These two trends are exemplified by the rise of tonnage tax. Economies of scope play a key role, providing opportunities for the creation of a new division of labour with combined specialisation skills. The post-Fordist era is characterised by a variation in public policies. These include incentives such as tonnage tax manipulated to meet national needs; applied by a variety of institutions at the level most appropriate – for example EU, IMO, national government, professional institution; and the use of a variety of governance mechanisms including the promotion of the free market principle as well as subsidies for shipping services and reduced taxation intended to mitigate the failures of the market. Such a policy framework that now exists in the EU contains neo-Fordist features which have been adapted and revised to be appropriate for a post-Fordist policy environment and to meet modern industrial arrangements and practices.

Post-Fordism as a policy framework is thus an inevitable force that will continue to affect the policy scenario, and particularly the relationship between policy levels, for the foreseeable future. There will, of course, eventually emerge a (post) post-Fordist era, but this is at present too far away to be identified. Meanwhile, the continued encroachment of post-Fordism and its significance for spatial policy relationships, derives from three driving forces which are vital to the shipping industry (Jessop, 1994):

1. The continuous rise of new technologies as a consequence of competitive pressures from newly industrialised countries. This has in turn focused attention upon the ability to be flexible in delivery and sensitive to customer needs.
2. The process of internationalisation. This has occurred rapidly and nations can no longer act as though borders were closed and markets domestic. Internationalised markets are already here and the post-Fordist approach has accepted and accommodated this.
3. A paradigm shift from Fordism. This has been illustrated by a move from demand driven economics (producing economies of scale) to one characterised by supply driven quality of service, accommodating individual desires and needs.

Shipping has a very close relationship to each of these three processes and as a consequence the activity of policy-making for the sector is closely related as well. Thus the increased flexibility and reduction in state involvement which characterises post-Fordism in turn affected the relationships within policy level between international and supra-national and supra-national and national, so that an inherent flexibility within shipping policies is now more apparent accompanied by a move towards less direction of policy detail by governmental organisations and more advice and encouragement. Post-Fordism is associated with new technology – a feature of the shipping sector – and internationalisation – something the shipping sector makes possible. Demand driven shipping services are also now characterised by increasing supply driven features and the need to raise quality of service. National shipping policies working within the framework of international and supra-national guidelines can achieve such post-Fordist ambitions in a way that Fordist driven shipping policies of the past could not.

The Fordist/Post-Fordist Debate and the Maritime Sector

We finish off the debate in this chapter on Fordism, post-Fordism and shipping policy by examining the way that a series of writers have seen the relationships that exist in the maritime sector. The work is dominated by examples from the ports industry but others have also introduced shipping and supply-chain management into the debate and shown that these models of policy-making are both appropriate and useful.

One of the earliest attempts to introduce the concept of Fordist models to the transport sector as a whole was provided by Rodrigue, Slack and Comtois, in their 1997 paper that examined the relationship between transportation and spatial cycles (Rodrigue et al., 1997). Interestingly, they took the maritime sector as the basis for their arguments and although there is no doubt that this application is late in comparison with other sector associations with the Fordist model movements, it does represent a relatively sudden and intense association. The authors examined the issues of change in freight markets and the impact that these cyclical changes have upon the maritime transport sector. Three issues were felt to be central to the debate – the constant contradiction between transport supply and demand; the rise and spatial diffusion of containerisation; and the capacity of transport networks to adapt to change. The issue of change itself was interpreted in the classical migration from Fordist to neo-Fordist to post-Fordist as we have discussed earlier – focusing on the changing role of the state in regulating; upon industry in adapting to variable demand; upon the continuous increase in sophistication of technology; and upon the flexibility inherent in a market-place demanding variation in supply.

This theme was taken up increasingly by analysts of the ports sector who viewed the Fordist models as offering a particularly useful means of interpreting maritime sectoral development. De Langen (1999) offered one of the first attempts at marrying port change with the Fordist economic models. He attempted to use the concepts of Fordism and post-Fordism to understand the implications for port management and policy-making. The interpretation focused on the shift from one to the other in the post-war period with an emphasis on how port policies would need to change to accommodate the move from Fordist stability to post-Fordist instability, flexibility and change.

Further port organisational studies using Fordist principles for analysis can be found in Chlomoudis et al. (2000, 2003) and more specific applications in Van de Loo and Van de Velde (2003), examining the role of small island ports. The latter provide a detailed discussion of the development of outsourcing and a post-Fordist interpretation of this process which has grown in popularity in recent years and which has helped to embed supply chain management into the maritime sector, providing the flexibility and specialisation needed in a post-Fordist market-place. The ports theme is continued by the work of Bonacich (2003) applying the principles of post-Fordism to an analysis of ports, labour relations and logistics.

Meanwhile the role of logistics and supply chain management in the development of the maritime sector had not gone unnoticed elsewhere. In particular Notteboom and Winkelmans (2001) were important in identifying the characteristics of logistics in the post-Fordist era, analysing three main trends:

- Outsourcing of the production of components, characterised by a large number of specialist suppliers organised on a global scale, providing components for global corporations.
- The rise of value added logistics requiring the integration of the supply chain into a single process so that benefits of global distribution are fully realised and the flexibility inherent in local logistics suppliers are also sustained.
- Outsourcing of transportation, warehousing and distribution. Third party (fourth party, even fifth party) logistics is now common. In the EU, the level of third party transportation is now commonly 50-60%; of warehousing, 20-30%.

Meanwhile Sanidas (2002) took the application of Fordist models even further in an analysis of the relationship between logistics, just in time, supply chain management and lean production methods in a study of industry in the USA and Japan.

The use of Fordist models in the maritime, transport and logistics sectors is thus well established even if it arrived a little later than elsewhere. It provides a sound analytical basis for understanding the complex relationships between supply, demand, globalisation, policy-making and the sector through the post-Fordism phase that will continue in the future.

CONCLUSIONS

This chapter has attempted to analyse some of the central features of today's shipping industry with particular reference to the European Union maritime sector and in the context of the models of Fordism and their subsequent development. It is clear that the present situation within the shipping industry is structured by both neo and post-Fordist elements. However, the post-Fordist tendencies are clearly dominant within this situation and form the driving force for the coming years. Shipping policy at all levels mirrors these model structures in having to accommodate increasing specialisation, flexibility in demand, developing technologies and rising quality of service.

The initial response to the crisis of Fordism did not immediately lead to anything like the post-Fordist state. On the contrary, it led to an intensification of some prime Fordist characteristics such as extensive flagging-out to Open Registries and subsequently to the neo-Fordist structure typified by significant changes in employment conditions along with a general pattern of cost rationality on behalf of shipping companies and ship-owners. The sharpest differences between neo and post-Fordism can be thus clarified following Jessop (1994). Neo-Fordism represents an adjustment to the problems of Fordism, but a way forward that in truth extends the life of Fordism. In contrast, post-Fordism represents a qualitatively new economic direction, and thus is a step beyond Fordism. As such, post-Fordism signals a new era, where regulation (and thus policy-making) moves towards a new flexible regime which targets global competition while at the same time aims to safeguard the national interests involved. As we have seen earlier, this is clearly reflected in the range of recent EU shipping policies and objectives.

In the final chapter, we draw these themes together and in particular attempt to examine the success of shipping policy-making at reconciling the conflicting interests and ambitions between international, supra-national and national authorities in the framework of an increasingly flexible and dynamic post-Fordist environment.

9. Conclusions

INTRODUCTION

This book has concentrated upon the significance of policy-making for the shipping sector with a particular emphasis upon the role of the nation state and its relationship with policy-making at jurisdictional levels which are (at least in theory) superior to it. We have seen that despite the advantages of co-ordinating policy between jurisdiction levels of (for example) international, supra-national and national, there is high potential for conflict which at times manifests itself with contrasting, conflicting and detrimental consequences for the sector. The current (late 2003) dispute between policy-makers in the IMO, the European Union and France over the banning of single-hulled tankers demonstrates these tensions well. On the other hand the widespread introduction of tonnage tax through most countries of the European Union has eased tensions as it has facilitated the translation of EU safety and environmental ideals to nation states through the use of specific financial regimes that allow national fleet recovery and flexibility whilst sustaining quality standards.

This chapter draws these issues together, with an examination of the future of the nation state in shipping policy-making at a time of increasing but conflicting trends of globalisation and national identity. In this way, the delicate relationships between jurisdictions and the need to ensure that arrangements between them can be agreed to satisfy most parties at least to a certain extent are made. Once again we can make good use of the Fordist, neo-Fordist and post-Fordist models (particularly the latter) to help provide a framework for the discussion.

NATIONAL POLICY-MAKING

Engels predicted that social and economic evolution must inevitably proceed through stages of conflict between economic classes, something known as dialectical materialism, whereby the dictatorship of the proletariat and the gradual atrophy of the state leads to the eventual emergence of a classless society (Vasiliou, 1996). In fact, it will be argued that the nation remains highly significant in policy-making in shipping despite the growth of supra-nationalism, internationalisation and globalisation in recent years. However, we begin with a discussion of nations in shipping policy and the role they increasingly will play.

Hollowing Out

Jessop (1994) analysed a process he termed as 'hollowing out', which referred to the condition and characteristics of nation states and their significance in policy development. We can use the same approach to understand the context for shipping policy-making in the coming years.

Two contrasting developments can be identified which are reflected in shipping policy-making activity at the national level. Firstly, the nation has become increasingly important as it is only by representation of nations in organisations such as the IMO and the EU that shipping policy ever emerges from these international and supra-national bodies. By the same token, it is the nation states that introduce specific legislation to enforce IMO and EU policy.   Secondly, and in contrast, the continued growth in globalised activity, international markets and flexibility in production has an opposite effect in weakening national impact. Jessop saw this 'loss of autonomy' as providing opportunities for the growth of supra-nationalism (typified by the EU from the 1990s) accompanied by the rise of regionalism within nations which would fill the gap created by the changed national role.

' . . . state capacities are transferred to a growing number of pan-regional [EU], pluri-national [OECD], or international [IMO] bodies with a widening range of powers; others are developed to restructured local or regional levels of governance in the national state' (Jessop, 1994) [authors' examples in brackets].

This process whereby the nation state retains influence through representation on supra-national and international bodies and through control of regional and local affairs was termed by Jessop, 'hollowing out' and we can see notable progression in the shipping sector. Thus IMO policies are put into effect by the EU which then dictates to member states that specific legislation is needed. The nation retains influence by making up the representatives on the IMO and EU policy-making groups but loses influence in handing over the over-arching policy production process to a higher authority.   Local and regional policies are dictated by nation states and commonly controlled through subtle financial linkages, but regionalism in particular has been growing rapidly in recent years, characterised by the creation and extension of influence of the EU's Committee of the Regions (now a formal part of the EU legislative process) and the European Regional Development Fund (ERDF), which in turn has played a significant role in directly financing aid from the supra-national (EU) level to the regional, whilst in many ways, omitting the national level.

This 'hollowed out' condition of the nation is essentially a post-Fordist response to a series of problems which have emerged and for which the shipping sector provides excellent examples. These include the Fordist tendency towards state interference – something Jessop calls 'maintaining employment in sunset sectors' – typified by the rise of tonnage tax in European Union member states. Tonnage tax thus provides an example of the slow move of the shipping industry to adapt to the inadequacies of the Fordist model as it is characterised by state subsidy and interference in the market. Hollowing out has yet to be fully implemented in the shipping sector and in many ways the changing policy priorities of the EU in this area at the turn of the century reflect a backward step which may eventually be detrimental to trading conditions and the industry's survival. Other economic sectors have not benefited from specific tax concessions and have made the step towards reducing (rather than increasing) state involvement, thus reacting to the failure of the Fordist model and the tendency towards hollowing.

Hollowing out also requires a move towards emphasis upon the supply side of the market in providing variety, flexibility and sensitivity to the needs of the consumer. Here we see the shipping industry adapting rather better to the post-Fordist era than the tonnage tax moves suggest, with the growth of logistics and supply chain management incorporating shipping service provision, tuned to company and market needs. Matching supply by ship operators to market forces helps to meet the post-Fordist dynamics identified by Jessop (1994).

Other characteristics of hollowing out are also reflected in the shipping industry. The introduction of new technology has moved on speedily in the sector with larger container vessels, faster ships and the continued application of IT solutions. The international competitive environment has also intensified with the growth of globalisation, and shipping has seen reactions to this in the form of joint ventures and mergers in liner shipping (for example P&O/Nedlloyd, Maersk/Sealand) and the continued trends towards shipping services sourcing from wherever is most efficient or economical. The latter is typified by the range and variability of nations involved in any vessel – built in Korea, financed in Germany, owned in Greece, manned by Filipinos, insured in London, maintained in France, chartered in Australia, etc. – this range and variability reflecting the internationalised market that exists. Tonnage tax is a result of this competition, although as we have noted above, in this case an example of state interference that clings rather more to Fordist than post-Fordist principles.

Policy-making in shipping must thus reflect this situation and the hollowing out of the nation state and its changed role has to be reflected in its policy activity. Thus national policies must reflect global trends, supra-national priorities and regional drift if they are to be successful in the post-Fordist era. Even tonnage tax in the EU can be seen in this way as, although the policy itself is retrogressive in its approach to the problems it aims to meet, its application is stimulated by a supra-national authority working within an international, globalised market, recognising essentially regional needs. As Jessop (1994) suggests, hollowing out can be seen as a reaction by nations to their inability to deal effectively with either too large or too small problems which used to be contained within state areas. Changes from the Fordist to the post-Fordist model have had to be mirrored by jurisdictional change for policy generation, leaving policy enforcement as the main national activity (Port State Control, ship inspections, ship registration, etc.). Hollowing out's contribution is to:

' . . . bring supply-side intervention closer than was possible for a national state [and] . . . to develop new state organizations and policies which are structurally and strategically better adapted to the emerging international economic order' Jessop (1994).

Neo-Liberalism, Neo-Corporatist and Neo-Statist Strategies

The post-Fordist model has to adapt to the political and institutional situation which exists and this varies considerably geographically. Three versions can be identified, each of which is reflected by shipping policy and its interpretation.

Neo-liberalism is perhaps the most advanced and developed post-Fordist approach to shipping policy and is characterised by market domination. Thus it is typified by moves towards port and shipping company privatisation around the world, liberalisation of the regulations and bureaucracy that interfere in shipping activities and also the adoption of commercial criteria in state shipping activities. The UK presents a fine example of neo-liberalism in that there is now no state-owned shipping sector, minimal state-owned ports, attempts to minimise state interference in maritime activities, and also commercialisation of state agencies such as the MCA (Maritime and Coastguard Agency) and the MAIB (Maritime Accident Investigation Branch) whereby commercial costs are recovered through fees for ship inspections and registration.

Inevitably it has to encourage competition and to the detriment of national dominance, this has to include competition from overseas. Thus shipping and ports may be sold overseas (for example the Port of Felixstowe is owned by

Hong Kong interests). Some commentators (for example Gardner and Pettit, 1999b) have suggested that this has created problems for other maritime activities (including the work of the City of London) which might rely upon national maritime market employment suppliers for future skilled and experienced workers.

Neo-corporatism reflects a move towards a post-Fordist society where the state is less involved than under Fordism but mainly acts to back-up the private sector rather than distancing itself radically from industry (as in neo-liberalism) or to be actively involved (as we shall see in neo-statism). Voluntary, industrial compliance with state guidelines is the main way forward involving organisations such as national ship-owning representative bodies in supporting and promoting the sector. Self-regulation is the dominant approach. This leaves the nation state with a role to play in monitoring this self-regulation and ensuring that broader national ambitions and wider supra-national demands are put into effect by the industry itself.

Shipping does not have the greatest track record of self-regulation, at least in part because of the internationalisation of the market and the pressures from other national interests. Thus safety and environmental standards have to be enforced rather than allowed to be regulated by the market and the industry itself. Neo-corporatism represents a half-way house between liberalisation and state control, and there are features of it in the shipping sector in most countries commonly directed by the national ship-owners' association. In terms of the post-Fordist scenario, it provides for only a limited role for the nation state in guiding, encouraging and monitoring the shipping industry in its own attempts to self-regulate.

Neo-statism, at a time when we have identified the reduction in national policy significance compared with a growth in international and supra-national importance, has curiously taken a senior role in the development of shipping policy in the EU. For it is here that we can locate the developments in tonnage tax that have taken place.

Tonnage tax represents a rise in state involvement in the shipping market but in a way that both facilitates the rise in supra-national influence, incorporates the need for international policy control, whilst providing a role for the nation state in all this in translating broader policy ambitions and objectives into national variants of a consistent and protective regime. Thus shipping within the EU receives protection from the international commercial shipping sector, maintains standards of quality which have been eroded elsewhere in the search for cost savings, sustains employment and fleet representation despite pressures to cut costs, and allows national variability to co-exist alongside international and supra-national demands for level playing fields. Neo-statism encourages the positive role of the state in monitoring and policing quality and competition in shipping and the EU approach to ship taxation has facilitated this in a way that is acceptable to all levels of jurisdiction.

This is, of course, not without criticism or deviation. We have seen in Chapter 7 how each EU country has its own variant of tonnage tax but each is regulated by the European Commission to ensure fair play and that the supra-national demands of the Treaty of Rome are met. The EU itself has agreed to operationalise all IMO regulations but in ways that facilitate the development of EU shipping whilst sustaining quality standards. Individual member states have also attempted to introduce policies that deviate from the international and supra-national – these include the 2003 decisions by France to ban single-hulled tankers in advance of higher authorities or other member states. But even here, the French decision did not conflict with those of the EU and IMO – it was just in advance of them.

All three strategies of neo-liberalism, neo-corporatism and neo-statism can be found co-existing and Jessop (1994) provides the example of the EU as clear evidence of this. If we take shipping policy as our specific example within the EU then Jessop's model is apparent. The application of the single market approach to shipping is inherently neo-liberal – including enforcing single models for seafarer qualifications, the development of EU cabotage rules, and access to shipping markets for all member states – and is characterised by 'liberalisation, deregulation and internationalisation'. Neo-statism is evident in Commission policing of competitiveness in the liner sector, in attempts to regulate competition in ports and in cross-governmental research strategies through Framework programmes for the maritime sector. Neo-corporatism is clearly evident in social policies that encourage worker mobility (seafarers and officers) to the benefit of flexible working practices in industry.

This variety in model can also be found between member states and their approach to shipping policy and it is here that the example of tonnage tax is most appropriate. Thus the mixed neo-liberalist, neo-corporatist and neo-statist approach of the EU towards state aids in shipping (including tonnage tax) has been interpreted differently by each member state to produce national policies that may reflect only one or two of these model strategies. In the UK we see a tonnage tax regime with neo-statist (detailed Treasury taxation regulations including training requirements), neo-liberalist (in that the tax is flag blind), and neo-corporatist (in that companies can choose whether to opt for the tonnage tax) characteristics. In other states (for example Greece) there is no choice but to enter the regime if the vessels are to be Greek flagged, but there is no associated training requirement. Tonnage tax thus fulfils a multi-functional policy need. As we have seen earlier, it facilitates the application of EU supra-national policies whist allowing the flexibility of member state interpretation of those policies to meet domestic needs. The demands of the

Treaty of Rome are matched by the member state needs to recognise political necessities which remain focused nationally. The flexibility in this process is mirrored in the neo-liberalist, neo-corporatist and neo-statist trends and priorities that vary between member states in their shipping policies.

IS THERE A ROLE FOR NATIONAL SHIPPING POLICY?

This book has concentrated upon the relationships between the jurisdictional levels of policy-making for the shipping sector. In particular it has attempted to understand the relationship between these levels of jurisdiction – and that of the supra-national and national level especially – in the context of the European Union and more specifically the development of shipping policy. Tonnage tax has been used as a prime example of policy conflict and co-ordination between these levels, including additional reference to the international policy level which, because of the nature of the shipping sector, has further significant influence.

Hollowing out is characterised by a changed role for the nation in policy-making in the shipping sector with a clear growth in the influence of the international and supra-national body. Some commentators would also claim that the regional role in policy-making has grown at the expense of the nation, but although there is some evidence of this in the EU as a whole (for example the Committee of the Regions), the influence of bodies like this in the shipping sector is far less significant.

Given these changes, can we still see a role for the nation in shipping policy-making or has the new globalised environment, characterised by increasing supra-national segmentation, made the nation an irrelevance?

Jessop (1994) is quite confident of the continuing importance of nations in policy-making and in particular its function in co-ordinating and managing linkages between the various jurisdictional levels. Thus in shipping the nation is still the origin of representatives at the international (for example the IMO) and supra-national (for example the EU) level of policy-making, and it is national constituencies to which these representatives ultimately have to return. Shipping companies, registers, ancillary businesses, ports and so on remain based within nation states where international and supra-national policy is ultimately applied. Thus the IMO and EU range of ship safety policies are implemented through nation states who apply ship inspections, Port State Control measures, passenger ferry regulation and the application of the ISM Code. Tonnage tax is regulated by individual member states and as we have seen, adapted by each (with the permission of the European Commission) to meet domestic requirements.

As a consequence the nation state remains the vital link in shipping policy between policy-making (increasingly taking place at the higher levels of jurisdiction) and policy implementation, and this situation is confirmed and determined by the make-up of shipping policy institutions for the foreseeable future whereby nation/member states constitute the fundamental framework upon which they sit. Tonnage tax provides an excellent example of this situation whereby the nation state formulates and implements policy within the constraints of national demands but also stimulated by higher jurisdictional ambitions. By compromising between the extreme desires of each, tonnage tax is an example of the virtuous policy circle that helps to ensure quality shipping, employment, domestic control, supra-national and international standards, competitiveness and ship-owner desires for profit, all held in place by a rigid framework of inspection, legislation and fines and at the ultimate expense of the Open Registry ship-owner, the low quality operator and the negligent and inadequate nation-state registry.

And the nation state will retain this role within the jurisdiction of shipping policy. As Jessop (1994) states:

'Unless or until supra-national political organization(s) acquires not only governmental powers but also some measure of popular-democratic legitimacy, the national state will remain a key political factor at the highest instance of democratic political accountability.'

KEY SHIPPING POLICY LESSONS

From this discussion a number of key themes have emerged which are outlined below and which will help steer policy for analysts in the shipping sector and guide understanding of the complex environment in which it has to develop and within which it has to work. Once again the discussion is directed towards and from the EU as a spatial focus, but many of the comments here could be applied to other regulators, in other areas.

- The national jurisdictional level remains central to policy development and effectiveness.
- Supra-national and international jurisdictions appear increasingly to direct policy but it must be remembered that in all cases they are constituted of national representatives with national priorities at heart and national constraints restricting their wider ambitions.
- The result is that a complex game of policy-making is played by all parties whereby the necessity of appearing publicly international or supra-national in scope has to be disguised domestically to meet

national demands, whilst at the same time the need to keep an international or supra-national control on the shipping sector has to be couched in terms that appear to be nationally advantageous even when not.

- Shipping policy is especially affected by these jurisdictional policy games because it is so international but retains distinct national dimensions.
- Meanwhile open dissent does occasionally occur evidenced, for example, by France and its unilateral implementation in banning single-hulled tankers in advance of the EU and the IMO, both of which it is a member. The EU also dissented from the IMO line in introducing its own ban in advance of the international body, despite having its own representatives at the IMO and being publicly committed to implementing IMO policy.
- Conflict between jurisdictions is also common even when implementing higher jurisdictional policies downwards – a process that is logical but often resented. This is different from the France, IMO, EU dispute whereby policy is being passed up the jurisdictional level and could lead to major conflicts between nations, supra-national authorities and international bodies. Here we are talking about interruptions to what is accepted as a logical practice of taking national views at an international level and deriving nationally implemented policies which are then resented. Thus derogations from policy initiatives are common – for example in the EU, cabotage in Greece, subsidy for some ship services and shipbuilding, national support for ports, etc. – which reflect the disagreement that may exist.
- In the majority of cases these disputes need to be reconciled or avoided and tonnage tax is an excellent example where the differing national needs of member states have been accommodated whilst paying attention to the supra-national and international policy needs.
- If there is essentially no agreement between jurisdictional levels then enforcement by international and supra-national bodies rarely works. Good examples come from the failure to implement the EU port services policy in 2003 and the European Ship Registry (EUROS) in the 1980s and 1990s.
- Thus increasing globalisation, which looks set to continue albeit in a framework of post-Fordism which attempts to encourage flexibility in supply characteristics to match varying demand, does not mean the end of the nation state in shipping policy formulation and implementation.

- So what comes next? The development of (post) post-Fordism is extremely difficult to envisage but may well see increasingly subtle and complex manifestations of the policy relationships between jurisdictions, which have been outlined above. It is unlikely to lead to the resurgence of the nation-state as the sole policy-making body in shipping as 'unlearning' globalisation is impossible to imagine. Thus international and supra-national bodies will remain with us in shipping and their continually increasing demands for policy-making power will have to be accommodated whilst nations remain the focus for individuals, company headquarters and even ships.
- Shipping policy is remarkably consistent at all jurisdictional levels and only really varies in degree of intensity or profile of ambition. Thus safety, protection of the environment, training skills, competitiveness and market accessibility are almost ubiquitous and their absence really suggests a failure in policy design.
- Shipping policy demands general consensus otherwise it fails. This does not mean that policy must be identical across policy-makers but the thrust of policy must be towards a conclusion that is desired at least in principle and by the majority.
- Shipping policy will also work only if there is a self-enforcing mechanism that makes it profitable for it to work for the majority of players. Tonnage tax achieves this in many ways and although it can be criticised from the point of view of equity (compared with subsidy given to other transport sectors), it does appear, by intervening in the market, to create a virtuous circle. Ship-owners are encouraged to register with a quality flag through national and supra-national approved subsidy. Quality is enforced through PSC, ISM code implementation and inspection, but the policy of quality works because financially it is popular. PSC has the potential to work in isolation, but would not as it is widely resented by low quality shipping (for obvious reasons). Result – quality shipping; national employment; nationally influenced fleets; happy, subsidised, good quality ship-owners; but at the expense of a distorted market and the EU Treaty of Rome principles broken. Overall, the judgement by supra-national and national shipping policy-makers is that the benefit exceeds the costs.
- Contradictions in shipping policy are common, especially within the EU. Thus there are active policies to reduce road traffic by promoting short-sea shipping at the same time as funding road corridor studies, and subsidies in port investment, through tonnage taxation shipbuilding and domestic cabotage, are permitted against Treaty of Rome principles;

- Shipping policy will not go away (and has a very long history – think of 'freedom of the seas') as market intervention will always be needed because shipping quality, as an international and commercial activity, will otherwise always drop to the lowest common policy denominator (and if there is none it will fall still further).

So this will not be the last word on shipping policy. In fact there will never be a last word as its character and application will continue to adapt and mutate as the jurisdictional boundaries continue to fluctuate under the continuous development of technology, political ambitions, commercial schemes and changing markets. And thank goodness for that, as it is only through policy migration that the industry can ever hope to achieve improving levels of quality shipping.

Bibliography

Aglietta, M. (1976), *A Theory of Capitalist Regulation: The US Experience*, New Left Books: London.

Aglietta, M. (1982), 'World capitalism in the eighties', *New Left Review*, **136**, 7-41.

Alderton, T. and Winchester, N. (2002a), 'Flag states and safety: 1997-1999', *Maritime Policy and Management*, **29**, 2, 151-162.

Alderton, T. and Winchester, N. (2002b), 'Globalisation and deregulation in the maritime industry', *Marine Policy*, **26**, 35-43.

Allan, T. (2000), *Flag State Implementation of Existing Rules Will Deliver Quality Shipping*, BIMCO Review 2000.

Allen, J. (1996), 'Post-Industrialism/Post-Fordism', in Hall, S., Held, D., Hubert, D. and Thompson, K. (eds), *Modernity: An Introduction to Modern Societies*, Blackwell: Oxford, 546-555.

Amin, A. (ed.) (1994), *Post Fordism, A Reader*, Studies in Urban and Social Change, Blackwell: Oxford.

Asheim, B. (2001), 'Localised learning and regional clusters', in Mariussen, A. (ed.), *Cluster Policies – Cluster Development?* Nordregion Report, Stockholm, 2001:2.

Aspinwall, M.D. (1995), *Moveable Feast; Pressure Group Conflict and the European Community Shipping Policy*, Ashgate Publishing: Aldershot.

Auchiney, J. (2002), *Tonnage Tax Scheme Sensible*, http://www.unison.ie

Banks, A. (2002), *Tonnage Tax Ruling a 'Catalyst for Renewal' Says Irish Minister*, http://www.tax-news.com

Barla, M.C., Sag, O.K., Roe, M.S. and Gray, R. (eds) (2001), *Developments in Maritime Transport and Logistics in Turkey*, Ashgate Publishing: Aldershot.

Beagley, T. (1973), 'Transport policy in the European Economic Community: the contribution Britain can make', *Chartered Institute of Transport Journal*, March, 99-115.

Behnam, A. (1994), 'The future of the shipping dialogue in UNCTAD', *Maritime Policy and Management*, **21**, 1, 15-28.

Belgian Shipowners' Association (2002), *Annual Report 2001*, Brussels.

Bergantino, A. and Marlow, P. (1998), 'Factors influencing the choice of flag: empirical evidence', *Maritime Policy and Management*, **25**, 2, 157-174.

Bergstrand, S. and Doganis, R. (1987), *Soviet Shipping*, Unwin Hyman: London.

BIMCO (2000), *BIMCO/ISF manpower studies: is balance nearer – or further away?* Annual Review 2000, 81-84.

Bonacich, E. (2003), 'Pulling the plug: labor and the global supply chain', *New Labor Forum*, http://qcpages.qc.edu/newlaborforum.html

Bonefeld, W. and Holloway, J. (eds) (1991), *Post-Fordism and Social Form: A Marxist Debate on the Post-Fordist State*, Macmillan: London.

Bredima-Savapoulou, A. (1981a), 'In search of a common shipping policy for the European Community', *Journal of Common Market Studies*, **XX**, 2, 95-114.

Bredima-Savapoulou, A. (1981b), 'The common shipping policy of the EEC', *Common Market Law Review*, **18**, 9-32.

Bredima-Savopoulou, A. and Tzoannos, J. (1990), *The Common Shipping Policy of the EC*, Elsevier: The Hague.

Brewer, S. (2000), 'Norway at crossroads', *DNV Magazine Forum*, **11**, 50.

Brooks, M.R. (1994), 'The impact of NAFTA on transportation companies: a Canadian point of view', *Transport Reviews*, **14**, 2, 105-117.

Brooks, M.R. (2000), *Sea Change in Liner Shipping*, Pergamon: Oxford.

Brooks, M.R. and Button, K.J. (1992), 'Shipping within the framework of a Single European Market', *Transport Reviews*, **12**, 3, 237-252.

Brownrigg, M. (1993), 'The British merchant fleet: a practical perspective', *Maritime Policy and Management*, **20**, 3, 177-180.

Brownrigg, M. (2000), *Implications for the UK flag*, Maritime Conference, Paris, 21st June: http://www.britishshipping.org/news/hold2.htm

Brownrigg, M., Dawe, G., Mann, M. and Weston, P. (2001), 'Developments in UK shipping: the tonnage tax', *Maritime Policy and Management*, **28**, 3, 213-224.

Button, K.J. (1993), *Transport Economics*, Edward Elgar: Cheltenham.

Cafruny, A. (1985), 'The political economy of international shipping; Europe versus America', *International Organization*, **39**, 1, Winter.

Cafruny, A. (1987), *Ruling the Waves – the Political Economy of International Shipping*, Studies in International Political Economy, University of California Press: Berkeley.

Cafruny, A. (1991), 'Toward a maritime policy', in Hurwitz, L. and Lequesne, C. (eds), *The State of the European Community; Policies, Institutions and Debates in the Transition Years*, Lynne Rienner: Boulder.

Calhoon MEBA Engineering School (2002), *Spain, Denmark to Implement Tonnage Tax*, http://www.mebaschool.org/03-15-02.html

Chlomoudis, C.I., Karalis, A.V. and Pallis, A.A. (2000), 'Transition to a new reality: theorising the organisational restructuring in ports', *Infomare*, November 7th, http://www.infomare.it

Chlomoudis, C.I., Karalis, A.V. and Pallis, A.A. (2003), 'Port reorganisations and the worlds of production theory', *European Journal of Transport and Infrastructure Research,* **3,** 1, 73-94.

Chrzanowski, I., Krzyzanowski, M. and Luks, K. (1979), *Shipping Economics and Policy; A Socialist View,* Fairplay: London.

Coleman, R. (2000), Maritime Policy, *BIMCO Review,* 34.

Colvin, M. and Marks, J. (1984), *British Shipping; The Right Course,* Policy Study 67, Centre for Policy Studies: London.

Commission of the European Communities (1976), *Communication from the Commission to the Council, Community Relations with Non-member Countries in Shipping Matters,* COM(76) 341 Final, Office for Official Publications of the European Communities: Luxembourg.

Commission of the European Communities (1989), *A Future for the Community Shipping Industry. Measures to Improve the Operating Conditions of Community Shipping,* COM(89) 266 Final, Office for Official Publications of the European Communities: Luxembourg.

Commission of the European Communities (1993), *A Common Policy on Safe Seas,* COM 93 (66), Office for Official Publications of the European Communities: Luxembourg.

Commission of the European Communities (1995a), *Concerning the Enforcement, in Respect of Shipping Using Community Ports and Sailing in the Waters Under the Jurisdiction of the Member States, of International Standards for Ship Safety, Pollution Prevention and Shipboard Living and Working Conditions (Port State Control),* 95/21/EC, Office for Official Publications of the European Communities: Luxembourg.

Commission of the European Communities (1995b), *The Common Transport Policy,* COM/95/302, Office for Official Publications of the European Communities: Luxembourg.

Commission of the European Communities (1996), *Towards a New Maritime Strategy,* COM (96) 81 Final, Office for Official Publications of the European Communities: Luxembourg.

Commission of the European Communities (1997), *Community Guidelines on State Aid to Maritime Transport,* COM 97/C 205/05, Office for Official Publications of the European Communities: Luxembourg.

Commission of the European Communities (1998), *Council Regulation on Aid to Shipbuilding,* 1540/98, Office for Official Publications of the European Communities: Luxembourg.

Commission of the European Communities (2000a), *Port Reception Facilities for Ship-Generated Waste and Cargo Residues,* 2000/59/EC, Office for Official Publications of the European Communities: Luxembourg.

Commission of the European Communities (2000b), *Maritime Safety: European Maritime Safety Agency, Activities of the European Union, Summaries of Legislation*, Proposal COM (2000), 802 Final COD2000/0327, Office for Official Publications of the European Communities: Luxembourg.

Commission of the European Communities (2001a), *European Transport Policy for 2010: Time to Decide*, Office for Official Publications of the European Communities: Luxembourg.

Commission of the European Communities (2001b), *Harmonised Requirements for the Safe Loading and Unloading of Bulk Carriers*, Directive 2001/96/EC, Office for Official Publications of the European Communities: Luxembourg.

Commission of the European Communities (2002a), *Improving Passenger Ship Safety: Memo*, Office for Official Publications of the European Communities: Luxembourg, http://europa.eu.int/comm/transport/themes/maritime/english/safety/index safety.html

Commission of the European Communities (2002b), *Maritime Policy. European Union Legislation and Objectives for Sea Transport*, Office for Official Publications of the European Communities: Luxembourg.

Commission of the European Communities (2002c), *Maritime Transport: the Commission Clears the Introduction of a Tonnage Tax in Ireland*, Press Release IP/02/1860.

Commission of the European Communities (2002d), *Maritime Transport, Common Transport Policy* http://europa.eu.int/comm/transport/themes/maritime/english/mt_1_en.html

Commission of the European Communities (2003), *Commission Gives Strong Support to European Maritime Transport Sector*, Press Release IP/03/1484, 30th October.

Cooper, J. (1994), 'The global logistics challenge', in Cooper, J. (ed.), *Logistics and Distribution Planning*, Dornier: London.

Danish Shipowners' Association (2001), *Maritime Regulations*, Annual Report.

De Langen, P. (1999), *Fordism and Post Fordism in Seaports; Implications for Port Policy and Management*. Paper presented at the Ports and Logistics Conference, Alexandria, Egypt.

De Palacio, L. (2002), *The EU shipping policy: Towards an open and quality-oriented market*, June 2nd, Posidonia Congress, Athens, Greece.

Despicht, N.S. (1966a), 'Transport and the Common Market', *Institute of Transport Journal*, January, 277-280.

Despicht, N.S. (1966b), 'Transport and the Common Market', *Institute of Transport Journal*, March.

Despicht, N.S. (1966c), 'Transport and the Common Market', *Institute of Transport Journal*, September, 475-478.

Despicht, N.S. (1966d), 'Transport and the Common Market', *Institute of Transport Journal*, November, 20-26.

Dickey, A. (1999), *Interview with Gerard Bos, managing director of Spliethoff shipping group,* Lloyd's List Focus: The Dutch Maritime cluster, A Network of Excellence, June 11th.

Dickey, A. (2000), 'More Dutch registered ships call on Rotterdam', *Lloyd's List*, January 27th.

Dickinson, M. (2001), *Is There a Better Way to Regulate the Shipping Industry? When is a Flag an FOC?* Oslo: Fockets Hus Conference centre.

Dirks, J. (2001), *Assessment of the Current Situation in the European Shipping Market in the Globalisation and World Market Context. Improving Employment Opportunities for European Seafarers – An Investigation to Identify Training and Education Priorities*, University of Bremen: http://www-user.uni.bremen.de/~jdirks/context.htm

Economic and Social Committee of the European Communities (1986), *Progress Towards a Common Transport Policy,* Communication and Proposals by the Commission to the Council, EEC Maritime Transport Policy, Brussels, June.

ECSA (2002a), *The Liberalisation of Maritime Trade in the European Community*, Publication 02-1, May.

ECSA (2002b), *Annual Report 2000-2001*, ECSA: Brussels.

Environment News Service (2002), *EU proposes maritime safety agency after oil, and chemical spills*: http://ens.com

Erdmenger, J. and Stasinopoulos, D. (1988), 'The shipping policy of the European Community', *Journal of Transport Economics and Policy*, September, **22**, 355-360.

Ernst and Young (2002), *Shipping Industry Almanac 2002*, Ernst and Young International Shipping Group: London.

European Parliament (1997), *The Common Maritime Policy,* Working Document Transport Series W14, Brussels.

European Tax Newsletter (2002), *Italian Tonnage Tax for 2002*, February, http://www.bakerinfo.com/newsletters

European Tax Newsletter (2003), *Overview of the Forthcoming Reform of the Italian Tax Regime: (g) Tonnage Tax,* May: http://www.bakerinfo.com/newsletters

Eyre, J. (1989), 'A ship's flag – who cares?', *Maritime Policy and Management*, **16**, 3, 179-187.

Fairplay (2000), EC approves UK tonnage tax, *Fairplay*, **339**, 17.

Farthing, B. (1987), *International Shipping; An Introduction to the Policies, Politics and Institutions of the Maritime World*, Lloyd's of London Press: London.

Flynn, M. (1999), 'PRC maritime and the Asian financial crisis', *Maritime Policy and Management*, **26**, 4, 337-348.

Forsyth, G.J. (1993), 'Transnational corporations: problems for study in the new international order for maritime shipping', *Maritime Policy and Management*, **20**, 3, 207-214.

Forum uber Shipping und Logistik (2001), *InforMare*, http://www.informare.it/news/forum/2001/ecsa/2de.asp

Frankel, E.G. (1989), 'Strategic planning applied to shipping and ports', *Maritime Policy and Management*, **16**, 2, 123-132.

Frankel, E.G. (1992), 'Hierarchical logic in shipping policy and decision-making', *Maritime Policy and Management*, **19**, 3, 211-221.

Frankel, E.G. (1999), 'The economics of total trans-ocean supply chain management', *International Journal of Maritime Economics*, **1**, 1, 61-70.

Gardner, B. (1999), 'Investment incentives for British shipping: a further comment', *Maritime Policy and Management*, **26**, 2, 195-200.

Gardner, B. and Pettit, S.J. (1999a), 'The land based jobs market for seafarers. Consequences of market imbalance and policy implications', *Marine Policy*, **23**, 161-175.

Gardner, B. and Pettit, S.J. (1999b), 'Seafarers and land based jobs market. The present UK situation'. *Marine Policy*, **23**, 103-115.

Gardner, B.M., Pettit, S.J. and Thanopoulou, H. (1996), 'Shifting challenges for British maritime policy; 10 years of decline', *Marine Policy*, **6**, 517-524.

Gardner, B.M., Naim, M., Obando-Rojas, B. and Pettit, S.J. (2001), 'Maintaining the maritime skills base: does the government have a realistic strategy?', *Maritime Policy and Management*, **28**, 4, 347-360.

Goergen, R. (1972), 'Transport policy in the European Community after the British entry', *Chartered Institute of Transport Journal*, March, 343-353.

Gold, E. (1981), *The Evolution of International Marine Policy and Shipping Law*, Lexington Books: Mass., USA.

Gordon, M.W. (1993), 'Economic integration in North America – an agreement of limited dimensions but unlimited expectations', *Modern Law Review*, **56**, 2, 157-171.

Goss, R.O. (ed.) (1982), *Advances in Maritime Economics*, Cambridge University Press: Cambridge.

Goss, R.O. (1987), 'Sense and shipping policies', *Maritime Policy and Management*, **14**, 2, 83-97.

Goss, R.O. (1991), 'Editorial: some challenges for British shipping', *Maritime Policy and Management*, **18**, 1, 1-9.

Goss, R.O. and Marlow, P.B. (1993), 'Internationalisation, protectionism and interventionism', in Gwilliam, K.M. (ed.), *Current Issues in Maritime Economics*, Kluwer Academic Publishing, Dordrecht, 45-67.

Goto, S. (1984), *Japan's Shipping Policy*, Japan Maritime Research Institute, JAMRI Report 3.

Government of Canada (1992), *North American Free Trade Agreement. An Overview and Description*, Toronto: Canada.

Grammenos, C. (ed.) (2002), *The Handbook of Maritime Economics and Business,* Lloyd's of London Press: London.

Grimaldi, E. (2001), *Foreword by the President, European Community Shipowners' Association*, Annual Report, 2000-2001, 5.

Gwilliam, K.M. (1979), 'Institutions and objectives in transport policy', *Journal of Transport Economics and Policy*, **XIII**, 1, 13.

Gwilliam, K.M. (1993), 'Transport policy in an international setting', in Polak, J. and Heertge, A. (eds), *European Transport Economics*, Edward Elgar: Cheltenham.

Hall, S., Held, D., Hubert, D. and Thompson, K. (eds) (1996), *Modernity: An Introduction to Modern Societies,* Blackwell: Oxford.

Hammer, H. (2000), *The Norwegian Shipping Industry*, ODIN, Ministry of Foreign Affairs, October 2000, http://odin.dep.no

Haralambides, H.E. and Yang, J. (2003), 'A fuzzy set theory approach to flagging out: towards a new Chinese shipping policy', *Marine Policy*, **27**, 1, 13-22.

Hart, P., Ledger, G., Roe, M.S. and Smith, B. (1993), *Shipping Policy in the European Community*, Ashgate Publishing: Aldershot.

Hawkins, J. (2001), 'Quality shipping in the Asia-Pacific region', *International Journal of Maritime Economics*, **3**, 1, 79-101.

Hawkins, J. and Gray, R. (1999), 'Making strategic choices for Asia-Pacific shipping', *International Journal of Maritime Economics*, **1**, 2, 57-72.

Hawkins, J. and Gray, R. (2000), *Strategies for Asia-Pacific Shipping*, Ashgate Publishing: Aldershot.

Heaver, T., Meersman, H. and van de Voorde, E. (2001a), 'Co-operation and competition in international container transport', *Maritime Policy and Management*, **28**, 3, 293-305.

Heaver, T., Meersman, H., Moglia, F. and van de Voorde, E. (2001b), 'Do mergers and alliances influence European shipping and port competition?', *Maritime Policy and Management*, **28**, 4, 363-373.

Hirsch, J. (1995), *Globalisation of Capital, Democracy and Citizenship*, October 1995, University of Frankfurt, Department of Social Sciences, Aalborg.

Holst, O. (1982), 'A long-term analysis of transport in Europe: some implications for transport policy and research', *European Journal of Operational Research*, **11**, 26-34.

Hoyle, B. and Knowles, R. (1998), *Modern Transport Geography*, Wiley: London.

ILO (2001), *29th Session of the Joint Maritime Commission Geneva, Final Report, 22-26 January 2001,* http://www.ilo.org/

ImarE Bulletin (1999), *Chamber of Shipping President Implores Government to Implement Tonnage Tax,* April, http://www.imarest.org

Institute of Shipping Economics and Logistics (2002), *SSMR Market Analysis 2002: Ownership and Patterns of the World Merchant Fleet*, University of Bremen: Bremen.

International Association of Independent Tanker Owners (2001), *Annual Review,* Intertanko: Oslo.

ISL (1996), *Shipping Statistics*, University of Bremen: Bremen.

Jaques, B. (1999), 'Government 'charts a new course'', *Seatrade Review*, March, 49-51.

Jessop, B. (1994), 'Post-Fordism and the State', in Amin, A. (ed.), *Post Fordism, A Reader*, Studies in Urban and Social Change, Blackwell: Oxford, 251-279.

Kellett, J. and Robinson, D. (2000a), 'Tax scheme promotes training', *Container Management,* October 17th.

Kellett, J. and Robinson, D. (2000b), *UK Tonnage Tax – Red Ensign or Red Faces?,* Maritime Review 2000, 21-23.

Kiriazidis, T. and Tzanidakis, G. (1995), 'Recent aspects of the EU maritime transport policy', *Maritime Policy and Management*, **22**, 2, 179-186.

Knoop, H.G. (2002), *GAUSS, Development of an Integrated and Internationally Applicable Incentive System for Quality Shipping,* Institute for Environmental Protection and Safety in Shipping, January 2002.

Kokuryo, H. (1985), *Korean Shipping and Shipping Policy; Shipping Industry Rationalisation Plan,* Japan Maritime Research Institute, JAMRI Report 8.

Kornegay, H.T. (1993), 'NAFTA. Impact on the maritime industry', *Worldwide Shipping,* September, 48-51.

Kouri, P. and Naniopoulos, A. (2000), *De l'opportunité de créer un observatoire Européen de l' emploi maritime at portuaire,* L'Orient Conference on maritime and port employment in Southern Europe, a challenge for the Mediterranean States: The case of Greece, 15-16th May, Palais des Congrés.

Kuiper, J. and Loyens, L. (2001), *New fiscal regime for the Dutch Antilles*, Practical Law, Volume V, Legal and Commercial Publishing Limited, http://www.plcinfo.com

Lalis, G. (1999a), *Maritime safety policy of the EU*, Maritime Cyprus Conference, 3-6th October.

Lalis, G. (1999b), *The Economist Conferences/British Embassy*, Second International Maritime Conference, International Shipping at the New Millennium, Athens, 18th September, http://europa.eu.int/comm/transport/themes/maritime/pdf/1999-11-athens.pdf

Lammont, N. (2000), *Work process knowledge in technical and organisational development, 1998-2000*, European Union Targeted Social Economic Research Programme Thematic Network, DG XII of the European Commission, http://www.education.man.ac.uk

Lazarus, P.E. (1978), 'The implications of EEC transport policy for the UK', *The Highway Engineer*, April, 2-7.

Ledger, G.D. and Roe, M.S. (1992), 'The decline of the UK merchant fleet: an assessment of government policies in recent years', *Maritime Policy and Management*, **19**, 3, 239-251.

Ledger, G.D. and Roe, M.S. (1993), 'East European shipping and economic change: a conceptual model', *Maritime Policy and Management*, **20**, 3, 229-241.

Ledger, G.D. and Roe, M.S. (1995), 'Positional change in the Polish liner shipping market', *Maritime Policy and Management*, **22**, 4, 295-318.

Ledger, G.D. and Roe, M.S. (1996), *East European Change and Shipping Policy*, Ashgate Publishing: Aldershot.

Lee, T. (1996), *Shipping Developments in Far East Asia*, Ashgate Publishing: Aldershot.

Lee, T. (1999), 'Restructuring of the economy and its impacts on the Korean maritime industry', *Maritime Policy and Management*, **26**, 4, 311-326.

Lee, T., Roe, M.S., Gray, R. and Shen, M. (eds) (2002), *Shipping in China*, Ashgate Publishing: Aldershot.

Li, K.X. and Wonham, J. (2001), 'Maritime legislation: new areas for safety of life at sea', *Maritime Policy and Management*, **28**, 3, 225-234.

Lipietz, A. (1987), *Mirages and Miracles: the Crises of Global Fordism*, Verso: London.

Little, W.M. (1962), 'Road to Europe', *Institute of Transport Journal*, July, 349-355.

Lloyd's List (1993), *Regional Deals Could Fuel New Trade War*, December 17th

Lloyd's List (1996), *Transport Commissioner Neil Kinnock's Maritime Strategy Document is the Most Tangible*, March 18th

Lloyd's List (1996a), *EC Backs Dutch Maritime Plan*, March 25th

Lloyd's List (1996b), *New Life for Dutch Shipping*, June 13th

Lloyd's List (1996c), *Italy Aims to Speed Box Lines Sell-Off*, June 27th

Lloyd's List (1997a), *Van Ommeren Gets Bolder: Dutch Group Looks for Takeover Targets and Alliances in Expansion Strategy*, June 17th

Lloyd's List (1997b), *Low Countries Letter: All Eyes on a Newcomer at Seat of Power*, September 12th

Lloyd's List (1997c), *Swedish Owners Prepare to Face Taxing Questions*, March 4th

Lloyd's List (1997d), *Swedish Ship-owners Call for Faster Action*, May 22nd

Lloyd's List (1997e), *EU Agrees to Swedish Shipping Subsidies*, June 6th

Lloyd's List (1997f), *Swedish Flag Warning as New Decline Reported*, July 9th

Lloyd's List (1997g), *Swedish Owners in Support Plea*, August 27th

Lloyd's List (1997h), *Argonaut Head Warns of Threat to Swedish Shipping*, September 10th

Lloyd's List (1997i), *Swedish Owners Near Accord with Unions*, October 2nd

Lloyd's List (1997j), *Sweden Set to Accept Foreign Seafarers*, November 14th

Lloyd's List (1997k), *Owners Seek More from Swedish Flag*, November 25th

Lloyd's List (1997l), *German Flag Fleet Under Threat from Tax Reforms*, February 14th

Lloyd's List (1997m), *German Bid to Boost Shipping*, July 2nd

Lloyd's List (1997n), *Owners Concerned Despite Possible Reforms*, July 11th

Lloyd's List (1997o), *German Owners Welcome Tax Move*, July 18th

Lloyd's List (1997p), *Bonn Relaxes Rules for Foreign Crews*, July 19th

Lloyd's List (1997q), *Owners Hit at German Shipping Budget Aid*, October 13th

Lloyd's List (1997r), *VDR Rejects Union Criticism of Minister*, November 1st

Lloyd's List (1997s), *Germany Set to Introduce Tonnage Tax*, July 23rd

Lloyd's List (1997t), *Finnish Owners Demand Tax Help*, August 28th

Lloyd's List (1997u), *Chamber Moves to Raise Lobby Profile*, January 20th

Lloyd's List (1997v), *Italy Proposes to Introduce a Second Register*, January 31st

Lloyd's List (1997w), *EU Plans Big Shipping Shake-Up*, May 6th

Lloyd's List (1997x), *Taxing Decisions*, May 26th

Lloyd's List (1997y), *Danish Diet is Keeping Ship Owners in Trims*, June 6th

Lloyd's List (1998a), *Dutch Solution Urged for Outflagging Dilemma*, June 25th

Lloyd's List (1998b), *Danish Owners Favour Tonnage Tax*, May 19th

Lloyd's List (1998c), *Danish Tax Talks*, May 22nd

Lloyd's List (1998d), *Shipping Industry Takes a Beating*, May 25th

Lloyd's List (1998e), *Swedish Orient Flag-out Move Threatens Jobs*, November 13th

Lloyd's List (1998f), *Shipping Faces Uncertain Future*, November 30th

Lloyd's List (1998g), *German Shipping Reforms Progress*, March 28th

Lloyd's List (1998h), *Reforms Test Old Assumptions*, April 14th

Lloyd's List (1998i), *Banking on Investment Funds*, May 8th

Lloyd's List (1998j), *German Register Set for Boost*, May 19th

Lloyd's List (1998k), *Germany Agrees to Tonnage Tax*, June 3rd

Lloyd's List (1998l), *Tax Choice for German Shipbuilders*, June 12th

Lloyd's List (1998m), *Industry in Merger Mania*, June 29th

Lloyd's List (1998n), *Harmony Over Latest Tax Moves*, June 29th

Lloyd's List (1998o), *German Call to Keep Reforms*, October 23rd

Lloyd's List (1998p), *New Leadership Must Come up With Some Fresh Ideas*, October 30th

Lloyd's List (1998q), *Reform of Tax Leads to Reduced Advantages*, November 11th

Lloyd's List (1998r), *Planned German Tonnage Tax Set to Cut Box Capacity*, November 14th

Lloyd's List (1998s), *EU Tax Moves Bring Threat to Finnish Flag*, March 11th

Lloyd's List (1998t), *Finnlines Join in Call for Tonnage-Based Tax System*, May 29th

Lloyd's List (1998u), *Finnish Shipowners Win Reforms*, June 11th

Lloyd's List (1998v), *Finland to Decide on Shipowner Reforms*, August 11th

Lloyd's List (1998w), *Reforms Setback as Finland Hit Owners*, August 15th

Lloyd's List (1998x), *Finnlines to Flag Out Two Ships*, October 16th

Lloyd's List (1998y), *Italian Owners Warn of Flag Exodus Over Register Issues*, February 20th

Lloyd's List (1998z), *Flag Vision*, February 28th

Lloyd's List (1998aa), *Opportunity Knocks*, January 12th

Lloyd's List (1999a), *Tax Choice Needs Great Care*, November 12th

Lloyd's List (1999b), *Ringing up the Changes*, November 12th

Lloyd's List (1999c), *Tonnage Tax Dilemma for German Shipping Funds*, November 29th

Lloyd's List (1999d), *Dr Peters Scores Victory in Golden Ocean Deal*, December 2nd.

Lloyd's List (1999e), *London Greek Maritime: Major Priority is Corrective Action on Flag*, November 4th

Lloyd's List (1999f), *Europe: Greece: Soumakis Will Not Act on Costs*, November 23rd

Lloyd's List (1999g), *How Tonnage Tax could Revitalise British Shipping*, December 12th

Lloyd's List (2000a), *Tonnage Tax Set to Attract Foreign Players Back to British Fold*, April 12th

Lloyd's List (2000b), *Dutch Tonnage Tax Blow to Netherlands Antilles Register*, October 4th

Lloyd's List (2000c), *Europe: Denmark is to Adopt Dutch Model for Tonnage Tax*, February 22nd

Lloyd's List (2000d), *Danes Rap Tax Plan*, September 9th

Lloyd's List (2000e), *State Sets Scene for Development*, March 24th

Lloyd's List (2000f), *'Dead' Flag on Verge of a Revival*, November 7th

Lloyd's List (2000g), *Tug Operator URS Heading for a Profit*, May 16th

Lloyd's List (2000h), *French Back Jospin on Flag Initiative*, March 1st

Lloyd's List (2000i), *Crewing: French Warn on Job Aims*, April 29th

Lloyd's List (2000j), *Owners Press Case for Tricolour*, May 19th

Lloyd's List (2000k), *Shipping Funds Losing Their Appeal*, January 6th

Lloyd's List (2000l), *Norddeutsche Puts a Brake on Ship Funds*, January 19th

Lloyd's List (2000m), *German Union Raps Shipping Tax Law*, April 13th

Lloyd's List (2000n), *Peterswerth Wewelsfleth Insolvency Steps Start*, June 20th

Lloyd's List (2000o), *Germany Set to Introduce Tonnage Tax*, June 23rd

Lloyd's List (2000p), *New German Tonnage Tax Proves a Magnet for 500 Owners*, June 23rd

Lloyd's List (2000q), *Grow or Die is the New Motto*, May 19th

Lloyd's List (2000r), *Ships Order Confirmation of Spending Spree Again*, August 7th

Lloyd's List (2000s), *Gdansk Shipyard Deal Puts Polish Stalwart in Leading Role*, September 1st

Lloyd's List (2000t), *Hapag-Lloyd Profits Soar*, September 14th

Lloyd's List (2000u), *New Appeal for German Flag Aid*, September 20th

Lloyd's List (2000v), *Tonnage Tax Introduction Arrests German Flagging Out*, October 23rd

Lloyd's List (2000w), *Reform of Tax System has its Advantages for Investors*, November 10th

Lloyd's List (2000x), *Nations Face Brussels Quiz Over Fuel Tax Cuts*, September 21st

Lloyd's List (2000y), *German Tonnage Tax Brings Fleet Back Home*, December 16th

Lloyd's List (2000z), *Finnlines Ships Set to Quit National Flag*, February 16th

Lloyd's List (2000aa), *Tax Moves Start Domino Effect*, February 22nd

Lloyd's List (2000bb), *Finns Go Dutch for Ro-Ro Ships*, April 17th

Lloyd's List (2000cc), *Long-Term Charters High but Actinor Has Flat First Quarter*, June 8th

Lloyd's List (2000dd), *Government Promise on Industry Changes*, June 9th

Lloyd's List (2000ee), *Shipowners Play a Waiting Game*, June 9th

Lloyd's List (2000ff), *Finland Opts for Tonnage Tax*, June 27th

Lloyd's List (2000gg), *Fortun Backs New Icebreaking Tanker*, July 3rd

Lloyd's List (2000hh), *Relief for Beleaguered Industry*, October 3rd

Lloyd's List (2000ii), *Viking Line Profits Tumble by 30%*, December 20th

Lloyd's List (2000jj), *Tight-lipped Shipping Firms Keep Their Options Open*, September 13th

Lloyd's List (2000kk), *British Unions Call for More Action on Crew Support*, September 13th

Lloyd's List (2000ll), *Fisher Gets Boost from Tonnage Tax*, September 13th

Lloyd's List (2000mm), *Northern's Star*, September 30th

Lloyd's List (2000nn), *UK Shortsea Pledge on Grants*, October 12th

Lloyd's List (2000oo), *Red Ensign Growth Faces Officer Dearth Block*, October 19th

Lloyd's List (2000pp), *Let's Confront Training Issues Properly Before it's Too Late*, October 25th

Lloyd's List (2000qq), *International Issues Claim Attention of the Think Tank*, November 1st

Lloyd's List (2000rr), *Relief for Beleaguered Industry. Nicolas Velliades Keeps Faith with City of London to Lead the Field as Contender for Velos Listing*, November 1st.

Lloyd's List (2000ss), *UK Tonnage Tax Has Boosted Cadet Seafarer Numbers*, November 17th

Lloyd's List (2000tt), *Tonnage Tax Prompts Cadet Training Boost*, November 20th

Lloyd's List (2000uu), *Tax Verdict May Revive Red Ensign*, December 2nd

Lloyd's List (2000vv), *Brighter Future for Euro Shipowner,* October 9th

Lloyd's List (2001a), *Governed by Brussels, Insight and Opinion*, May 23rd

Lloyd's List (2001b), *Knudsen Encourages Common Sense*, March 30th

Lloyd's List (2001c), *Sense and Insensibility*, March 28th

Lloyd's List (2001d), *Bugsier Calls for Competitive Ports*, February 16th

Lloyd's List (2001e), *Brussels to Launch Formal Enquiry into Dutch State Aid for Tugs Sector*, July 10th

Lloyd's List (2001f), *AP Moller under Pressure at AGM*, May 8th

Lloyd's List (2001g), *Danish Tonnage Tax Pressure*, May 8th

Lloyd's List (2001h), *Pontoppidian Issues Battle Cry Against Protectionism*, May 21st

Lloyd's List (2001i), *Owners' Leader Pontoppidian to Push for More Competitive Fleet*, June 13th

Lloyd's List (2001j), *In a Buoyant Mood*, June 13th

Lloyd's List (2001k), *Should Investors be Seeking Bargains in Europe*, July 11th

Lloyd's List (2001l), *Danes Hail Tonnage Tax Breakthrough*, August 27th

Lloyd's List (2001m), *Pay Plan a Marine Turning Point*, January 16th

Lloyd's List (2001n), *War of Tugs Levelling Out*, October 17th

Lloyd's List (2001o), *Tonnage Tax Set for Green Light*, October 17th

Lloyd's List (2001p), *Pressure for French Flag Reforms*, February 7th

Lloyd's List (2001q), *French Owners Urge Registry Reforms*, April 4th

Lloyd's List (2001r), *Owners Flag Need for Reform*, June 5th

Lloyd's List (2001s), *Early Hopes for French Tonnage Tax Dashed*, September 26th

Lloyd's List (2001t), *French Owners Resigned Over Tonnage Tax Failure*, November 8th

Lloyd's List (2001u), *Shipping Bosses Look for Turn to the Right,* December 18th

Lloyd's List (2001v), *German Market Ahead of Politicians*, January 8th

Lloyd's List (2001w), *Hansa Mare Owners to Go Separate Ways*, January 15th

Lloyd's List (2001x), *Hansa Treuhand Share Sales Down*, January 31st

Lloyd's List (2001y), *HCI Reshapes After Merger with HST*, February 8th

Lloyd's List (2001z), *Box Arm is Key Driver in Hapag-Lloyd Record Year*, April 11th

Lloyd's List (2001aa), *German Maritime Sector Faces Up to Tough Labour Market*, May 1st

Lloyd's List (2001bb), *Hansa Treuhand Sees Rates Hike*, May 31st

Lloyd's List (2001cc), *Schröder Keeps Vow on Aid for Owners*, June 19th

Lloyd's List (2001dd), *Norddeutsche Plans Fleet Surge*, June 26th

Lloyd's List (2001ee), *Fresh Finance Challenges*, October 12th

Lloyd's List (2001ff), *Call for Clarity in Depreciation Rules*, October 30th

Lloyd's List (2001gg), *Crewing Regulations Keep Home Flag Numbers Down*, October 30th

Lloyd's List (2001hh), *German Owners to Get Aid Incentive*, November 7th

Lloyd's List (2001ii), *Viking Finds Finnish Flag a Hindrance*, June 8th

Lloyd's List (2001jj), *Viking Line Says Sweden has Left Finns Flagging*, September 7th

Lloyd's List (2001kk), *Fears for Irish Shipping after Government Snub*, February 27th

Lloyd's List (2001ll), *Irish Shipping Body Attacks Confused Tonnage Tax Plan*, April 20th

Lloyd's List (2001mm), *Irish Continental Group Calls for Tonnage Tax as Disease Hits Profits*, June 29th

Lloyd's List (2001nn), *Government Takes a Fresh Look at Shipping*, July 27th

Lloyd's List (2001oo), *Economy Confounds the Sceptics*, July 27th

Lloyd's List (2001pp), *Tonnage Tax Proposal Averts 'Disaster' for Irish Companies*, December 7th

Lloyd's List (2001qq), *Registering a Renaissance*, June 14th

Lloyd's List (2001rr), *New Italian Government Offers Hope of Tonnage Tax*, June 15th

Lloyd's List (2001ss), *Tonnage Tax Letdown 'Will Sink Italian Fleet' Claims Clerici*, October 15th

Lloyd's List (2001tt), *Montanari Co-owner Wins Leadership of Confitarma*, October 22nd

Lloyd's List (2001uu), *Owners Cheer Greek U-turn on Tonnage Tax*, April 4th

Lloyd's List (2001vv), *Greece Set to Slash Tonnage Tax in Half*, September 7th

Lloyd's List (2001ww), *Flag Policies to Boost Industry*, November 22nd

Globalisation, Policy and Shipping

Lloyd's List (2001xx), *Union Takes on UK Government Over Ratings' Employment Woes*, February 8th

Lloyd's List (2001yy), *Bollore, Sterling Warn Shipowners*, February 8th

Lloyd's List (2001zz), *Skills are Key for British Ratings*, February 9th

Lloyd's List (2001aaa), *CP Ships Eyes UK Tonnage Breaks*, February 15th

Lloyd's List (2001bbb), *Brown to Keep UK Shipping Sweet*, March 5th

Lloyd's List (2001ccc), *Brussels to Shake Up Euro Ship Tax*, March 5th

Lloyd's List (2001ddd), *Firm's Queue Up for Britain's Tonnage Tax*, March 23rd

Lloyd's List (2001eee), *Salt Water Horses*, March 26th

Lloyd's List (2001fff), *Challenge Over Call of the Sea*, May 1st

Lloyd's List (2001ggg), *Not Entirely Open*, May 2nd

Lloyd's List (2001hhh), *UK Still Rules the Waves as Top Maritime Centre*, May 2nd

Lloyd's List (2001iii), *Prescott Fumes as Numast Flags Up Crew Agreements*, May 2nd

Lloyd's List (2001jjj), *FT Everard Decides Not to Opt for Tonnage Tax*, May 8th

Lloyd's List (2001kkk), *Tonnage Tax No Use to Us Say UK Seafarers*, May 8th

Lloyd's List (2001lll), *URS Faces Service Tug-of-war*, May 18th

Lloyd's List (2001mmm), *Companies Undecided as Tonnage Tax Deadline Looms*, May 21st

Lloyd's List (2001nnn), *Allaying the Doubt on Flying the Flag*, May 21st

Lloyd's List (2001ooo), *Body Counting*, June 29th

Lloyd's List (2001ppp), *The Secrets of the Industry's Success*, July 9th

Lloyd's List (2001qqq), *Tonnage Tax Rides to Rescue Princess*, July 27th

Lloyd's List (2001rrr), *586 Ships Signed to UK Tonnage Tax*, August 1st

Lloyd's List (2001sss), *UK Unions Call for Social Dialogue in Shipping*, September 11th

Lloyd's List (2001ttt), *UK Tonnage Tax Regime Puts Accent on Competency*, September 25th

Lloyd's List (2001uuu), *UK Intake Far Behind Cadet Target Figure*, October 10th

Lloyd's List (2001vvv), *Lloyd Triestino May Switch New Ships to UK Flag*, October 15th

Lloyd's List (2001www), *Shift of Emphasis Pays Dividends for MCA*, October 16th

Lloyd's List (2001xxx), *Latest Two Evergreen Ships to Fly Red Ensign*, October 16th

Lloyd's List (2001yyy), *New Look UK Flag Pulls Off a Major Coup*, October 17th

Lloyd's List (2001zzz), *Critical Mass*, October 22nd

Lloyd's List (2001aaaa), *Evergreen Leads with Top Class Sea School*, October 25th

Lloyd's List (2001bbbb), *RMT to Fight as P&O Nedlloyd Axes Last British Ratings*, November 13th

Lloyd's List (2001cccc), *UK Union Seeks Clarification on Crewing of MoD Ro-ros*, March 30th

Lloyd's List (2001dddd), *Brussels Spouts*, June 16th

Lloyd's List (2001eeee), *FoCs Face Curbs in Europe*, April 5th

Lloyd's List (2001ffff), *CSG to Seek US Allies in Opposition to Jones Act*, May 4th

Lloyd's List (2001gggg), *De Palacio Blueprint Wins Owner Support*, July 13th

Lloyd's List (2001hhhh), *European Owners Warn of Deepening Crisis*, October 23rd

Lloyd's List (2002a), *Incentives Needed to Rebuild the National Fleet, Interview with Pieter van Agtmaal, Managing Director of KVNR*, June 24th

Lloyd's List (2002b), *Denmark Delivers Financial Fillip to Owners in Bid to Spur Trade*, January 25th

Lloyd's List (2002c), *Paris Gives Go-ahead for Creation of Tonnage Tax*, December 31st

Lloyd's List (2002d), *German Flag Hit by Plan to Axe Tonnage Tax Next Year*, October 21st

Lloyd's List (2002e), *Germans Hope that Tonnage Tax will Survive*, October 22nd

Lloyd's List (2002f), *Elastic Taxes*, October 24th

Lloyd's List (2002g), *German Opposition Starts Battle to Save Tonnage Tax*, November 8th

Lloyd's List (2002h), *German Tonnage Tax Set for Reprieve*, November 12th

Lloyd's List (2002i), *Crisis Avoided as Tonnage Tax is Saved*, December 31st

Lloyd's List (2002j), *Finland Stands by Unpopular Tonnage Tax*, October 3rd

Lloyd's List (2002k), *Bearing the Weight of Tonnage Tax Policy*, October 18th

Lloyd's List (2002l), *Nordo-Link Buy Whets Finnlines Appetite*, October 18th

Lloyd's List (2002m), *Small Shipowners Chalk Up 50 for Cargoship Association*, October 18th

Lloyd's List (2002n), *Cavalry Arrives in Form of New Tonnage Tax Regime*, February 6th

Lloyd's List (2002o), *Brussels Approves Irish Tonnage Tax System*, December 11th

Lloyd's List (2002p), *Reprieve for Flag as Italian Owners Win Tax Rebates*, January 10th

Lloyd's List (2002q), *Greece Cuts Tonnage Tax to Help Flag*, January 25th

Lloyd's List (2002r), *Evergreen Boss Hints at Transfer of 40 Ships to UK*, January 8th

Lloyd's List (2002s), *Maersk Adds More Vessels to Red Ensign*, January 28th

Lloyd's List (2002t), *Red Ensign and Italy Prove the Flags of Choice for Evergreen Renewal*, February 6th

Lloyd's List (2002u), *UK Flag Reaps New Dividends From Changes in MCA Practice*, February 6th

Lloyd's List (2002v), *Evergreen Flies Another Red Ensign*, February 7th

Lloyd's List (2002w), *Political Deadlock Drives Evergreen from Taiwan*, February 11th

Lloyd's List (2002x), *Cafin is Latest Italian Owner to Pick-Up UK Flag*, November 1st

Lloyd's List (2002y), *Montanari Threatens Italian mass Exodus to Red Ensign*, November 7th

Lloyd's List (2002z), *UK Under Fire for Secrecy Over Tonnage Tax Owners*, December 11th

Lloyd's List (2002aa), *Guidelines on State Aid 'Not Used'*, January 25th

Lloyd's List (2002bb), *Tonnage Tax Not the Cure for All Industry's Ills Danish Owner's Told*, May 23rd

Lloyd's List (2002cc), *Tonnage Tax Bandwagon Rolls Along*, November 28th

Lloyd's List (2003a), *Denmark's Smaller Owners Feel Pinch*, January 23rd

Lloyd's List (2003b), *Torm Shareholders Bear Bulk Losses*, March 3rd

Lloyd's List (2003c), *Tonnage Tax Swells Norden Profit*, March 27th

Lloyd's List (2003d), *Sweden's Heart Beats Stronger*, January 29th

Lloyd's List (2003e), *Belgian Tonnage Tax Plans Partly Approved*, March 20th

Lloyd's List (2003f), *Brussels Pledges Global Approach to Liner Law*, April 2nd

Lloyd's List (2003g), *Belgium Ready to Revive National Flag*, May 8th

Lloyd's List (2003h), *A Good Year for German Shipping Companies*, January 27th

Lloyd's List (2003i), *V Ships Sees Rosy Future in Germany*, March 7th

Lloyd's List (2003j), *Confidence Returns in Germany*, April 9th

Lloyd's List (2003k), *German Ship Investors Could Lose Tax Gain*, May 23rd

Lloyd's List (2003l), *Brussels Rules for Basque Tonnage Tax*, February 7th

Lloyd's List (2003m), *Schröder Waits for Owners' Warm Applause*, May 29th

Lloyd's List (2003n), *Belgian Flag Revival is at Expense of Luxembourg*, May 26th

Lloyd's List (2003o), *Royal Seal of Approval Marks End of Long Battle for Shipowners*, May 29th

Lloyd's List (2003p), *Luxembourg's Loss Could Result in a New Benelux Register*, May 29th

Lloyd's List (2003q), *Schröder in Tax Subsidy Vow to Revive German Flag*, May 28th

Lloyd's List (2003r), *Belgian Shipowners Ready to Fly the Flag*, May 19th

Lloyd's List (2003s), *Bank of Ireland Establishes Green Shoots in Maritime Scene*, April 9th

Lloyd's List (2003t), *Now The Job to Build on Past Four Year's Achievements*, July 21st

Lloyd's List (2003u), *Revitalised Maritime Sector is Emerging*, July 21st

Lloyd's List (2003v), *Irish Vessel Registration Faces Major Overhaul*, July 30th

Lloyd's List (2003w), *Tonnage Tax Postponement is Blow for Italian Owners*, October 17th

Lloyd's List (2003x), *Move Back to Belgian Flag to Save $1.18m*, June 17th

Lloyd's List (2003y), *New Greek Owners' Leader Pushes for Flag Initiatives*, March 19th

Lloyd's List (2003z), *Shortsea Boost in European State Aid Rules*, October 31st

Lloyd's List (2003aa), *Dutch Maritime Interests Fear the Worst from Budget*, September 15th

Lloyd's List (2003bb), *Dutch Budget Disappoints*, September 17th

Lloyd's List (2003cc), *Passenger ships May Quit Finnish Flag Says Lawyer*, September 3rd

Lloyd's List (2003dd), *Germany's Financiers Face New Challenges*, June 25th

Lloyd's List (2003ee), *Germans in Loyalty Pledge to Cyprus*, October 27th

Lloyd's List (2003ff), *KG Investment Bandwagon Shows No Sign of Rolling to a Stop*, October 28th

Lloyd's List (2003gg), *Repatriation Drive Heralds Return of Flag*, October 23rd

Lloyd's List (2003hh), *Belgian Flag Bags Safmarine*, November 11th

Lloyd's List (2003ii), *Tonnage Tax Switch 'Could Drive Ships from UK Flag'*, January 9th

Lloyd's List (2003jj), *Changes Stop the Slide from the Red Duster*, February 10th

Lloyd's List (2003kk), *Financiers to Feel Effect of Anti-avoidance Laws*, February 10th

Lloyd's List (2003ll), *Too Many Trainees for UK Shipping to Handle*, November 11th

Lloyd's List (2003mm), *Fulfilling Two Needs*, February 14th

Lloyd's List (2003nn), *Noble Launches Abbey Shipping in Rare Enterprise Investment*, February 25th

Lloyd's List (2003oo), *A Single Step for Abbey, a Giant Leap for London*, February 26th

Lloyd's List (2003pp), *James Fisher Well Placed for Expansion*, March 5th

Lloyd's List (2003qq), *Arison Wins Over the Princess Faithful*, June 25th

Lloyd's List (2003rr), *Zodiac Maritime Poised to Give Huge Boost to UK Flag*, July 25th

Lloyd's List (2003ss), *Bright Future is Forecast for Star-Quality Zodiac*, July 31st

Lloyd's List (2003tt), *More Jobs Under Threat*, August 19th

Lloyd's List (2003uu), *Look at Basel II*, August 20th

Lloyd's List (2003vv), *Tonnage Tax Boost for UK Register*, September 1st

Lloyd's List (2003ww), *Hyundai Goes for 6,800teu Quintet*, September 29th

Lloyd's List (2003xx), *Parker Criticises 'Misguided' Government*, September 30th

Lloyd's List (2003yy), *UK Fleet of Merchant Tonnage Up Almost 30%*, October 9th

Lloyd's List (2003zz), *Proposed Reforms 'Would Threaten the Attractions of British Tonnage Tax'*, September 30th

Lloyd's List (2003aaa), *Brussels in Blitz on Ship and Port Security*, May 9th

Lloyd's List (2003bbb), *ICS Accuses Brussels of Undermining Marpol*, May 15th

Lloyd's List (2003ccc), *Industry a 'Poor Relation' to EU Rivals Warns Andersen*, June 4th

Lloyd's List (2003ddd), *European MPs Vote for Faster Phase-Out*, June 6th

Lloyd's List (2003eee), *Brussels Poised as Single-Hull Talks Begin*, July 14th

Lloyd's List (2003fff), *Russia Rules Out Bilateral Tanker Talks with Brussels*, October 24th

Lloyd's List (2003ggg), *O'Neil Goes to War on EU's Single-Hull Ban*, October 24th

Lloyd's List (2003hhh), *Wedge Driven Between EU and the World*, November 13th

Lloyd's List (2003iii), *EU Has No Wish to Undermine IMO Over Single-Hull Says Karamitsos*, November 20th

Lloyd's List (2003jjj), *French Tanker Ban Stays Until IMO Deal*, May 1st

Lloyd's List (2003kkk), *Shortsea Aid Tops EU Agenda*, May 28th

Lloyd's List (2003lll), *Look at Basel II*, November 28th

Lloyd's List (2003mmm), *Recurring Accidents Call for New Approach*, May 7th

Lloyd's List (2003nnn), *Time to Answer Big Questions*, May 7th

Lloyd's List (2003ooo), *O'Neil Urges IMO Flag Power*, May 15th

Lloyd's List (2003ppp), *Economists Get to Grips with Maritime Realities*, May 16th

Lloyd's List (2003qqq), *Class Under Threat from IMO Plans Says Gavin*, May 22nd

Lloyd's List (2003rrr), *Towards Global Wage Parity*, June 1st

Lloyd's List (2003sss), *IMO Must Retain Power – IAC's Head*, June 5th

Lloyd's List (2003ttt), *WTO Boss Calls on China to Use Its Influence to Get Talks Back on Track*, November 11th

Lloyd's List (2003uuu), *IMO Powers 'Must be Extended'*, November 25th

Lloyd's List (2003vvv), *IMO Urged to Think Global on Environmental Issues*, December 1st

Lloyd's List (2003www), *Italian Owners Hail Success of Tonnage Tax Campaign*, December 31st

Lloyd's List Focus (1997), *Netherlands, A Strategy for Growth*, October.

Lloyd's List Focus (2000), *Norway, Surprisingly Steady Growth*, May.

Lloyd's Maritime Information Services (1994), *Vessel Database, 1994*, Lloyds Maritime Information Services: London.

Lloyd's Register (2002), *World Fleet Statistics, 2001*, Lloyds Register of Shipping: London.

Lloyd's Ship Manager (1995), *Supplement; A Solid Base for Shipping, the Netherlands Antilles' Ship Register*, July 3-5th.

Lloyd's Ship Manager (1997), *Time for a (modest) change*, **27**, 3.

Lloyd's Ship Manager (2000), *Flying the Dutch flag, The Netherlands and Belgium*, **30**, 25-26.

Lloyd's Shipping Economist (2000), *What Future with Paragraph 2b?*, May: http://www1.shipecon.com

Lloyd's Shipping Economist (2003), *Re-assessing the fundamentals*, **25**, April, 22.

Lomas, U. (2002a), *Swedish Ship-owners Press for Tonnage Tax Regime*, January 24th: http://www.taxnews.com/asp/story/story.asp?storyname=7082

Lomas, U. (2002b), *Spanish Tonnage Tax Given Go-Ahead by EC*, http://www.tax-news.com/asp/story/story.asp?storyname=7609

Lu, C.S. (1999), 'Strategic groups in Taiwanese liner shipping', *Maritime Policy and Management*, **26**, 1, 1-26.

Lyons, P.K. (2000), *Transport Policies of the EU*, Business Intelligence Report, EC Inform, January.

Marlow, P., Pettit, S.J. and Bergantino, A. (1997), *The decision to flag out and its impact to the national economy*, Maritime Transport and Economic Reconstruction, Roundtable Conference, Institute of Maritime Transport and Seaborne Trade, University of Gdansk, 17-18th October.

MCA (2000), *Seafarer Standards*, http://www.mcga.gov.uk/survey/surv.htm

McConville, J. (1999), 'Editorial: shipping policy', *Maritime Policy and Management*, **26**, 2, 103-104.

McConville, J. and Glen, D. (1997), 'The employment implications of UK merchant fleet's decline', *Marine Policy*, **21**, 267-276.

McKenna, T. (1972), 'Towards Europe', *Chartered Institute of Transport Journal*, November, 5-10.

Milne, P. (1996), *Comments on the Communication from the Commission to the European Parliament, the Council, the Economic and Social Committee and the Committee of the Regions on 'Towards a New Maritime Strategy'* COM (96) 81 Final, http://www.amrie.org/docs/mar_stra.htm

Mimiran, S.M.R. (1994), *Iran's National Shipping Policy*, Unpublished MSc Thesis, University of Plymouth.

Moyer, R.C. (1977), 'Maritime subsidies: problems, alternatives and trade-offs', *Journal of Industrial Economics*, **25**, 3.

Nasiru, I.S. (1994), *The Nigerian National Shipping Policy; Aground or Afloat?*, Unpublished MSc Thesis, University of Plymouth.

Navigator (2001), *Shipping is Necessary*, http:/www.seacompanion.com/fi

Norton Rose (2002), *Greece Tonnage Tax Regime*, Norton Rose Shipping Group, London.

Norwegian Shipowners Association (1996), *Annual Report 1995-96*.

Notteboom, T. and Winkelmans, W. (2001), 'Structural change in logistics; how will port authorities face the challenge?', *Maritime Policy and Management*, **28**, 1, 78-89.

Odeke, A. (1984), *Protectionism and the Future of International Shipping*, Martinus Nijhoff: Dordrecht.

OECD (2002), *Regulator Issues in International Maritime Transport*, Directorate for Science, Technology and Industry, Division of Transport, OECD, Paris, http://www.oecd.org

Omosun, A.Y. (1987), *A Consideration of the Means of Attaining the Nigerian Shipping Policy Objectives,* Unpublished MSc Thesis, University of Plymouth.

Osler, D. (2002), Can UK count on the Red Ensign?, *Lloyd's List*, June 20th.

Paixao, A. and Marlow, P. (2001), 'A review of the European Union shipping policy', *Maritime Policy and Management*, **28**, 2, 187-198.

Pallis, A. (1997), 'Towards a common ports policy? EU – proposals and the ports industry's perceptions', *Maritime Policy and Management*, **24**, 4, 365-380.

Pallis, A. (2002), *The Common EU Maritime Transport Policy, Policy Europeanisation in the 1990s*, Ashgate Publishing: Aldershot.

Parker, M. (1999), 'Globalisation; shipping seeks new global role', *Lloyd's Shipping Economist*, November, **21**, 11, 7-10.

Peeters, C., Verbeke, A., Declerq, E. and Wijnholst, N. (1995), *Analysis of the Competitive Position of Short Sea Shipping; Development of Policy Measures*, Delft University Press: Delft.

Peters, H.J. (2001), 'Developments in global seatrade and container shipping markets: their effects on the port industry and private sector involvement', *International Journal of Maritime Economics*, **3**, 1, 3-26.

Porter, M. (1998), 'Clusters and the new economics of competition', *Harvard Business Review*, November-December, **76**, 77-90.

Posidonia Congress (2002), 'Dynamism of an industry based on human factor', *Seatrade and Naftiliaki*, 12.

Randay, T. (2001), 'Internationalisation and foreign direct investment in shipping: a study of Norwegian firms', *International Journal of Maritime Economics*, **3**, 3, 298-317.

Rochdale Committee (1970), *Report of the Committee of Inquiry into Shipping*, Cmnd 337, UK Government.

Rodrigue, J., Slack, B. and Comtois, C. (1997), 'Transportation and spatial cycles: evidence from maritime systems', *Journal of Transport Geography*, **5**, 2, 87-98.

Roe, M.S. (1997), *Reconstruction and development in the UK shipping industry – Is there any future?*, Maritime Transport and Economic Reconstruction Roundtable Conference, Gdansk, 17-18th October, University of Gdansk.

Roe, M.S. (1998), *Commercialisation in Central and East European Shipping*, Ashgate Publishing: Aldershot.

Roe, M.S. (2002), 'Shipping policy in the globalisation era: the interrelationship between international, supra-national and national shipping policies', in Grammenos, C. (ed.), *The Handbook of Maritime Economics and Business*, Lloyds of London Press: London, 495-511.

Roobeck, A. (1987), 'The crisis of Fordism and the rise of a new technological paradigm', *Future*, **19** (2).

Ryoo, D.K. and Thanopoulou, H.A. (1999), 'Liner alliances in the globalization era: a strategic tool for Asian container carriers', *Maritime Policy and Management*, **26**, 4, 349-368.

Sanidas, E. (2002), *Organizational Innovations of Firms from the 1850s in the USA and Japan,* University of Wollongong, Department of Economics, Working Paper Series 2002, WP 02-06.

Schrier, E., Nadel, E. and Rifas, B. (1985), *Outlook for the Liberalization of Maritime Transport*, Trade Policy Research Centre: London.

Seatrade (2002), *Reputation Flies High*, Netherlands Shipping and Dutch Maritime Network.

Selkou, E. and Roe, M.S. (2001), 'The UK register of shipping; recent trends and tax concessions', *Naftika Xronika,* November, 92-93.

Selkou, E. and Roe, M.S. (2002), 'UK tonnage tax: subsidy or special case?', *Maritime Policy and Management,* **29**, 4, 393-404.

Slack, B., Comtois, C. and McCalla, R. (2002), 'Strategic alliances in the container shipping industry; a global perspective', *Maritime Policy and Management,* **29**, 1, 65-76.

Sletmo, G.K. (2001), 'The end of national shipping policy? A historical perspective on shipping policy in a global economy', *International Journal of Maritime Economics,* **3**, 4, 333-350.

Sletmo, G.K. and Holste, S. (1993), 'Shipping and the competitive advantage of nations', *Maritime Policy and Management*, **20**, 3, 243-255.

Sletmo, G.K. and Williams, E.W. (1981), *Liner Conferences in the Container Age: US Policy,* McMillan: New York.

Song, D.-W., Cullinane, K. and Roe, M.S. (2001), *The Productive Efficiency of Container Terminals*, Ashgate Publishing: Aldershot.

Strom, H.K. (1966), 'The "Common Market" and discrimination in transport', *Transportation Journal*, 16-23.

Sturmey, S.G. (1962), *British Shipping and World Competition*, Oxford University Press: Oxford.

Sturmey, S.G. (1975), *A Consideration of the Ends and Means of National Shipping Policies,* Shipping Economics: Collected Papers, MacMillan Press: New York.

Sun, G. and Zhang, S. (1999), 'General review of the Chinese shipping policy for the contemporary era', *Maritime Policy and Management,* **26**, 1, 93-99.

Sun, G. and Zhang, S. (2000), 'Comment. The APEC future maritime policy and its evaluation', *Maritime Policy and Management,* **27**, 2, 209-213.

Thanopoulou, H. (1995), 'The growth of fleets registered in the newly-emerging maritime countries and maritime crises', *Maritime Policy and Management,* **22**, 1, 51-62.

Thanopoulou, H.A., Ryoo, D.K. and Lee, T. (1999), 'Korean liner shipping in the era of global alliances', *Maritime Policy and Management,* **26**, 3, 209-230.

Tradewinds (2003), 'EU boost to shipping', *Tradewinds,* 30th October.

Trainer, T. (1999), 'The limits to growth case now', *The Environmentalist,* **19**, 19.4, 325-336.

UK Chamber of Shipping (1999), *Maritime Britain, Charting a New Course,* http://www.british-shipping.org/maritime/introduction.htm

UK Chamber of Shipping (2001), *Annual Review 2000,* The Chamber of Shipping: London.

UK Chamber of Shipping (2002), *Annual Review 2001,* The Chamber of Shipping: London.

UK Chamber of Shipping (2003), *Annual Review 2002,* The Chamber of Shipping: London.

UK Department of the Environment, Transport and the Regions (1998), *Tackling the issues,* Shipping Working Group, http://shipping.detr.gov.uk

UK Department of the Environment, Transport and the Regions (1999), *British Shipping, Charting a New Course,* http://shipping.detr.gov.uk

UK Government Department for International Development (2000), *Eliminating World Poverty: A Challenge for the 21st Century,* White Paper.

UK House of Commons (1988), *Transport Committee, First Report, Decline in the UK-registered Merchant Fleet, Volume 1, Report and Minutes of Proceedings,* HMSO: London.

UK Inland Revenue (2000a), *City F Large Office, Tonnage Tax in the UK, a Brief Guide,* H.M. Treasury: London.

UK Inland Revenue (2000b), *Statutory Instruments, Income Tax. The Tonnage Tax Regulations 2000,* No. 2303.

UK Inland Revenue (2000c), *Tonnage Tax in the UK, a Brief Guide,* H.M. Treasury: London.

UNCLOS (2001), *Oceans and Law of the Sea,* Office for Ocean Affairs and the Law of the Sea, Office of Legal Affairs, United Nations: New York.

UNCTAD (1991), *Review of Maritime Transport 1990*, United Nations: New York.

UNICE (2002), *Priorities for the New European Commission*, Globalisation – International Agreement, October, http://attac.org/fra/libe/doc/unice.htm

Van de Loo, B. and Van de Velde, S. (2003), *Key Success Factors for Positioning Small-island Sea Ports for Competitive Advantage*, Erasmus University, Rotterdam.

Van der Linden, J. (2001), 'The economic impact study of maritime policy issues: application to the German case', *Maritime Policy and Management*, **28**, 1, 33-54.

Vasiliou, G. (1996), *The Role of the State and the New Global Financial, Business and Technological Environment*, The Greek Economic Almanac, Banking Insurance Industry.

Veenstra, A.W. (2002), 'Nautical education in a changing world: the case of the Netherlands', *Marine Policy*, **26**, 133-141.

Walenciak, A., Constantinou, A. and Roe, M.S. (2001), 'Liner shipping between East and West Europe; competitive developments on the Poland-United Kingdom trade', *Maritime Policy and Management*, **28**, 4, 323-338.

Walter, A.E.M. (1960), 'European transport policies', *Institute of Transport Journal*, September, 370-376.

Walter, A.E.M. (1963), 'Transport in the Common Market', *Institute of Transport Journal*, January, 33-42.

Wang, S. (1993), *European Community Shipping Competition Policy*, Unpublished MSc Thesis, University of Plymouth.

Watkin, C. (2000), *UK Tax Authorities publish draft legislation*, Sinclair Roche and Temperley Shipping Finance.

Whitehurst, C.H. (1983), *The US Merchant Marine; In Search of an Enduring Maritime Policy*, Nautical Institute Press: Annapolis.

Womack, J.P., Jones, D.T. and Roos, D. (1990), *The Machine That Changed the World*, Rawson Associates: New York.

Wrona, A. and Roe, M.S. (2002), 'The Polish maritime sector under transition', *Maritime Policy and Management*, **29**, 1, 17-43.

Yannopoulos, C.N. (2003), *Taxation on Vessels and Shipping Enterprises. Greece Tax Deskbook. International Tax Deskbook*, Zepos and Yannopoulos Law Firm: Athens.

Yannopoulos, G.N. (1989), *Shipping Policies for an Open World Economy*, Routledge: London.

Yercan, F. (1999), *Ferry Services in Europe*, Ashgate Publishing: Aldershot.

Yercan, F. and Roe, M.S. (1999), *Shipping in Turkey*, Ashgate Publishing: Aldershot.

Index